300/101

STATES AND MORALS

STATES AND MORALS

A STUDY IN POLITICAL CONFLICTS

by T. D. WELDON

Whittlesey House

McGRAW-HILL BOOK COMPANY, INC.

NEW YORK : LONDON

Preface

IT is painfully clear that political conflicts are common in these days and that the results of them are likely to be exceedingly unpleasant. What these conflicts are really about is not equally clear and is not explained by describing them as ideological differences. The position is that few people are quite certain whether the major Powers are at odds with one another over economic advantages or political organization or something more vague but equally important which may be called the claim of the individual to determine his own life and conduct; and there is no agreement as to whether these are separate questions or are so intimately connected that they can profitably be considered only as a single problem. In other words, it is extremely hard to say whether the U.S.A., the U.S.S.R., and Great Britain are quarreling primarily about the ownership of oil wells and trading facilities, about the best method of controlling the means of production in a well-ordered community, or about the importance of freedom of speech and freedom of political association.

It may well be admitted that we have here three different kinds of ground for disagreement and also that there are important connections between them. But it is important to discover how they are related to one another, if only because military and strategic advantages are obviously pursued as a means of extending or protecting economic, political and moral claims. The chief concern of political philosophy is with the third claim, namely with that of human beings to liberty or freedom within the States to which they belong, and there are two serious mistakes to which it is especially liable. The first is that of Plato and his modern disciples who suppose that philosophy leads to the discovery of eternal Ideas or Values and that anyone who is acquainted with these must know beyond any possibility of doubt how all States ought to be organized and what the relation of States to one another and to their own members ought to be. This special insight into the nature of reality makes the philosopher the final court of appeal on all kinds of important practical problems such as education, birth control, and the proper use of atomic bombs.

This does not seem to me a very sensible view. Political conflicts of the kinds with which we are all familiar arise because people and nations are genuinely at variance about principles, and there is no ground whatever for supposing that such disagreement can be disposed of by a course of philosophy. Furthermore, there is no evidence for the contention that Platonic or other philosophers do possess any special knowledge which qualifies them to act as consultants on actual political and economic affairs, nor have their incursions into these departments been particularly fortunate.

At the other end of the philosophical scale are those writers who see clearly that the Platonic philosopher king is a dangerous delusion and who therefore attempt to divorce political philosophy completely from practical considerations of every kind. Theories about the nature of the State are then regarded simply as logical problems. All that the philosopher can properly do about them is to ask whether they are internally consistent and whether they fit in with some more general view about the nature of God, the self and the universe which is regarded as acceptable on other grounds.

This method of treatment would be defective even if it were not doomed to failure by the nature of the facts concerned. Consistency is indeed a virtue and philosophers are not likely to underestimate it. But it is not enough. The time and labor needed to achieve it are well spent only when the problems considered are of real importance, and few people are likely to consider the expenditure justified unless this importance is fairly evident. But the need for reflection about theories of the State is not obvious at all unless those theories are recognized as having some direct bearing on actual political conflicts. In the absence of such connection they appear to be nothing more than empty speculations on rather trivial verbal points.

The aim of this book is not to produce a new political theory but to consider theories which are already well established. Its primary purpose is to show that the views put forward by such writers as Locke, Hegel, and Marx are neither gospels whose eternal truth cannot be challenged except by criminals or lunatics, nor mere quibbles about the meanings of terms like "State," "freedom," or "democracy." They are important simply because they formulate in reasonably clear and intelligible language the political principles which are the basis of the practical policies of statesmen in different kinds of State. In other words, these theories are derived to a considerable extent from acquaintance with the observable characteristics of actual States and their value as well as their limitations depends on recognition of this. It is impossible to understand the points about which the Russians, the Americans, and the British are disputing without a clear idea of the divergent political beliefs on which much of their practical thinking is founded, and it is equally impossible to recognize the character and importance of those beliefs without relating them to the conflicting policies in which they find expression. This should not be taken to mean that economic actions and political institutions depend entirely on beliefs about political freedom. To suggest this would be as foolish as to hold the opposite view, namely that economic factors completely determine political beliefs. The prevailing tendency, however, is to misunderstand and therefore to undervalue the moral sentiments which political theories formulate, and it is desirable that this tendency should be corrected.

The point on which I wish to concentrate is not the consistency of the main political theories but their status. If democracy and its competitors are none of them capable of making out a claim to be regarded as revealed truths, what are we to say about them and, more particularly, what warrant have those who believe in one of them for attempting to impose this belief on other people? What I shall try to show is that these theories closely resemble scientific theories or hypotheses invented to explain observed facts. In the case of political beliefs, however, the nature of the facts to be explained is peculiar and presents special problems. In the end they are convictions or sentiments about the value and purpose of individual human beings which cannot immediately be removed or even seriously modified by argument or discussion. They must simply be accepted. Hence they are not suitable or even possible objects for indiscriminate export. All this does not make very easy reading. Although I have tried to avoid the use of technical philosophical terminology, I have not aimed at producing a popular exposition. The subject is not one which can be grasped without an effort. If it were there would be less misunderstanding about it than there is. And to write about it as if it were easy when in fact it is nothing of the kind would merely add another to the existing sources of confusion. I have aimed at showing not merely how political theories are connected with the facts and problems of internal and international politics, but also at giving some indication of their connection with other branches of philosophy. The interrelation between the problems of political and those of moral philosophy is too evident to be in any doubt. But the dependence of political theories or special views about logic and the theory of knowledge, to say nothing of psychology, is equally important but less frequently noticed.

The connection of politics with morals is so close that I have been unable to avoid a fairly technical discussion of some of the problems which the latter involves. I should like to say that the sections in which this happens (especially in Chapter 5) are not essential to political philosophy and may therefore be omitted by those whose interest is limited to it. But this would be merely untrue. These passages are already over-simplified and there is nothing for it but for those who want to understand the view I am putting in the rest of the book to make the best they can of them. It is a pity, but it is not my fault. Philosophy, even though it has no private revelations to offer, is still quite an exacting subject.

To end this Preface, I must express my thanks to Mr. W. J. M. Mackenzie, for reading the book both in manuscript and in proof, and for contributing valuable ideas as well as many suggestions for improvements in detail; to Mr. C. E. Stevens for reading and correcting the proofs, and to Mr. L. H. McDonald for many useful comments and amendments. I also acknowledge with gratitude the patience and good-will of pupils, both British and American, to whom I expounded my views on these subjects in the interval between the wars.

T. D. WELDON

Contents

		PAGE
PREFACE	. . . .	V

CHAPTER

1	THE AIM OF POLITICAL PHILOSOPHY	1
2	POLITICAL THEORIES	26
3	POLITICAL PHILOSOPHERS	62
4	STATES IN THEORY AND IN PRACTICE . . .	146
5	POLITICS AND MORALS	216
6	THE PRACTICAL PROBLEM	281
INDEX	. . . .	297

The Aim of Political Philosophy

Nothing universal can rationally be affirmed of any
moral or any political subject.—BURKE.

THE AIM OF political philosophy is to discover the grounds
on which the State claims to exercise authority over its members. To achieve this, it examines the nature of the State and
attempts, as a result of this examination, to reach conclusions
about the rights of individuals, the rights of the State to control the behavior of its citizens and the relation of States to
one another. Most political philosophers have also held that
their investigation is concerned with ideals as well as with facts,
and there is clearly a case for supposing that we cannot hope to
deal satisfactorily with the problems raised unless we know,
not merely what the State is, but also, what it ought to be.

This program may suggest that political philosophy is in the
end a study in abstract and highly general terms of the aims
and policies of political parties. It might conceivably be this.
In practice, it is usually nothing of the kind. It is true that in
this book we shall consider a number of theories which inevitably suggest party political catchwords, and I shall show that
those catchwords have a definite and important connection
with political philosophy. At the beginning, however, it is
essential to guard against premature identifications which lead
to confusion and not to enlightenment.

The point I have in mind is this. Generally speaking it is
not the case that political parties in Great Britain or in any
other country are at odds with one another because they differ

about political philosophy. Much more commonly they share a philosophy and quarrel about particular applications of it. Unfortunately those who organize political campaigns are firmly, though mistakenly, convinced that electorates will respond only to slogans and that the political colorvision of their publics is restricted to the distinction between white and red. This leads them to represent their opponents as standing for a species of political philosophy which is essentially opposed to that which most of the electors are known or believed to hold. In England at the present time, it is not seriously questionable that the vast majority of the electorate are in favor of what are vaguely described as democratic institutions or that they hold some sort of democratic political theory. Hence it was thought expedient by the leaders of every party at the general election of 1945 to suggest that the other parties were in fact not democratic at all but believed in some antidemocratic philosophy which the public would naturally reject. All of them, therefore, claimed to be supporting the same view in principle, but each argued (*a*) that his program alone was truly consistent with that view and (*b*) that no other party genuinely believed in it.

This does not mean that there are no serious differences of opinion on political philosophy or that all the citizens of any country at a given time hold exactly the same view about it. Certainly there are some people in Great Britain who honestly believe that a so-called totalitarian regime of the right or of the left, that is, a fascist or communist State, would be an improvement on what we now have, and it is true that a genuine opposition of political philosophies is here involved; but, provided the number of such dissentients is small as compared with that of the total population, this controversy has little importance. Only when the stage is reached in any community at which more or less equally balanced political parties are disputing, not about questions of application, but about political principles, is it safe to assume that a revolution or a civil war is fairly close.

There is another possibility which needs watching in this connection. I have said that political parties do not usually differ about political philosophy nearly as much as their propagandists would lead us to suppose that they do; but this is not to be taken as meaning that their differences are merely trivial. It is quite common for a body of men to be in complete agreement as to the kind of government they want but to be violently at variance as to who shall be the governors and who the governed: and we may all hold that rights given by the Constitution are sacred and still fight one another because we cannot agree as to what those rights are.

It must be emphasized that disputes of this kind, however important they may be and however disastrous their consequences, are not strictly speaking disputes about political philosophy. All or nearly all of them are capable of being avoided or settled by patience and a reasonable display of good will and common sense by the parties concerned. Genuine differences about principles, on the other hand, can seldom, if ever, be dealt with peacefully, though their worst consequences may be postponed, perhaps indefinitely, if their character is generally understood.

What this means will, I hope, become clear in the course of the following discussion. All I want to establish at the start is that much care is necessary in distinguishing between political philosophy and party programs, since the latter are usually concerned not with political principles but with questions of application, and these, although they may be of extreme importance, are by no means necessarily so. The distinction is one which has to be constantly borne in mind because it is not always easy to make and it is possible to be mistaken and also to be deliberately cheated about it. The American Civil War provides a good instance. There is little doubt that it involved a real conflict between irreconcilable political doctrines; but it can be argued perfectly reasonably that this was not the case, and that different points of view about issues even as vital as those of slavery, secession and economic policy could have been and ought to have been settled by intelligent men without recourse to war.

At this point it will no doubt be asked, Is political philosophy really as important as that? I think that it is and shall devote the rest of this chapter to giving briefly my reasons for holding this opinion.

Most people admittedly have views about the nature of the State, and many of those views are highly confused and self-contradictory. At first sight this may not seem to matter a great deal. They are just theories, it may be said, which can be discussed and argued about in the same sort of way as relativity or theology, without anybody being noticeably the better or the worse for it. Political philosophy, inasmuch as it is concerned with the study of the State and of its relation to the individuals who are members of it, is clearly an academic and highly abstract subject which the ordinary citizen has little or no reason to trouble his head about, though it is quite a good topic for debating societies.

Is this a sensible view to hold?

Political philosophy is certainly academic. This means simply that it is the kind of subject which is studied at universities, not that it can safely be left to the experts to deal with and that the rest of the world should wait until the answers have been found and presented in a simplified form before taking any serious interest in them. Still less does it imply that those answers are certain to be unimportant in the sense of being irrelevant to practical affairs. Some academic theorizing is unimportant and even futile, and an often-quoted instance of such futility is the medieval speculation as to the number of angels who could dance on the point of a needle; but others less notorious and equally remote from daily life could easily be produced.

It is not advisable to make too much of this and to suppose that theorizing is always merely an intellectual exercise, or that academic speculation is just a pleasant pastime for those who enjoy that kind of pursuit. There are plenty of historical and scientific inquiries which, although they appear and are thought by those who make them to be of no importance, are none the less highly relevant to the lives and happiness of ordinary people.

For instance, any inquiry at the present day into the aims and methods of President Wilson at the Versailles Peace Conference is academic. Wilson is dead, and whatever he may have wished or tried to do can make no difference now. For the same reason and to a much greater extent one might argue that what Aristotle thought about the nature of the State in the fourth century B.C. and what Hobbes and Locke wrote about it in the seventeenth century A.D., can have nothing but "examination value" for us. But these are mistaken arguments. The conditions of peacemaking in 1947 are very different from those of 1919. We should, therefore, be stupidly optimistic if we assumed that it is necessary only to find out and avoid the mistakes which a post-mortem shows to have been made at Versailles in order to ensure that the present peace will be better and more permanent than the last one was. But we ought to be able to avoid this sort of credulity without falling into the opposite delusion, namely that there is nothing important in common between the two situations. There is a great deal. And anyone who takes the trouble to find out what it is will be to that extent qualified to have a view as to the practical steps now required to produce the result which is wanted. In the same way, the political philosophies of Aristotle and Hobbes are out of date, in the sense that the actual political situations with which they were concerned have long ceased to exist. But they may none the less express important general truths which it is most unwise to forget. In other words, they may be far less remote from present-day problems than they appear to be on a casual inspection.

Much the same may be said of the objection that political philosophy deals only with abstractions. All theory does that. Few studies are more "abstract" in the sense of "remote from daily life" than modern physics, and many can remember wondering at the to-do which occurred in learned circles in the 1930's over Rutherford's experimental work on the disintegration of the atom. It became quite a well-established joke of a mildly intellectual kind. But since this work has already led to the invention of an operationally effective uranium bomb which can devastate with a single explosion, five square miles of a thickly populated industrial area, it is not easy to deny that in this case an essentially abstract research has given rise to exceedingly practical results.

To put the matter shortly, the test of whether this kind of inquiry is worth while or not is whether the conclusions which it tries to reach can reasonably be expected to be important. If anyone can show ground for believing that it matters whether ten or ten thousand angels can in fact dance on a needle's point, then there is some sense in attempting to decide whether either of these answers is correct. Otherwise there is none.

So we must ask whether reasonings about the State, which inevitably include its relations both to individuals and to other States, seem on the whole likely to be helpful or futile. On the face of it there seems to be something to be said for the latter view. For after all, it may be said, the political questions to which we really want to know the answers are all essentially practical. Social security, nationalization of coal mines, banks and transport, how to deal with Russia, Germany, and Japan so as to avoid, if possible, another catastrophe at least for the next thirty years or so: these are the problems we ought to be thinking about. And it is hard to see that abstract inquiries about the State will get us any nearer to solving them. There is a little truth in this, but not very much. It is possible for a discussion about the nationalization of mines to be conducted on a strictly practical and economic level, at least in its opening stages. One can sensibly ask how much capital is required to modernize plant and equipment, buy out and close down redundant pits and generally to effect an economic reorganization of the industry. One can also ask whether it is probable that the necessary sums of money would be likely to be obtainable from private sources, and, if not, whether the continued existence of the coal-mining industry on a big scale is a condition without which this country would not, as far as can be foreseen, enjoy any reasonably high standard of living. These are factual and perfectly rational inquiries. Inevitably, however, unless disputants are agreed on something quite different, namely "abstract political principles," they will and can lead to no conclusion. No one who believes as an article of faith that any compulsory taking over by the State of what has previously been a legitimate form of private property is an outrage against the natural rights of man, can possibly approve of such proceedings, even if he is convinced by argument that the community as a whole would gain an economic advantage if they were permitted; and equally no one who believes that private property in the means of production is an infringement of the natural rights of man, can possibly approve of its continuance, even if he is satisfied that the owners had a workable scheme for doing what is necessary which they would really have carried out if given the chance to do so.

This is the main reason why so many arguments which start in a harmless way on matters which appear to concern only practical expediency, arrive quite quickly at a condition of hopeless deadlock from which there seems to be no escape except by physical contest or abandonment of the discussion. So even if statements like "The State ought not to interfere with free competition," "The State ought to control the use of the raw materials essential to production which exist within its borders," are really nonsensical or trivial, it is still important that as many people as possible should know that they are irrelevant and also why they are irrelevant to any serious discussion. For no one wants to fight about nonsense statements, even though it is hard to deny that plenty of people have inadvertently done so before now. It is also pretty clear that when an argument gets tangled up in a dispute of this kind, neither side has usually the faintest idea of what, if anything, is being talked about. For these propositions, whether true or false, sense or nonsense, are statements which involve political philosophy. They assert in a muddled way opposite theories about the relation of the State to the Individual and they are, even though this also is often not noticed, entirely abstract. It is unfortunately true that important practical decisions are sometimes made on the strength of views about political philosophy which would certainly be rejected by those who act on them, if only their meaning and implications were understood.

Discussions on international politics usually involve so many empty statements which purport to be about hard facts but are really fragments of bad political philosophy that it is difficult to select particular instances. However, the most popular in recent months have unquestionably been those current about Germany, and a few samples will suffice.

The war was a war between States. We have no quarrel with the German people, who had as little responsibility as we had for its happening. . . .

We are not trying to destroy either the German people or the German State. When the Nazi Party is eliminated, it will be our duty to rehabilitate the real Germany as quickly as possible. . . .

All Germans are fully responsible for what the Nazi Government has committed in the way of aggressions and atrocities. We ought therefore to shoot the lot—or at least to ensure that they are so weakened and kept under for a long period as to be incapable of causing trouble to anybody.

It is hardly necessary to point out that these propositions, about which venomous discussions are still in progress, though most people are already extremely tired of them, are practically important. They are all slogans in common use by those who wish to advocate or to put out of court concrete suggestions for dealing with pressing international problems. Yet anyone who thinks about them for a moment can see that they are unhelpful unless definite meanings are given to the words "State," "Party," "Government" and "People." Furthermore, they make sense only if some more abstract statements about the relations of the State both to its own citizens and to other States are assumed to be true. But here again we have come up against the problems of political philosophy.

Finally, there are endless discussions, not confined by any means to "academic" circles, about forms of government. This, it is argued in almost any war nowadays, is not just another war between States; it is a war of ideologies. In other words it is a sort of crusade by democratic peoples against the tyranny of fascism. Now, on the face of it, democracy and fascism have no moral or religious meaning whatever. They are just names for different methods of organizing human beings and, as such, are as unsuitable to crusade about as limited liability or public utility corporations. Few people would be prepared to shed their blood in order to substitute proportional representation for our present electoral system, or to obtain a decimal currency. So one is led naturally and rightly to suppose that "democracy" and "fascism" in this context really mean something quite different from what they seem to mean. It is not easy to say exactly what this highly important meaning is, and statements that it is the British, American or German way of life that is in question have done nothing whatever to clear up the difficulty. They merely suggest that the war had something to do with Bank Holidays, German sausages, or refrigerators, and evoke much enthusiasm without shedding any light. This is not surprising since "fascism," "democracy," "communism," "socialism" and similar terms, are all of them significant only in relation to a system of political philosophy; and they stir the emotions because of the moral principles which such systems involve.

From all this it follows that anyone who attempts to discuss any practical political question without a background of political philosophy is usually talking rather at random. That is to say, he is using words without attaching any definite meaning to them. Statements made in this way may make sense by accident, especially if, as frequently happens, they are moderately accurate recollections of more authoritative pronouncements, since the "source" may have had a coherent philosophy and have been able to say what he meant even though his imitator is incompetent to do so. But this is at best an unhappy and dangerous situation. Obviously I do not have to parade and expound my political philosophy whenever I make a statement which takes it for granted. That would be intolerably tedious. I do not find it necessary to prove the whole of Euclid in order to make a special application of the problem of Pythagoras when I wish to calculate the diagonal of a field. In both cases, however, the disadvantage of not being able, if necessary, to do the demonstration is twofold. In the first place, I am poorly placed if my special application is challenged, and it is just at this point and for this reason that political disputants tend to reach for their revolvers; and in the second, unless I know the theoretical background I can never be sure whether any two propositions in geometry or politics are consistent with each other or not. That is why it is often possible for a newspaper to run simultaneously campaigns whose underlying political principles are completely incompatible with one another, and to get away with it. It is not obviously foolish to maintain simultaneously that the Government ought to remove all wartime controls to give proper opportunities for free enterprise, that it ought to ensure that employment and houses are available for all, and that cartels and combines ought to be prevented from cutting out the small trader. It requires at least an elementary study of political philosophy to show that no one consistent doctrine of the position of the State in relation to the individual can possibly cover these requirements. They are equally inconsistent from an economic point of view. But that is another question.

Possibly it may be thought that it is pedantic and unreasonable to expect consistency in principle from the daily press, but unfortunately this kind of rubbish can lead, if not to action, at least to demands for action. The demands cannot all be met, because they take for granted fundamental principles which are incompatible with one another; but the fact that all are not met can be used quite unfairly as a stick with which to beat the authorities. This too is not important in itself or in an isolated case. But when it occurs again and again, it is perfectly possible that the resulting irritation and disillusionment with successive governments may lead to a widespread feeling of contempt for the existing system of government as a whole. An excess of muddled thinking about bureaucratic incompetence, especially as some of it is always certain to have a practical ground, may contribute substantially to producing the kind of situation in which revolutions occur.

All this is not intended to lead to the conclusion that the big words of political philosophy are unimportant. Certainly they have a great emotive power, at least in some communities. In the United States, and in England only to a slightly smaller

extent, "liberty" and "democracy," in spite of the disillusionment of the last peace, are still rousing war cries and it would
be rash to suppose that they are merely catchwords. There is
much wisdom in Lincoln's conviction that you can't fool all the
people all the time, and, although the patent medicines and
beverages which are most heavily advertised are not necessarily
all that their authors claim for them, it is safe to assume that
they are not actively harmful. Without a foundation in truth
advertisement is seldom quite successful. Now it is undeniable
that belief in something to which the names "liberty" and
"democracy" refer has been a strong enough motive to impel
large numbers of people to risk and lose their lives. This in
itself is valuable though not completely satisfactory evidence
for supposing that, although no very clear account of what they
mean is usually forthcoming even from their strongest supporters, there is still some important reality to correspond to
them. It is also, I think, reasonable to suppose that in them
we have at least a reference to ideals as well as to facts. In
other words, they may and often do refer to beliefs about what
the State and its relation to its citizens ought to be rather than
to what they actually are.

So far I have argued that the study of political philosophy
is important because questions concerned with the relation
of States to individuals are often involved in what appear to
be discussions about quite other matters. It is not always easy
to see that this is so, and the peddling of slogans by political
adventurers in all countries makes the difficulty much greater
than it need be. But we ought to know what it is that we are
arguing about, and I do not see how anybody can hope to do
this on political issues without taking the trouble to discover
and to understand what the competing doctrines are.

This is not all. We should not underestimate the value of
political philosophy as a contribution to efficient thinking on

practical politics, but we should not exaggerate it either. For what matters most about such philosophies is that they are intimately concerned with the great moral issues for which people are prepared to make extreme sacrifices. How this comes about will be explained more fully in Chapter 5, but it is a good thing to be conscious of our destination from the start. What we are asking is "Does the State exist for the individual or does the individual exist for the State?" Everybody knows in a general sort of way that both views have been and are held, and even that the difference between them is of some importance. But it would be optimistic to pretend either that most people are fully alive to the practical implications of them, or that those implications are obvious. In 1917 an English political philosopher who had watched an early (and rather ineffective) German air attack on London wrote as follows: "In the bombing of London I had just witnessed the visible and tangible outcome of a false and wicked doctrine, the foundations of which lay, as I believe, in the book before me (Hegel's *Philosophy of Right*). . . . Hegel himself carried the proof sheets of his first work to the printer through streets crowded with fugitives from the field of Jena. With that work began the most penetrating and subtle of all the intellectual influences which have sapped the rational humanitarianism of the eighteenth and nineteenth centuries, and in the Hegelian theory of the god-state all that I had witnessed lay implicit." [1] This may be an overstatement and in any case the blame may lie not primarily with Hegel for holding his view but with the Germans for accepting it. But it cannot be denied that his political philosophy has at least stimulated and encouraged them to attack the cities of other people and has thereby eventually led to the complete destruction of their own.

[1] L. T. Hobhouse, *The Metaphysical Theory of the State*, p. 6. Compare K. R. Popper, *The Open Society and Its Enemies*, Chap. 12.

Reflection on this aspect of political philosophy ought to make us careful in attributing strong feelings about it either to ourselves or to other people. If we mean that a particular party or individual is fascist or Marxist or democratic, then we mean something important. If we do not mean it, we had much better not say it, since we are talking about states of mind which tend to produce violent and sometimes destructive action. But this is a counsel of perfection which is unlikely to be much observed in practical affairs, at least while the efficacy of catchwords remains an unchallenged belief in so many quarters. "However just these sentiments will be allowed to be, we have already sufficient indications that it will happen in this as in all former cases of great national discussion. A torrent of angry and malignant passions will be let loose. To judge from the conduct of the opposite parties, we shall be led to conclude that they will mutually hope to evince the justness of their opinions, and to increase the number of their converts by the loudness of their declamations and the bitterness of their invectives. An enlightened zeal for the energy and the efficiency of government will be stigmatized as the offspring of a temper fond of despotic power and hostile to the principles of liberty. An overscrupulous jealousy of danger to the rights of the people, which is more commonly the fault of the head than of the heart, will be represented as mere pretence and artifice, the stale bait of popularity at the expense of the public good." [2] The reckless propaganda for and against the adoption of the Constitution of the United States which Hamilton anticipated and which duly occurred, is, as he says, unfortunately typical of such political discussions. Nobody in 1788 wanted the United States to become either an absolutist tyranny or an extreme kind of democracy. But each side, by attributing to its opponents a political philosophy

[2] HAMILTON, *The Federalist*, No. 1.

which they did not hold, did what it could to turn a rational discussion into a shooting match.

THE METHOD OF POLITICAL PHILOSOPHY

Having decided that political philosophy is important, we must next consider how it is to be studied, and since it is concerned with the relation between States and individuals, our method will depend on what we think about the way in which definitions of these terms can best be gained. There are two possibilities. We may claim that some revelation or intuitive insight into the nature of reality enables us to say with complete confidence what the correct definitions are. They are then guaranteed beyond any possibility of doubt, and political philosophy will consist simply in analyzing them in order to find out the inferences which can be drawn from them. This method, which was widely approved and followed in philosophical and theological studies before the seventeenth century, is known as rationalism.[3] Alternatively, we may hold that no such certainty is to be expected but that political theories and the definitions they include are, as one might expect from their name, working hypotheses.[4] That is to say, they are not, as they stand, necessary truths but simply suppositions whose only claim to validity rests on the possibility of confirming or refuting them by an appeal to the facts. This is the method of observation and experiment known as empiricism.

To illustrate this distinction, consider for a moment the character of the individual human being. It may be claimed

[3] "Rationalism" is also used as the opposite of "supernaturalism" or "superstition." As I do not propose to employ it in the latter sense, there should be no danger of confusion arising from this ambiguity.

[4] Although "theory" and "hypothesis" have the same meaning, "theory" is frequently employed with at least a suggestion that it refers to a system of demonstrated truth rather than of supposition. I shall use "theory" and "hypothesis" as synonyms.

(and many reputable authorities have asserted it without any appeal to evidence to support their case), that there is no motive which will move anybody to act except a desire to promote his own material advantage; and from this assertion a good many important conclusions about human society can be deduced. This is a rationalist procedure. By contrast, however, I may suppose that human nature is like that and attempt to verify my hypothesis by referring to psychological research; and I shall not accept as proved any conclusions which can be inferred from my supposition until the supposition has itself been verified.

Now it may be thought that the choice between these methods is obvious. But this is not so. Quite a good case can be made out for either of them, and, consequently, what is only too likely to happen is a confusion of both. For rationalism, it can be argued that both politics and morals are concerned, not with what is, but with what ought to be. Psychology, it will then be maintained, has the task of discovering how people do normally behave, and sociology deals with the actual relations of human beings to one another in society. Moral and political philosophy, however, are not concerned with these questions except in a quite incidental way. They must deal with ideal relationships and need no appeal to actual facts to confirm their conclusions about good societies and right actions. I do not myself agree with this view, though it is by no means a negligible one. It appears to me that, unless our definitions both of States and of individuals are grounded on something more solid than guesses, we may well find in the end that our views on what ought to happen are empty and meaningless. To my mind it makes no sense to conclude that all men ought to be democratically governed if experience convinces me (as it does) that large groups of human beings are, for whatever reason, so made that they do not want a constitution of this kind and could not work it if they had it.

But I should make it clear at once that I am in a minority on this point. Although the practice of political philosophers has been far from consistent, their official view is generally that their definitions are not hypotheses but are self-evident truths about the real world, and this has frequently committed them to a greater confidence in the value of their conclusions than appears to me to be warranted by the facts. As this distinction between rationalism and empiricism in political theory is important, I will attempt to make it clearer by a rather more technical statement. This, however, may be omitted without any serious loss by readers who do not care for that kind of thing. What is essential is to notice that there are alternative methods of approaching the subject and that a good deal of obscurity arises in the works of the standard authors because they did not clearly distinguish between these methods. In other words, they failed to ask themselves "What is the status of the definitions from which political philosophy is derived?"

RATIONALISM AND EMPIRICISM

It is not difficult to see that definitions occupy a different position in Euclidean geometry, the most familiar study in which rationalist procedure is followed, from that which they hold in the empirical sciences of zoology and physiology. Geometry begins with definitions. The empirical sciences seek to formulate them. To put it differently, when we want to find out truths about the frog, we proceed by examining particular frogs. These are observed, measured, and dissected, and, as the outcome of this investigation, an account of "the frog" is gradually built up. This account, which is an empirical definition, enables us to predict with a high degree of probability the behavior and contents of other frogs which we have not specifically examined. Plenty of problems arise about this procedure when we begin to ask ourselves *why* we are confident that unexamined frogs will behave in the same way as examined frogs have done, and also when we try to decide how much confidence it is reasonable to place in results obtained by this method. But these are problems of inductive logic which do not concern us here. What has to be remembered is simply that we do extend our knowledge by studying particular instances and by subjecting them to measurement and analysis. In this process definitions are an important element. But they are always provisional and subject to correction in the light of new facts. They make no claim to be more than this.

The case of geometry is not at all similar. We do not find out about the triangle by drawing large numbers of triangles and then subjecting them to measurement and analysis. We might conceivably do this, and, if we did, we should discover empirically that the internal angles of all of them add up to approximately 180°, and that such of them as contain an angle which is approximately a right angle have the squares on their hypotenuses approximately equal to the sums of the squares on their other two sides. The qualification "approximately" would need to be inserted at every stage, since measurements can never in practice be perfectly accurate. We could, however, predict with a high degree of probability that anybody who took the trouble to construct a figure of that kind would find that its angles actually added up to approximately 180°. What we do in geometry, however, is to rely entirely on our definitions and to say that any figure which conforms to our definition of a triangle must have the characteristics mentioned and must have them precisely and not approximately. The definitions are not built up as the result of observation tested by experiment. They are taken for granted. This does not mean that geometrical results were never empirically obtained. People knew that the theorem of Pythagoras was approximately true long before the geometrical proof of it was discovered. But when the proof was discovered, it did not depend for its validity on previous observations. It is a wholly rationalist demonstration which owes nothing to the study or analysis of particular instances, and the definitions from which it is derived are based, not on actual experience, but on a special insight into the nature of Euclidean space.

What is to be said, in the light of this distinction, about the status of definitions in political philosophy? At first sight it would certainly appear that this status should be empirical, since it would surely be highly optimistic to suppose that we have the same sort of insight into the nature of human relations as we have into the nature of geometrical figures. We should, therefore, expect that the definition of the State would be built up gradually and would be conceived as a provisional hypothesis requiring verification and confirmation from experience before further use is made of it. But when we inquire into the method which political philosophers have employed, we find that, from Plato onward, they have been predominantly rationalist in their approach, though they have seldom been quite consistent about it.

The historical grounds for this attitude are clear enough. The Greeks, who laid the foundations on which western thought has mainly been constructed, were remarkably proficient in geometry, whereas hardly any progress was made with empirical science until the possibilities of experiment and induction were taken seriously with the help of improved mathematical technique in the seventeenth century. Indeed, it was self-evident to Plato, and Plato's view as developed by Aristotle was dominant through the Middle Ages, that true knowledge could never be achieved except by the rationalist method of which geometry was the type, and also that the definitions from which true conclusions about States and frogs as well as about triangles could be deduced were the product of an intellectual insight into the nature of the real and not of the dissection of particular instances.

As a result of this attachment of political philosophers to a rationalist outlook, they have commonly set out with a definition of the State and have proceeded to infer conclusions from it without any very careful consideration of the source from which it was derived. It is worth while to indicate the lines along with this process develops before we inquire whether it is justified by the subject matter or not. Suppose that, as Plato and his descendants have done, we define the State as a special kind of organic unity. From this definition alone it follows that the parts of the State, that is its citizens, must be related to it in a specifiable way. We do not need to look for instances to prove this, but simply assert that, in any organism, the parts are subordinate to and dominated by the whole. They therefore necessarily lose their essential character when they are separated from it. They may continue to exist in an incomplete and mangled way, but they lose all meaning and importance. The full implications of this view do not matter at this stage. The point is that if the method is accepted and the definition unchallenged, I can deduce important consequences about the status of the individual without considering the actual organization of existing States at all.

Equally, I can define the State not as a kind of organism but as a kind of machine. Again important consequences follow about the individual, but they are of an entirely different kind, since a machine is made up out of a number of separate bits each of which exists before it is put into the machine and each of which can be taken out and used in a different machine without any loss of reality or, except by accident, of importance. A machine, in fact, is an artificial [5] whole, and the pieces of it are what they are in their own right and not simply because they belong to a whole which is more comprehensive than they are themselves. Now on this definition, in contrast to the previous one, it is clear that the individual is real while the State is just a combination of related individuals. It exists, presumably, in order to get something done, and, in Professor Laird's phrase, may be called "The Device of Government." [6] But this, too, would be something which could be inferred from a definition and not established by any reference to observed facts.

It is not always easy to see at a glance whether a particular author is developing his explanation of the nature of the State on rationalist or empiricist lines, and two points especially deserve attention in this connection. The first is that definitions do not determine facts. My immediate insight into the nature of Euclidean space does enable me to formulate a number of true propositions about that space. But it does not assure me that actual space is Euclidean, and modern experimental evidence has given strong grounds for holding that it is not Euclidean. In the same way I cannot turn States into organisms or into machines simply by defining them as organisms or as machines. If I am to be certain which they are, I must have some evidence, other than my definition, which will convince me of it. The second point to be noticed is that definitions of the State have frequently been put forward not as the product of impartial investigation, but primarily in order to provide intellectual backing for a line of political

[5] It is nevertheless a mistake to think that an organic State is in any relevant sense more "natural" than a mechanical one. It is just as natural for me to build a house as it is for me to consume food. Clearly any State is "natural" in some sense of that much-abused term; but the one question at issue here is whether States just happen to us, or whether we make them.

[6] LAIRD, *The Device of Government: An Essay on Civil Polity.*

action. This does not mean that they cannot be supported by empirical evidence, but it renders them suspect. And the suspicion naturally deepens when we find that their supporters ostensibly derive such definitions, not from observation of actual States, but from historical fictions about the origin of society. Suspicion, finally, may well turn to positive mistrust when it is discovered that the historical fictions are themselves based on nothing more solid than arbitrary assumptions about human nature of the kind to which I have already drawn attention.

As these points will arise repeatedly in the subsequent discussions, I do not propose to go into them further at this stage. They are mentioned only as a preliminary warning of what is to be expected.

The aim of this book is to show grounds for believing that the idea of political philosophy as a body of demonstrated truth is deceptive. I am convinced that no single statement of what the State is or of what it ought to be can command universal assent. This is not because most people are too stupid or too pigheaded to recognize elementary truths when philosophers point them out; it is due to the fact that different and incompatible political philosophies, or, as I prefer to call them, political theories are sincerely held, and in spite of their incompatibility with one another they are all logically defensible. It would be nonsense to say this if we held that the definitions involved in such theories were the products of intuition or of revelation. But on the more modest assumption that they are practical working hypotheses, it constitutes no fatal difficulty. This is the assumption on which I shall proceed. My reasons for accepting it will, I hope, become clear in the following chapters.

In Chapter 2 the three main theories which have been propounded about the nature of the State will be stated in a very

general way, and a few of their implications as well as the chief
objections which can be brought against them as theories will
be discussed. This examination is mainly concerned with the
meanings of words in common use and may, therefore, seem to
be superfluous. It appears to be lexicographical work, and since
an excellent dictionary of the English language already exists,
the reader may feel that it would be advisable to use this.
If what we want to know is the meaning of "State," "Society," "Community" and "Individual," we should surely do
better by looking them up than by puzzling our heads about
them.

Unfortunately it is not as easy as this. The trouble is that
all these words are currently employed not merely in a vague
but also in an ambiguous manner. When a Marxist uses the
word "State," he consciously and deliberately uses it with a
different meaning from that of the ordinary man or of authors
who do not hold the Marxist political theory. This ambiguity
infects all the related terms, and, unless it is clearly recognized and guarded against, all subsequent inquiry is confused
and all arguments at cross purposes. It is, therefore, worth
while to begin by considering the bare outline of the main
theories.

When this has been done, we can proceed in Chapter 3 to
examine some of the more detailed theories which leading
authorities have put forward. These are considerably less abstract, since every writer of importance has made some effort
to adapt his fundamental hypothesis to the conditions of the
time and place in which he was primarily interested. This investigation will show that, in spite of rationalist assumptions
and rationalist procedure, practically all outstanding political
philosophers have modified and compromised their initial
definitions in order to avoid conclusions which would have
conflicted both with established morality and with accepted
facts. This tendency indicates that the theories were im-

plicitly admitted, even by their advocates, to be working hypotheses and not systems of unalterable truth.

In Chapter 4 we shall inquire whether it can be plausibly maintained that any actual existing States correspond either to the general theories or to the more specific views discussed in Chapter 3. This leads to the conclusion that no "Theory of the State" will fit all the facts as we find them today. States, it will appear, are essentially different from one another, and the moral ideals of the individuals who impart their character to different types of State show corresponding divergencies.

There is manifest difficulty in accepting this conclusion as the final word on political philosophy. The main problem is this. If it were true that, although some States are very imperfect, there is only one political ideal which a rational man can embrace, we should be confronted with a difficult but not insoluble practical problem. Suppose, for instance, that Plato was right in holding that the organic State is the only ideal of a human community which can be accepted by a mature mind, then it would follow that nothing but defective education and defective political institutions stands in the way of its universal acceptance; and we could maintain with complete confidence that educational methods and political institutions calculated to speed up such acceptance were always to be commended. But if it is rather more than doubtful whether the organic (or any other) definition of the State is ever going to be generally approved as an ideal, we are faced with a much more serious difficulty. For it is no longer so easy to say that all States ought to be of a certain type or to be clear as to what people whose State is agreed to be in a bad way ought to do about it. We may simply say, "Well, some States are like that and there is nothing to be done about it at all." That, however, is rather a counsel of despair and should not be accepted without demur. I do not think we ought to accept it at all, but I do believe that the question, "What ought we to do about it?" is enormously more difficult to answer than is sometimes supposed. While not admitting that human nature is immutable, any more than that it is uniform, I am confident that we cannot change it either by wishing that it were different or by telling it that it ought to be different.

This is the point at which political and moral philosophy merge into each other. Political theories are accepted and acted upon not primarily because of their internal consistency but because they conform to moral beliefs about the importance or unimportance of the individual: and therefore, although we can formulate them and, to some extent, identify them in existing States, we cannot assess their merits except in the light of the moral sentiments which they presuppose. It is not my intention to write a treatise on morals, but to make the situation clear I shall devote Chapter 5 to consideration of the moral beliefs which political theories are more or less consciously designed to satisfy, and, in particular, to the somewhat different moral outlooks which seem to me to underlie the forms of democratic political theory dominant in Great Britain and the United States.

As a result of this investigation it is possible to achieve a reasonable view on two important questions, namely (1) are political theories, and especially democratic theories, suitable articles for export; and (2) if they are not, is it inevitable or probable that nations which believe in democracy will find themselves again committed to an ideological war against nations which do not? These problems are the concern of Chapter 6.

CHAPTER 2

Political Theories

Half the wrong conclusions at which mankind arrive are reached by the abuse of metaphors, and by mistaking general resemblance or imaginary similarity for real identity.—PALMERSTON.

IT IS IMPORTANT to realize exactly what the limitations of this inquiry are. Our final aim is to understand the relation of the State to the individual, and, as a preliminary, we have to get as clear a view as possible of the nature of the State. To do this, we have to examine the leading theories about the State which have been put forward, and those theories are unintelligible except in the light of the definitions of the State which they either formulate or take for granted.

All theories of the State fall, as I have already indicated, into two main groups. Some define it as a kind of organism, others as a kind of machine. The machine hypothesis again is subdivided. Within it, the theory of government by consent associated in practice with the name of democracy defines the State as an instrument created by and at the disposal of all members of Society, while the force theory associated particularly with the names of Thrasymachus,[1] Hobbes and Marx, conceives it as an instrument employed by some members only in order to control and exploit the remainder. The question here is whether consent or force is asserted to be the basis of the State.

At this stage it is no part of our purpose to decide either

[1] The Sophist in PLATO's *Republic*.

which of these views is morally best or whether any of them can actually point to unquestioned instances of realities which correspond to their definitions. Our aim is simply to take each of them to pieces in order to see how they are made, and thus to show the kind of thing reality would have to be in order to make them operative.

To see exactly what this means we may consider a parallel case. Suppose that instead of asking what is the relation of man to the State we were to ask, What is the relation of man to the dragon? To find out exactly what a dragon is, we look it up in the dictionary and find the following definition: "A huge and terrible reptile, with strong claws, like a beast or bird of prey, and a scaly skin; it generally has wings and sometimes breathes fire." From this definition it is possible to deduce a perfectly sensible theory as to the best way of hunting and destroying the dragon. A frontal attack, for instance, would be ill-advised, unless the attacker possessed special fire-fighting equipment. And so on. We do not, however, discover from this investigation whether any animal corresponding to the definition of the dragon actually exists or not. This is a matter for quite a different kind of inquiry. But we cannot usefully start on that inquiry until we know the character of the thing about which we are asking. So we have first to understand the definition and, next, to ask whether anything exists in the world to correspond to it. Then, in the case of the dragon, we can add to the definition the further statement that the dragon is a mythical monster, or, more simply, that there are no dragons. Possibly there are no States either, but that remains to be seen.

It is useful to remember this illustration, because in what follows I shall fairly often refer to facts in order to make clear exactly what the definitions under discussion really imply. It is possible to avoid such references and to deal throughout with abstract theory. This would have the advantage of making clear that, for the moment, theory only and not facts are our concern. It would also be subject to the fatal disadvantage of obscurity. Abstract argument is hard to follow, especially for people who do not ordinarily have to use it. I shall therefore use illustrations to help it out. This does no harm, provided it is remembered that these are only illustrations, not proofs. The consequences of the main political hypotheses, in so far as they are valid, follow not from illustrations but simply from definitions.

ELEMENTS COMMON TO ALL THEORIES

To produce a definition of the State at all we have to begin by thinking about a collection of people, and the most rudimentary collection of people is just a crowd. This is defined as meaning simply "a large number of persons"; there is in it no suggestion of arrangement or organization, in other words there are no rules but simply an unregulated multitude. As soon as there is organization, however simple, what we have is by definition no longer a crowd but a society, community, or association, all of which are, for purposes of this discussion, interchangeable terms. It must be added that by organization, in this connection, is meant an arrangement deliberately imposed by someone and understood as such by the creatures organized. An antheap and a beehive are, therefore, not organizations, except metaphorically, unless we assume either (a) that the insects are conscious or (b) that God (or Nature) has thought out the rules according to which they behave and recognizes them as rules. Organization, then, is merely subjection to deliberately formulated rules of behavior. An organized body of people is a community. The only important implication here is that of a distinction between those who arrange the planning or organizing and those who follow out their decisions, that is, between rulers and ruled. Nothing whatever is asserted as to how rulers get to be rulers, how many of them there are, or what the purpose of the society is. The definition is completely general and fits a patrol of Boy Scouts as well as the U.S.S.R.

The next stage, then, is to define Society or the Community, and here, while there is no longer complete agreement, differences are not sufficiently important to matter much. Generally speaking, Society is conceived as an organization of a special kind, namely one which is independent of all other forms of association and which therefore does what it likes to its own members. In more technical language, Society or the Community has complete control over its own members, and, as a consequence of this, it has to possess clearly recognized geographical boundaries. One of the many troubles about Hitler was that he claimed to control Germans outside Germany, in other words he extended the definition of the German Community to cover people of German origin anywhere in the world and acted on this hypothesis. Beyond these extremely vague and general definitions we cannot go without becoming involved in the distinction between the two fundamental hypotheses which offer to explain the relation between State and individual. This distinction is as follows: What I propose to call the organic theory defines the State as Society organized as a sovereign political body and conceives it as a natural individual, superior to and more valuable than the individuals who are its citizens. Opposed to this theory is the mechanical hypothesis, in which the State is not a natural-grown but an artificial product. It is a device made by men for a particular purpose and is of value only because it serves that purpose. This theory requires a sharp distinction to be drawn between the State and Society. Instead of being identical with politically organized Society, the State is now defined rather as what we ordinarily call the Government in the widest sense of that term. There are two subforms of this mechanical theory, since government may be thought of either as imposed on the governed by force or as created by their consent. But before these theories are considered, there are several important points of terminology which demand attention.

WORDS AND NAMES

The words "organic" and "mechanical" have been used fairly commonly to describe the kind of State which the two main branches of political theory have assumed. They are not altogether satisfactory but, on the whole, they are less open to objection than are any available alternatives. Their value lies in the fact that they do suggest the true line of demarcation between the theories under discussion, namely between the conception of the State as something for which man exists and the State as something which exists for man. For what is organic is alive, and the parts or organs of things which are alive are commonly conceived as being in some sense, not always very clearly defined, subordinate to the animal or plant to which they belong. Machines, on the other hand, are not alive. They derive their unity and importance from the purposes of the individuals who put them together.

This, however, is not the whole story. As we have already seen, the distinction is liable to suggest that a State corresponding to the machine definition would be less "natural" than one whose character was organic. There is no force in this suggestion, and, since "nature" [2] and "natural" are more variable in their meanings than any of the other words in common use in political theory, it may be regarded as a unimportant objection. "Natural" in this context is contrasted with "artificial" and has no moral implications.

There is a more serious difficulty in the appropriation of the word "organic." Certainly organisms are living things. But few biologists would agree that plants or animals are organic in the sense in which the term is being defined for pur-

2 See below, p. 72.

poses of this theory. If nothing more were going to be maintained than that organic connection implies some sort of general subordination of the part to the whole, there would be no objection. But, as we shall see very shortly, something much more drastic is entailed. In other words, most scientists would doubt whether particular dogs and rabbits could truly be said to be organic in the sense required. We might get out of this by calling our hypothesis "superorganic," but this would not make things better for the ordinary reader and would hardly pacify the scientist. "Organic" will not mislead provided it is understood to start with in a general and not very precise sense. A similar sort of misunderstanding may be caused by the term "mechanical." It has inevitably a suggestion of automatic action about it, and we are liable to get the idea that anything which could sensibly be called a machine State would have to be a "slave society" or "community of robots." This is an error. All that is meant is that the State is something created by man and not something that grows. A more general word like "artifact" would perhaps be preferable to express this idea. But "artifact" is clumsy and unfamiliar, and this constitutes a strong reason for avoiding it.

On the whole, then, with some slight misgivings, I propose to retain "organic" and "mechanical." Available alternatives, such as "collectivist" and "individualist," are at least equally misleading and the coining of new terms which would be entirely unambiguous and have no associations whatever is seldom to be recommended in studies of this kind.

There is another difficulty which arises largely from terminology and which the reader will probably find rather troublesome. We are going to consider three different theories about the State, which it is easy but misleading to identify with the views held, or supposed to be held, by members of political parties in this country. There is a tendency for parties of the political center to favor the hypothesis that the State is an organization deliberately invented and consented to by the governed and for parties of the right and of the left to prefer either the organic theory or the theory that all States depend only on force. But this is by no means invariable and it is most unsafe to assume that anything like the following equation holds good:

Organic theory	=	Right wing party	=	Fascist
Consent theory	=	Center party	=	Liberal
Force theory	=	Left wing party	=	Communist

The fatal objection to any tidy identification of this sort is that, although members of political parties do sometimes share a political theory, all that they need to share is a political policy; and one policy may be, at any rate in the short run, consistent with more than one theory. The nationalization of particular undertakings, Imperial Preference and Prohibition are all of them policies which may be supported by people whose political theories are diametrically opposed.

This is obvious in the United States, since neither the Republican nor the Democratic Party has for many years pretended that its members agreed about principles. It is perhaps still too soon to say that the same is true of parties in Great Britain. In view of the possibility for misunderstanding to which this situation gives rise, it might seem wise in formulating theories to avoid names which inevitably suggest that parties and theories are closely linked together. It would be wise, if it were possible, but history is all against it. Again, we might invent new names or even designate our theories simply as "Hypothesis A," "Hypothesis B 1" and "Hypothesis B 2." But I do not think that this would help. The name "Liberalism" is too firmly joined in popular thought to the political theory of consent to be detached from it by a mere pronouncement; and most people in these days can recognize the Marxist theory, even under a new alias.

All the same, it is helpful to remember that the theories are theories, and they are neither improved nor weakened by the fact that the statesmen and writers who have held them were, in our opinion, saints or sinners. And, since there is a discoverable connection in England at the present time between theories and parties, it may help if I show diagrammatically what it is:

A		B	C	
Conservative		*Liberal*	*Labor*	
(1)	(2)	(3)	(4)	(5)
Right wing	Left wing	Consent	Right wing	Left wing
Organic theory	Consent	theory	Consent	Organic theory
or	theory with		theory with	or
Force theory	bias to right		bias to left	Force theory

Liberal-democratic theory

Although this diagram is too simple to do justice to the facts, it will not mislead provided that its limitations are recognized. The most important point to be remembered about it is that it represents beliefs about political theory, not about economic policies, and these are not always easy to reconcile with one another. Some right-wing conservatives, for instance, at present preach an extreme form of economic individualism combined with a political theory which assumes that the British Empire as a whole is an organic State controlled by a single will: and some labor politicians favor an economic policy which is at least not obviously capable of being carried through by democratic methods, and have argued that it ought to be carried through nevertheless. These, however, are minor if well-advertised eccentricities. They do not affect the accuracy of the general picture. It is also true that some small elements who conceive the State simply as an apparatus based on pure force should, strictly speaking, be extracted from (1) and (5) and put into separate compartments. But to do this and to label those compartments fascist and communist would be very deceptive. Fascism and communism, as we shall see later on, have long ceased to be serviceable terms.[3] They are useful only for rousing strong but confused passions.

The point of all this is that a lot of patience is needed here and indeed throughout this book to keep parties and theories distinct and at the same time to remember that in particular countries at particular times there are close affiliations between them. But every case needs to be investigated on its merits. It would be most hazardous to assume that members of the Radical Socialist Party in France between the wars held a revolutionary political theory.

THE ORGANIC THEORY

An independent community organized as government and governed and supreme within a defined geographical area constitutes a genuine individual or person and is known as the State. The first and most important point to notice about this definition is that the words "person" and "individual" are not used metaphorically. The State is not defined as being "like an individual" but actually as being one, and it is from the identification of the State with the community conceived in this way that the consequences of the organic view, for better or worse, are derived. It is also to be observed that the description of the State as an individual or as a person really understates rather than exaggerates the importance which the theory gives to the State as compared with its members. For the State is by definition not merely as real as, but more real than, are the individuals who belong to it.

This theory of the community and of man's place in it is at first sight so repugnant to common English and American ideas that it is very likely to be rejected out-of-hand as plain nonsense. It looks not only unpleasant but silly. For it is surely obvious, whatever anybody may say about hands and

3 See below, pp. 211 and 214.

bodies, that the individual man is a unity and is real in a sense in which no society or corporation conceivably can be. One has only to look in order to be assured about this, if there is any serious doubt on the subject.

But this firm line, though it is attractive, will not really do. We have got used to regarding the individual man as a single being, but this may well be only a matter of custom and convenience depending largely on the kind of eyes we happen to have. It is highly unlikely that our essential unity is as apparent to a microbe as it is to ourselves. And if we say that by the individual person we mean not the body, which is admittedly "one" only for convenience, but the mind or soul, it has to be allowed that there are plenty of expert psychologists who believe that the unity of the mind is no better established than that of the body. From the other side, too, it is hard to deny that the movements of organized bodies of men when seen from the distance, especially from an aircraft, look very much more like the movements of individuals than like those of collections or multitudes. A body of men moving along a road looks, from a suitable height, like a snake and not like a lot of separate beings. Finally, if it is said that the behavior of individuals is at least more or less unified and coherent, it may be answered that the behavior of communities is unified too. If it were not, we should find that the standard personifications (John Bull, Uncle Sam) had no significance.

And so we cannot justifiably deny the organic view a hearing, however little we may like the look of it; and the more closely it is examined, the more unpleasant and the more plausible it tends to become. Let us look at some of the results which follow from it. The State is a real individual. This entails its having some sort of organizing control, corresponding to the central nervous system of the body. There must be in it something which determines the behavior of the parts which make it up. This, then, is what we mean by government, and the government of the State is seen to be not a device or gadget for doing something, but an entirely natural arrangement which any community is bound to have. It is one of the characteristics without which a community degenerates into a crowd.

It also follows that the State has a single unified interest on all matters. This also is something real. It is not to be thought of as an artificial result of compromise and arrangement between different and conflicting interests of individuals, groups or classes. For these by definition have no real interests of their own. It is nonsense to say that it is not to the interest of my tooth to be drilled, stopped or taken out. It is better for me as an individual that it should be, and that is all there is to be said about it. Hence the laws of the State are designed to promote the interests of the State, and government is there to formulate and enforce laws which do this. It must on this definition be foolish even to ask whether a subordinate individual has any right to break a law of which he disapproves; it is indeed just as foolish as to ask whether my foot has a right to refuse to go on walking when it gets tired.

Thus the State has jurisdiction in all cases. The individual except in obeying the State is essentially subordinate, incomplete and, in the last resort, unreal.

This rather paradoxical consequence of the organic hypothesis deserves a little more elucidation, especially as it is seldom emphasized by those who support the theory. Plato, a very consistent organic thinker, has stated it more bluntly. than any of his successors, and his words are worth quoting: "Our aim in founding the State was not the disproportionate happiness of any one class, but the greatest happiness of the whole; we thought that in a State which is ordered with a view to the good of the whole we should be most likely to find justice, and in the ill-ordered State injustice; and having found them, we might then decide which of the two is the happier.

. . . And therefore we must consider whether in appointing our guardians we would look to their greatest happiness individually or whether this principle of happiness does not rather reside in the State as a whole. But if the latter be the truth, then the guardians and auxiliaries, *and all others equally with them, must be compelled or induced to do their own work in the best way*. And thus the whole State will grow up in a noble order, and the several classes will receive the proportion of happiness which nature assigns to them." [4] What this amounts to, however odd it may sound, is that the happiness of a community is not identical with the sum of the different happinesses of its members. They may come to much the same thing, but they probably do not, and in any case this is quite unimportant. For Plato, the State is happy when a particular type of political organization is realized in it, and if we want to know whether a particular State is a happy State, we must inquire into the extent to which that condition is satisfied. We should get absolutely nowhere by discovering that the individual citizens were happy.

What this view does is to open a gap between the notion of what may be called the general or common interest of a community regarded as a single individual, and the joint or several interests of its members considered as separate people. The former is not the sum of the latter and may be extremely different from it.

This is a very helpful idea for those who wish to persecute their political opponents. It is always impossible to prove that the good of the community (in this highly specialized sense) will not be promoted by the liquidation of selected members of the population. It is a good deal simpler to be reasonably sure that the sum of the joint happiness of all the members will be reduced by torturing some of them. But that, to a strict organic theorist, is, as Plato points out, not evidence.

4 PLATO, *Republic*, 420. Jowett trans. My italics.

There are other implications of the organic theory which are hardly less fundamental than these. All States, on this view, are not necessarily equally good. That is to say, they are not equally States. In the same sort of sense a lunatic is not really a man. The general idea is that, in so far as central control is absent, we have only a low-grade community. The reality or the goodness of a State depends simply on the degree to which the elements are integrated into a single individual. From this admission, it might be thought that a high-grade or well-integrated man who is unfortunate enough to be a member of a low-grade or weakly integrated State would have the right to disagree with that State and, if necessary, to start a revolution in it. But this is a complete mistake. There is no sense in talking about a man as being good except in relation to his own State. A good hand is one which meets my requirements, not one that would suit a violinist or an agricultural laborer. A good man is one who meets the requirements of his own State, that is, a good citizen. Good citizens are not all equally important, since their goodness depends on their carrying out their function in the State and not on any inborn merit. But all functions are not equally necessary. There are plenty of outlying parts of the body which can be sacrificed without the efficiency of the whole suffering noticeably by their disappearance. There are other parts of which this cannot be said. So it follows unavoidably on the organic hypothesis that the bricklayer, however well and conscientiously he does his job, is not as important to the State as the Prime Minister. Neither has any rights at all against the State, but the State will be correct if it gives them unequal treatment in standard of living and in other ways. It is sensible and proper for most people to take more care of their eyes than of their toes.

The organic hypothesis is thus essentially in conflict with any idea of human equality as an ideal; and this is no accident. It is implied by the definition. On this theory the relations of men to one another and to the State depend, in legal terminology, on status not on contract. This does not necessarily mean that inequalities are inherited, and therefore finally settled at birth, although the theory may well be developed in this way. It does mean that the equality of man is not a self-evident fact but a dangerous delusion. What is real is the State, and within the State men are equal to precisely the extent to which the interest of the State requires that they should be equal and no more. Outside the State, there is no equality since there is no existence.

Obviously Christianity as developed since the Reformation, and especially in Puritan England during the seventeenth century, can have nothing whatever to do with this as a political theory. It may be noted in passing, however, that the hypothesis, except in its extreme practical application, is not equally repugnant to the Church of Rome. Provided it is agreed that the fundamental inequality of individuals is restricted to secular Society and that the equal importance of souls in the sight of God is firmly maintained, the theory in general is quite congenial to Roman Catholicism. Indeed, it is necessary since no other view of Society will accord with the Aristotelianism which the Church accepts. Hence it is not surprising that organic doctrine is a great deal less objectionable to Catholics as a body than is any form of the mechanical view to which it is opposed. Marxism and liberalism are both necessarily more alarming to the Vatican in principle than is organic theory.[5]

The obvious criticism to be leveled at the organic hypothesis is that, although ostensibly not based on force, it is essentially undemocratic, fascist and totalitarian in its consequences, and

5 See MARITAIN, *Scholasticism and Politics*. The author rejects National Socialism but favors "Organic Democracy" (pp. 98–117). This "democracy," however, does not involve government *by* the people in any real sense. It is, in fact, the ideal of a good organic State. Cf. p. 230 below.

this alone appears to be enough to discredit it as a basis for political thinking. Clearly there is something in this criticism. If democracy demands equality of political status for all human beings, then no organic theory of society can be brought into harmony with it. For the whole idea of an organism is that the elements in it have different functions to perform and that these functions are not equally important for the maintenance of the whole. Hence, since the interest of the whole has priority over any supposed private interests of the parts, no claim for general equality of treatment can be upheld. It should, however, be noted that, although on the organic theory government *by* the people is inevitably discarded, government *for*, that is, in the interest of, the Community as a whole is definitely asserted. The matter, therefore, again involves definition, and, as will appear later, "democracy" is not a term whose definition is obvious and free from dispute. On this issue, then, it is wise to suspend judgment for the time being. It is unnecessary, and it would be foolish, to deny that totalitarian regimes, especially those of Germany, Italy, and Spain, have all been founded at least officially on the organic theory. *Ein Reich, ein Volk, ein Führer* had no significance except as the expression of a thoroughgoing organic doctrine. But it does not follow that the organic view is always more likely to breed concentration camps and massacres than are the alternative political theories. Any political hypothesis is liable to be invoked to justify tyranny, and the fact that the atrocities in whose support this one has been cited are particularly horrible does not constitute a condemnation of the view. At the same time it cannot be completely ignored. There may be no necessary connection between organic theory and fascist practice, but the familiar link-up between them is nevertheless something which needs explanation. But no such explanation can be given at the purely theoretical level with which for the moment we are concerned.

Much the same reply must be given to criticisms of the organic theory which maintain that it is inconsistent with the recognition of natural rights, for these are as ill-defined as is democracy. It must be agreed that if the unqualified right of every individual in society to his life, liberty, and property is self-evident and untouchable, then there is no room for such "natural" rights in any organic theory. On the other hand, it must not be overlooked that the rigid form of the mechanical theory on which the constitution of the United States is based has proved unable to retain these rights in practice except in a somewhat qualified way. In their extreme form they are incompatible with the existence of any government, and even of any organized community whatever. It may thus reasonably be doubted whether the failure of the organic theory to accommodate them is very much of an argument against it. But here again caution is necessary. Whatever the theoretical position may be, it will rightly be remembered that "natural rights," even if they are not accepted as absolute, are treated with much more respect under democratic systems based on consent than under fascist regimes. There may not be any necessity about this, but it needs examination.

A more awkward objection to the organic hypothesis is the complete preeminence which it confers on one particular form of human community. The State is all-important, and, in comparison to it, all wider and narrower communities are reduced in status almost to vanishing point. This is certainly a fair criticism of the views expressed by leading exponents of the doctrine, Hegel in Germany, Bradley and Bosanquet (though with some reservation [6]) in England. For them neither a Trade Union nor a Church nor a League of Nations can in the end be permitted to compete with the State for the loyalty of the individual. The State is the highest form of reality with which we are acquainted, and that is the end of the matter.

6 BOSANQUET, *Philosophical Theory of the State.* Introduction, p. lix ff.

When Hegel talked about the State as "the march of God on earth" he really meant it, and Hitler, as head of the organic German State, was, on his own theory, entitled to the semi-divine honors he gave himself. This development of the organic theory, however, really is a misconstruction based on a special piece of definition. There is no logical reason for the absolute finality of the State. I might just as well start by defining the human race as a whole as the organic unity in which particular nation States are just members. The idea of a League of Nations [7] is capable of being either that of an organism or that of a machine, in just the same way that the idea of a State may also be either of them. The same is possibly true of other kinds of community. It is plausible to argue that membership of a World-State or of a Nation-State really absorbs and gives reality to all the potentialities of the individual. And if this can be established, then it can be argued that there is no place left in his life for any other loyalty. Trade Unions and so on exist, and are thought to be important only because existing States are not completely integrated. Such inferior societies obviously do not embrace the whole of a man's life and activity, and, inasmuch as the interest of the whole community is supreme, they cannot justly claim to operate in conflict with it. This argument was worked very heavily during the General Strike of 1926 and was the basis of the Trades Disputes Act of 1927 which in effect prohibited strikes as a method of bringing pressure on the State and restricted them to strictly nonpolitical action. While it is not quite clear that any organic theory of the State is logically bound to deny the existence of subordinate organizations within itself, except as inferior types of organism with limited and restricted aims, it is certainly true that all leading supporters of the theory have actually done this. Nor could they have avoided it without sacrificing that identification of the

7 See below, p. 277.

State with a self-sufficient society, which is an essential point of their theory. It would not be necessary to make this sacrifice in order to maintain the organic character of a Superstate or League of Nations, though the claim of the Nation-State to complete authority over the lives and liberties of its own members would have to be given up to permit this being done.

These difficulties all arise from a common source, or rather, they are different expressions of a single principle. This principle is ultimately the claim of the Protestant Reformation that in matters of faith and of conduct the final court of appeal is the conscience of the individual, and no authority can be morally entitled to control or even to interfere with the operation of that conscience. This doctrine has had its ups and downs. Like the doctrine of natural rights, with which it is very closely connected, it has an obvious tendency to lead to anarchy if pressed to extremes. If my conscience means simply "my intuition," and if nothing must be done to control acts done in obedience to that intuition, then no rule of law and no organized community is possible at all, and this was one of the major problems with which political theorists of the seventeenth century had to grapple. But the importance attached in the Protestant countries of the world to the individual's conscience cannot be either overlooked or explained away, and this is exactly what the organic theory of the State claims to do. Whatever the practical position may be, it is theoretical nonsense to hold *both* that I ought in the last resort always to do what I think right, *and* that the State, as one of its essential functions, must formulate laws which it is my duty to obey, irrespective of what my personal opinion on their rightness may be. No State based on an organic theory can accept the defense of conscientious objection. To do so would be to deny the assertion of superior reality on which its definition rests. Equally no Protestant doctrine of conscience can conceivably permit Society to claim the right to dictate to the individual what he ought to do.

Broadly speaking, all the difficulties of the organic view arise from its incompetence to make place for the conscience of the individual. And this difficulty, both in theory and in practice, seems to be insurmountable. It is not an answer to say that the individual, if he really understood the actions of Society, would accept them as his own and thus avoid conflict. What is involved is the question of right. Free speech and free association within Society are either rights which individuals can justly claim, whatever the views of Society as a whole may be, or they are not rights at all. There seems to be no theoretical compromise possible on this point, and the following quotation from a British supporter of the organic view may help to make the position clear. Professor Lord [8] writes as follows: "We must insist on the reality of the State and of its absolute right. It is impossible justly to understand human political experience if we reduce the State to a mere convention, an artificial device of individuals to secure their own rights or the objects of their desires, or if we fail to appreciate the sense in which the State is a necessary and natural being, and even prior to the individuals themselves. It does not merely follow from the good pleasure of its citizens: neither do its rights depend solely upon their permissive agreement." If, however, we start our inquiry, not from the point of view of Society but from that of the individual, the difficulty is reversed. We begin now by asserting the reality of the individual and the consequent supremacy of his conscience and his natural rights. The question then becomes "How do we escape from perpetual anarchy?" To put it differently, is any theory of the State really compatible with the recognition of the supremacy of conscience which Protestant theory requires? Of the two main forms of the mechanical theory of the State,

8 *The Principles of Politics*, p. 283.

one, namely the consent theory or democracy, claims to provide a satisfactory answer to this problem; the other, whose modern representative is Marxism, would not agree that it is ultimately important. It is, then, to the mechanical hypothesis that we must now turn for further enlightenment on this subject.

THE MACHINE THEORY

The fundamental principle of the organic theory is that Society or the State is actually and not metaphorically an individual person; and that, as such, it has the same unqualified control over its subordinate members as is sometimes allowed to reside in a biological organism. All this is denied by the machine theory. Sometimes, indeed, this denial is not quite obvious. Hobbes, for instance, describes his State as *Leviathan* and talks of it in terms which suggest that he is putting forward an organic theory. It is "this mortal God" and so forth. But these suggestions are quite misleading. Very little examination is needed to show that *Leviathan* is not a natural growth but an entirely artificial product of human invention. At most, it is a contrivance which acts as if it were human and might therefore be mistaken for a real person although it is only an ingenious mechanical device. It is not altogether easy to detect this practice, which is common in the mechanical school of political theorists. Which side of the fence a particular writer is on can usually be discovered by asking whether his conclusions require that his personification of the State should be taken literally, or regarded as a metaphor in order to make intelligible what he says about it. But even this is not quite conclusive, since some writers, whether by accident or design, are seriously confused on this essential point. Rousseau, for instance, held a mechanical theory of the origin of the State linked uneasily with an organic theory of its nature when once it had come into existence. He tried, as many others have done, to be on both sides of the fence at the same time.

In spite of this practical difficulty, the distinction in theory between the competing views is straightforward. Either the State is real and the individual is only an abstract element in it, or the individual is real and the State is some kind of device which the individual produces and which depends on him for its creation and subsequent existence. All mechanical theories, whether based on force or on consent, distinguish sharply between the State and Society, whereas any distinction which an organic theory makes between these ideas is necessarily artificial and of practical, not theoretical importance. Mechanical theory may either take the existence of organized human society for granted, or, as is frequently attempted, consider that this, too, is a product of human invention of whose origin and purpose some preliminary investigation is needed. This point is, for our present purpose, not important. We need notice only that the State is now to be defined, not as something coextensive with Society, but as a special form of organization within it.

The first point which strikes us about this definition is that it is *prima facie* acceptable, whereas the organic theory, whatever may be said about it in the end, is *prima facie* unattractive. As far as Britain and the United States are concerned, we are accustomed to thinking of the State as meaning vaguely "they" rather than "we." This idea is not usually analyzed, and too much importance should not be attached to it. It does indicate an outlook which is common to Englishmen and Americans and unfamiliar to Germans.

On the other hand, the idea of the State as a machine is liable to be challenged on the ground that, even if it can be formulated as a theory, it is so manifestly at variance with obvious facts as to be undeserving of further consideration. It may be urged that people do not construct States, but are born into them just as they are born into families. Admittedly there are a few instances in which this appears not to be the case. The New England colonists certainly intended to create States of an entirely different type from those which they had left, and some of them drew up a kind of social contract on which their new State was to be based. But, in spite of this, a little reflection shows that no assembly of men can really start with a blank sheet to invent a new form of political association. They must always be too deeply imbued with beliefs and traditions about government for this to be practicable. They may indeed produce a much-improved version of the type of State with which they are already familiar, but if they set out to do more than this, they may easily achieve less. It may well be maintained that the history of the U.S.S.R. since 1917 is a case of this. And so it may be said that, when a new State comes into being, as the succession States in Europe did after the 1914–1918 war, they are not manufactured as motor cars or airplanes are, but emerge as the result of a process of organic development. To suggest that old-established States are machinery or devices of government is not even plausible. Hence it is surely pointless to discuss a theory of the State which all experience refutes at the outset.

There is something in this objection. If there were not, the organic theory would not have gained much currency. But there is not enough in it to show that any mechanical theory is so far-fetched as to be undeserving of serious study. Whatever may be believed about Society, government is not something which just happens. It has to be "laid on" by somebody. This process, though it seems to differ from that of manufacture, seems also to have a good deal in common with it. The machine hypothesis can most easily be made to look dubious if we fail to distinguish the idea of the State from that of Society. Even if the latter is in the end admitted to be "natural" and not "artificial" there is a good case for suggesting that the former, as an organization within it, may be properly defined as a machine.

We must therefore discover what is implied by the definition of the State as a machine and what are the theoretical problems which such a definition involves.

A machine is something put together by somebody in order to do a particular job; here, as with the organic theory, it is of importance to remember that we are not supposed to be speaking metaphorically. What is being asserted is not the commonplace that some kinds of association behave in much the same way as the machines with which we are familiar. If this were all, no theory would follow. We should merely be talking figuratively and meaning nothing in particular. But the proposition we are considering is quite different from this. It is that there exists within Society a special piece of actual machinery which it is convenient to call "the State." What, then, is the purpose of this machine? It would be generally agreed that it is to govern, and this is not affected by widely divergent views as to its origin and composition. Perhaps the general theory can best be stated like this: Society, though we may not believe that it is an organism, is in some sense a natural growth. Men do tend to live in groups or herds. Possibly they do this because they like living together rather than in isolated families or in even less sociable ways than that. Possibly they do not like it at all but are constrained to do it because they are not strong enough to survive at all unless they get together in comparatively large herds. However this may be, existence in herds implies some rudimentary sort of organization. If the herd is going to provide any comfort or security superior to those obtainable in solitude, there has to be some division of labor. At a very primitive level this may be done by simple agreement between members. If two people have to use the same bathroom, they can normally agree to go to it at different times and so avoid any particular inconvenience; and much more complex arrangements than this are perfectly practicable without the invention of any special machine to cope with them. Nevertheless, there comes a point at which, even with good will on all sides, mutual understandings are no longer enough to enable the community to function smoothly. In common language, some authority is necessary to make things happen which otherwise would either never happen at all (because no one took the trouble to arrange for them to do so) or would happen only after futile wrangling and discord.

This account of the State is not quite satisfactory from the point of view of mechanical theory. It covers the essential point, but it puts the emphasis in the wrong place. In fact, it is superficially indistinguishable from that put forward by many organic thinkers from Plato downward as the basis of their doctrines. The trouble lies in the suggestion that State organization or the apparatus of government is something evolved by the common or general will of the community to promote a common good or to avoid a common evil. This is just what does not happen on any mechanical theory, since, for such theories, there is no common good in the sense in which the organic theory takes it for granted that there is. My good is one thing, your good is another. They may or may not be interdependent. But, even if they are, it is neither necessary nor sensible to introduce the idea of a third, or common good, conceived as somehow fusing and absorbing them into a single whole.

The State must not be thought of as arising as the result of a common aim or purpose, for there is no such thing. It may be the product of a joint requirement by a number of different people, but that is quite a different matter. All passengers on railway trains want to get somewhere. But it is not helpful to say that railway services are arranged to cater for a common or general will to move from place to place.

It is possible that all the individuals in a community might simultaneously recognize that their affairs had gradually become too complicated to be dealt with efficiently by means of separate voluntary agreements between individuals, and they might thereupon decide to set up a central governing body to control and organize them. This process, if carried out by a Society having the necessary characteristics of independence and territorial unity, would certainly constitute a State. But it is not the only or the most probable method of producing this result. A section or class within the community may just as well decide that such an organization would be to its private advantage and impose it on the remainder either by force, or, at best, with the passive acquiescence of those who are to be governed. A conqueror, similarly, may impose it on his victims, either by naked force, that is, by military occupation, or by the imposition of a puppet regime supported at only one remove by bayonets. Such institutions may be called independent States by courtesy or for purposes of legal convenience. But, in so far as they have organized government, they are parts of some State or other, namely of the occupying or controlling power.

The distinguishing mark of the State is simply the exercise of compulsory organizing power by a selected body of individuals within the community. It does not matter for the moment how these individuals achieve this position or how many of them are there. Theoretically they may equally well be either the entire population or a single individual. Nor is it yet relevant to ask whether they have moral authority as well as effective force to impose their decisions on anybody. Neither the moral nor the legal basis of State control is yet in question.

This conception of the State, whether in the end it is found to be satisfactory or not, has, at least, much to be said for it on historical grounds. Modern research gives convincing evidence that human beings actually did exist in social groups for enormous periods of time before any apparatus of government was necessary to organize them. Indeed it seems likely that the origin of the State as a form of human organization is contemporary with and dependent on the development of settled agricultural communities with fixed geographical locations. This, if correct, would put it somewhere about 4000 B.C., that is, later by 100,000 years or so than the known dates at which fairly human creatures were already in existence, and would relate it to a particular need. Obviously an agricultural community with fixed habitations and allotments requires more complicated arrangements for the protection and disposal of person and property than hunting or pastoral communities would do.

This merely indicates that some form of the machine theory may, after all, be found to fit the facts, and gives that hypothesis an initial plausibility. It does not prove anything about the internal consistency of the hypothesis or about its applicability to actual States, and should certainly not be taken to imply that any State which is not organic must be based on consent.

A. THE FORCE THEORY

We must now distinguish between the two main forms of the machine hypothesis. The State may be defined as the product either of force or of consent. The first of these possibilities, though it has had many advocates and is of great practical importance, requires little theoretical elaboration. Force creates no right, and therefore, if force and force only is the determining factor in political relations, no alternative explanation to that offered by the organic hypothesis of the moral authority of the State to control its members can be produced by the force theory. On the contrary, any such theory must in the end entail a denial that such authority exists. All that could be claimed is that the ruled, if they think it out, will come to the conclusion that it pays them better to obey their rulers than to attempt a revolution. But to say this is not to explain but to annihilate political obligation.

B. THE DEMOCRATIC THEORY

The theory which defines the State as an organization based on consent is evidently on a level entirely different from this. It is a genuine attempt to answer the question "Why ought I to obey the State?" and to do so without reducing the individual to the level of a mere adjective of the community. The individual is to be regarded as real, while the State is simply a contrivance produced by one or more human beings to control and govern the community within which it is created. From this it clearly follows that whatever right of coercion any State possesses is conferred on it by individuals and is not generated automatically just by the fact that it is a State. The State is actually, and not metaphorically, a joint-stock company, though with an important difference. State and joint-stock company are alike in that their aims depend on the joint [9] (not common) purposes of their members, and that their right to penalize members depends solely on what is explicitly conferred on them by their Constitutions. But by our present definition States, unlike companies, obviously have to exercise control over everyone within their territorial boundaries, and this must either be accepted as the exercise of naked force for which no claim of right can be made, or some theory must be invented to prove that a State is morally entitled to bring compulsion to bear on those whom it controls. To bring it into line with the joint-stock company seems to require that some contract or compact to which all concerned have given their assent should be able to be quoted in its favor.

[9] See above, p. 36.

This leads to a difficult question. Even if the general theory of a social contract as justifying State compulsion is accepted, it is always possible that legislation which is contrary to individual consciences may be passed. The Constitution of the United States is most carefully designed to prevent this from happening. But even so, no success can be guaranteed. Prohibition was enacted and had later to be repealed. The problem is: When such accidents do happen, what is the individual affected to do about them? The answer which follows from the theory of consent is perfectly clear and is diametrically opposed to that put forward by the organic theory. There can here be no identification of the good man with the good citizen. A man who obeys the rules of his joint-stock company and who shows uncommon zeal and ability at furthering, within those rules, the objects which the company has been created to promote, is a good member of that company. There can be no other test of goodness in this capacity. But in joining such a company the individual does not surrender his claim to individual judgment of what is right and what is wrong except to a strictly defined and limited extent. He binds himself by contract to accept decisions with which he personally may disagree, within a certain specified range of subjects. In doing this he believes that, in the nature of the case, either subjects within the specified range cannot be immoral (because they involve only nonmoral questions, like rules of the road) or that the line adopted by the company on moral issues will always be one with which he will agree. Furthermore, he knows that, if his expectations on these points are falsified by events, he can always resign from the company and thus recover complete freedom of decision. But it seems at first sight nonsense to maintain that anybody can surrender to a corporation or to a majority precisely that capacity which makes him a genuine human being, and it is worth noticing that this is just the difficulty which organic theorists find in admitting that the State (which they regard as a moral individual) can surrender *its* claim to independent judgment on moral issues to an international assembly. On the consent theory, then, the individual has not merely a right but a duty to challenge, and, in the last resort, to disobey State legislation if it transgresses the limits laid down in the articles of association.

A further implication is that no articles of association which sanction immoral institutions, such as slavery, can have any authority. The State may have the force but it can have no right to maintain these, and if it does maintain them, it is a tyranny which ought to be overthrown. No State based on consent can be conceived except within a theory of moral rules which bind its members; and the essential rule is that people should admit an obligation to keep contracts. Unless, however, this is the only rule, occasions are always possible in theory and probable in practice, in which a man will feel, and therefore be, obliged to break his contract or to terminate it in order to avoid committing an even worse offense.

All consent theories are thus committed to the idea of equality as a matter of principle. In theory the large shareholder, like the small one, has the rights prescribed by the rules of the company and no more. He gets no special privilege. A doubtful point, and one which the abstract theory cannot settle, is whether the influence which an individual is permitted by the rules to exercise ought to depend on his importance to the undertaking or on the importance of the undertaking to him. In other words, should political influence be proportionate to a man's "stake in the State," that is, to his property, or to his contribution to its success, that is, to his ability and zeal as a citizen? Whichever answer is given, the principle of equality is preserved. The question is simply, What is the characteristic which must be equally possessed by those who are to have an equal say in the operation of the State? If the answer is just "Humanity" or "being a human being," we get equal votes. If it is "Property" or "Ability," then the administrative arrangements are different. But provided the principle of equality is maintained, the requirements of the general definition are fulfilled. No man, however, will agree to a contract whose terms he recognizes as being unfair to himself.

There is some obscurity as to the aim of the State on this view. Obviously it is meant to promote some interest or other. If it were not, nobody would invent it or be a member of it. On no mechanical view is there any common interest of the community which can be promoted by it, and therefore it must be held, in so far as it is genuinely a voluntary association based on contract, to aim at promoting the several interests of its members. These can be combined if compromises are accepted, and we can thereby reach a kind of lowest common denominator which may be called the joint interest of all concerned. But this is the point at which agreement ceases. Except on the basis of a general view about morals, it is quite impossible to say which of all the possible and conflicting human interests the State is devised by its inventors to promote, and even when, as in the case of the American Constitution, an attempt is made by the authors to specify what is intended, the result is bound to be vague and controversial. Such terms as "liberty" and "the pursuit of happiness" give very little information about practical matters until they are themselves defined. And if anything is obvious, it is that no definition of them will win general, let alone universal, approval. Anyone who doubts this should attempt to get an agreed assessment among any body of people of the relative importance of alcohol, jazz, opera and religious experience as ingredients in happiness.

CONCLUSION

Regarded simply as theories, both the organic hypothesis and the force hypothesis have much to recommend them. They are simple, tidy and comprehensive. There are no loose ends about them, and there are very few political problems which cannot be answered in terms of them merely by reference to the accepted definitions. One may, perhaps, reasonably doubt whether human relations, which at least look extremely complicated, can really be sorted out in this comfortable and straightforward way, but it must be admitted that, on the purely theoretical level, these hypotheses achieve without difficulty a very high degree of consistency. In both cases, however, this is gained at the cost of the individual. On the organic view, he is entirely subordinated to the State and can claim no rights other than those which the State, as a superior being, is prepared to concede him. His position, on a force theory, especially as developed by Marx, looks rather better, since the State has no rights against him. The difference, however, is apparent rather than real. For unless he happens to belong to the ruling class, he has no choice except that between perpetual exploitation and revolution. He may also note that, unless the ruling class is quite exceptionally incompetent (as it was in Russia before 1917), his chances of successful revolution are negligible. The State, by definition, has a monopoly, not merely of armed force, but also of all the machinery of organized publicity and propaganda. The individual may have a lot of justice on his side, but the State has a lot of guns. Indeed all that Marxism can promise is that, in the long run, a revolutionary situation will necessarily arise in any capitalist State, and it will then be possible for the workers (if they are well organized and led, but not otherwise) to seize power and reverse the position. They will then set up a State which will exploit for their benefit the previous exploiters. That is all very well, but naturally there is nothing in the theory to say how long the run is going to be. And, as Lord Keynes has pertinently remarked, in the long run we are all dead. In fact, neither the organic nor the Marxist theory can really be called a cheerful one from the individual's point of view, and, in spite of their theoretical opposition to one another, the distinction between them in practice may not be considerable. A man may prefer Marxism on the ground that, if the State is going to coerce him without restriction, he would prefer this process to be carried out by the exercise of naked force rather than as the alleged performance of a moral duty. But, apart from this, there would seem to be very little in it.

The consent theory, on the other hand, while it claims to protect to the full the rights of the individual conscience, gets into difficulties as soon as it attempts to reconcile these rights with the minimum claim of the State to govern. For, if the State is simply a man-made product, what can be meant by saying that I owe it a duty or that I ought to obey its laws? The answer, we are told, is that my relation to it is contractual and that I ought to keep my contracts. This raises two awkward problems. In the first place, we must ask whether "contractual" is here used in a literal or in a metaphorical sense. Literally, I have not made any contract with or promise to the State at all. But it may be held that there is at least a close resemblance between my relationship to the State and my relationship to other institutions which are admittedly contractual. This may be true, though a little examination suggests that the differences here are no less important than the resemblance. For, even if we overlook the fact that I never join the State in the sense in which I join a club, it is perfectly clear that I cannot get out of it and join another one by a simple voluntary act. Furthermore, while it is true that if I break the club rules the committee can impose minor penalties on me and, if I go on doing so, they can expel me, they cannot hang or imprison me. This seems quite an important difference, though theoretically it may be irrelevant.

But, if these points are ignored or explained, our second main problem still remains. It is that the consent theory is not self-contained. For let it be granted that I have somehow promised to obey the State, I can nevertheless ask, ought I always to keep that promise, and, if not, in what circumstances does it cease to be binding? Within the limits of political theory, this question cannot be answered. If I say, as some would do, I ought always to keep this promise, whatever the claims with which it may conflict, then surely the claim of the consent theory to uphold the individual's private conscience is abandoned. If, on the contrary, the claim of conscience is unchallenged, it may be impossible for the State to govern. But whether we accept either of these alternatives or effect some sort of compromise between them, it is apparent that we are here dealing with a problem in moral philosophy. Loyalty to the State thus no longer stands on its own feet. It has to rest on some other basis of obligation. This necessity is generally admitted either explicitly or tacitly by democratic theorists, and too much need not be made of it, but unquestionably it adds a complication to which the other hypotheses are not subject.

Democratic theory, however, is by no means out of the wood, even if its doctrine of consent based on a moral obligation to keep promises is granted. For it is evident that, in a State of any size, unanimous decisions as to what laws are to be enforced are unobtainable, and this raises the problem which has always been seen as inevitable, namely that of the position of minorities within the State. If is difficult to hold either that these have no rights against majority decisions or that they have complete rights to disavow such decisions and to organize disobedience to laws of which they disapprove. Here again, no satisfactory theoretical solution can be offered.

The organic State claims a right to "force people to be free," if necessary by sending them to concentration camps. But no consent theory can possibly accept this doctrine. It must be argued that, while my promise to obey the State is binding, it is also conditional, and the condition is that the State should not require me to act in a manner which my conscience forbids. It is as imperative for democratic theory to admit the rights of minorities as it is for organic theory to deny them. But, when they are admitted, the right of the State to suppress what is now a legalized revolt against its authority looks rather dubious.

Finally, there is the problem of the relation of the State to other forms of community, whether wider or narrower than itself. To a great extent, the latter is already covered by the previous discussion. On any consent theory the claim of the State to interfere with such bodies as Churches or Trade Unions is exceedingly precarious. Its force may be superior to theirs, but its claim to the loyalty of its members is not. Indeed from this point of view, all other communities have a distinct advantage over the State, since they are voluntary, at least in theory, and can point to a definite act of consent made by their members on joining. The moral position of the State is weakened by its involuntary character. Nor is the theoretical position of democracy much better in relation to the League of Nations or any other association wider in extent than itself. On the only moral theory which will justify its controlling of its own members, it cannot deny that the decision of a majority in the end ought to carry the day. It is based on a doctrine of the natural rights of man and cannot deny them without sawing off the branch on which it is sitting. To admit these rights without qualification, however, appears to reduce the State to an absurdity. Its internal sovereignty has already been rendered limited and doubtful by the necessary admission of the rights of individuals and groups within it to dispute

its authority; and in its international dealings it is now sub-
jected to the overriding condition that majority rights ought
not to be violated. It certainly looks as if the hopeful start of
democratic theory leads, in the end, either to complete theoretical bankruptcy or to the adoption of a Marxist view in
which force, not consent, is accepted as the basis of the State.

The truth is that, if we begin by defining the State as a
voluntary association of independently real persons, each of
whom retains his right of private judgment unrestricted except for any limitations which he may choose to impose on
himself, the conclusions we can get from our definition are so
vague and hedged about with qualifications as to amount to
practically nothing. For in the end, all questions have to be
referred back to the moral standards of the individual, and
it has to be admitted that the answers to political questions
have to be looked for outside political theory. Whether the
answers lie in morals, or, as many would say, in religion, makes
little difference, since, on either view, politics is not an independent study but a branch of some other investigation.

All this is rather discouraging; but there is worse to come.
For, as soon as the three views are considered with any care,
it is perfectly clear that their main principles are completely
incompatible with one another. We cannot, without con-
tradicting ourselves, combine the organic theory of the State
as an object of patriotic loyalty either with the Marxist theory
of it as a mere means of exercising force or with democratic
claims to the rights of the individual. As they stand, these views
cannot be reconciled. If one is substantiated, the others are
false, and that is an end of it.

So much for the theories.

It is at this point, however, that we have to remember not
merely their consequences, but also their limitations. They
are theories only, and it remains to be seen whether any of
them can establish a claim to explain reality except in a very

partial and abstract way. Theories are often dangerous to entertain unless their credentials are very carefully examined, and the welcome which has been so generously extended to political ideologies has already proved extremely costly. It would be equally unwise, even if it were possible, to throw them all out without further inquiry. For, even if none of them is right, the fact remains that all of them have been more or less consistently held by many people who, in general, have known fairly well what they were talking about. Such views may well be imperfect or even wrong, as many other hypotheses about the world have proved to be. But they are not likely to be just ridiculous.

CHAPTER 3

Political Philosophers

*If anyone thinks there are such innate ideas or propositions, which by their clearness and usefulness are distinguishable from all that is adventitious in the mind and acquired, it will not be a hard thing for him to tell us which they are.—*LOCKE.

BEFORE WE can regard any theory as satisfactory, we must make sure that it fulfils two conditions. In the first place, it must not be self-contradictory, and in the second, it must be applicable to the facts which it claims to explain. This is a very rough and inadequate statement, but anything like a complete account would require a more elaborate inquiry into philosophical and scientific method generally than would be in place here. It is worth pointing out, however, that self-contradiction is not always blatant. If it were, it would be much simpler to detect and avoid than in fact it is. Thus, "Suppose that a triangle has four sides" is evidently a meaningless form of words; but "Suppose that the diagonal of a square is commensurate with its sides" is not. In the former instance it is necessary only to substitute "three-sided figure . . ." for "triangle" in order to recognize that this is a senseless supposition; the substitution required in the latter is considerably more complicated.

There is no case for maintaining that any of the three political theories outlined in Chapter 2 break down in this way. It is possible to state them carelessly, and consequently to become involved in contradiction by accident: and this tends to happen when an attempt is made incautiously to combine pieces of all of them in a single doctrine. But it is not at all necessary to do this. Hence it is at first sight rather surprising to find that those writers who are generally regarded as the leading theorists in the subject are by no means incapable of putting forward, as parts of their views, statements which, when carefully examined, do involve inconsistencies and even contradictions. None of them, with the possible exception of Hegel, is completely faithful to the political theory which it is his primary purpose to expound. This does not occur accidentally or as a result of mere carelessness on the author's part. To understand it, we must attend to the second essential of a satisfactory theory, namely, capacity to fit the facts. In a subject like politics where the facts are especially difficult to determine, any theory, if ruthlessly applied, can make a good attempt at doing this. But the writers whose theories we shall consider in this chapter were on the whole not disposed to adopt this method. All of them had in mind a definite type of State and knew perfectly well the relations between rulers and ruled which held good in it. Taking this as their starting point, they formulated what they took to be the essential element in that relationship and thus developed their ideas of the relation between *the* State and *the* individual. Normally, however, they did not accept the full implications of their own theories when these conflicted sharply with well-established and strongly held beliefs. Now it is the plain truth that in actual States greater importance has always, or nearly always, been attached to the dictates of the individual conscience and to the sanctity of law than a consistent organic theory can countenance, and also that actual States have normally expected and received a greater measure of loyalty than a purely mechanical theory would appear to justify. Serious writers have generally accepted these facts (though attempts have sometimes been made to explain them away in the interests of the theories) and have accommodated them by hedging a good deal about their definitions. It has seemed preferable to them to accept some untidiness in doctrine (though I doubt whether any of them except Locke would have admitted this) rather than to admit an open breach or an unplausible reconciliation between theory and fact. This is quite sensible, since none but the most tiresome doctrinaires adhere to their hypotheses at all costs.

But the matter cannot be settled quite as easily as this. For, even if we accept the contention that the organic and mechanical theories are working hypotheses about the relation of States to individuals, and not, as writers on political theory have frequently assumed, true statements about the nature of things, it still seems rather odd that, after more than two thousand years of concentrated thought, we should be quite uncertain which of them works and which ought to be discarded as inappropriate to the facts.

It would indeed be odd, if all States were, as has often been assumed without question, identical in principle. It is surely more reasonable to suppose that leading thinkers have disagreed with one another mainly because this is not the case. If the States which they have dealt with have not been identical but radically different, it is no longer surprising that the hypothesis which fits one of them is inappropriate to another. It is exactly what we should expect to happen.

We may put the matter thus: Perhaps one of the three main theories is entirely right and the others are entirely wrong. That is to say, the facts, when carefully examined, may really accept the one and reject the others. This would imply that some alleged facts are not facts at all but illusions, and that those writers who have allowed such illusions to cause inconsistency in their theories have, in spite of their reputation as thinkers of the first rank, been careless or gullible. This is rather hard to swallow. The rights of the State (as actually recognized by the Germans) and the rights of the individual (as actually recognized by the English) are, at any rate to all appearances, very solid facts indeed. Still we cannot be too dogmatic about this. It is wise to remember that beliefs in other "facts," such as ghosts and magic generally, were also regarded as exceedingly firmly based in their day. But in the end, they proved ill grounded and have been mostly abandoned. If, however, the facts remain, as far as our present knowledge will take us, unshaken, we have no alternative but to admit that none of the conflicting hypotheses can finally make good its claim against the others; and we might further admit that the great theorists have been at odds with one another, not because any of them were careless or prejudiced, but because they were studying genuinely different things. Waxworks look pretty much like living people, but one would not expect agreement on human anatomy from two students, one of whom had worked in a hospital and the other at Madame Tussaud's. Nor, on the other hand, could it be said that their findings were completely unrelated to one another.

The writings of standard authors on political theory are, therefore, not simply a matter of historical interest. Their disagreements are not merely fortuitous. They are themselves important evidence as to the nature of the subject matter which is to be studied. And that subject matter is so elusive that no evidence about it can safely be neglected.

Two further points must be mentioned before we go on to consider particular authors. In the first place, no analysis of a political theorist's work can take us very far unless it is read in the light of a general acquaintance with the time at which he lived and the type of community which was most prominently before his eyes as he wrote. Aristotle was dealing with the only type of State of which he had any expert knowledge, namely, the Greek City-State of the fourth century B.C.;

Rousseau was largely restricted to the absolutist monarchy of France and the Calvinist State of Geneva in the early eighteenth century, and so on. Hence it is impossible to understand completely the position of any political theorist without a thorough study of the history and character of the political institutions which were his prime concern and from which his facts were derived. I have not attempted to provide material for such a study, and what is said here is certainly quite inadequate to make the aim and outlook of the writers discussed intelligible to anyone who does not know their works. My second point is that I am not trying to give a full and balanced summary of the theory of each of the authors named. My purpose is to show the issues on which the impact of observed or accepted facts led them to modify their main theory and so to achieve credibility at the expense of consistency. This means that what is offered is more like a caricature than a portrait of the writer's work. It presents, not the whole man, but a special characteristic of him. It is a deliberate oversimplification, and to that extent a falsification of the original, but this is a perfectly legitimate and useful undertaking, provided we recognize what it is that we are doing. For instance, the late Mr. Neville Chamberlain was honestly devoted to the cause of maintaining peace; his umbrella, in contrast with the warlike panoply of the dictators, was quite a good symbol of this tendency. And so the Chamberlain-with-umbrella cartoons of the Munich era, though rather unkind, were not essential falsifications of his character. But they became disastrously misleading when taken to represent the whole truth and to imply (as the dictators and their advisers thought they did) that Mr. Chamberlain would in no circumstances do anything not calculated to appease the Axis Powers. Similarly it is quite reasonable to concentrate for a particular purpose on the inconsistencies of political theorists. This, too, may lead to false conclusions if it is taken uncritically to suggest that these inconsistencies were their only or their most important contributions to political philosophy. They were not always, or even usually, in a state of confusion and self-contradiction.

This seems obvious, but it deserves a little emphasis. It is too easy to argue that, since no writer has been quite free from inconsistency, all ideologies are equally futile and all can equally be ignored with a clear conscience by the practical man. The result of this attitude is usually the unconscious and enthusiastic acceptance of the most nonsensical and self-contradictory of all the political theories available in the contemporary market.

Finally, it may be argued that, although differences between States may well be fundamental, it is still not necessary to plunge into past theories with all their added complications of historical research in order to find out about them. There are, as I shall myself try to show in Chapter 4, good specimens of the main types available for study in the contemporary world, and we should therefore surely do better to stick to these and to the works of modern authors who theorize about them. This is a reasonable suggestion, but I do not think that it can be realized in practice. The trouble is that the contemporary State crowds in upon us so much and is so complex in its structure and operations that it is extremely difficult to analyze it with complete confidence. Not that we should abstain from attempting to do so. To admit that such an undertaking is hopeless or even unprofitable would make nonsense of political theory. But we shall be better equipped to tackle this problem if we start on the simpler and more abstract puzzles set by the established authors. For, however the matter may have appeared to them, the States they were contemplating appear to us to be relatively simple and easy to classify.

This may well be a delusion, but, if so, it is quite a useful one. There is a further merit. For the States of today embody or at least are supposed to embody the political theories of the past. The United States and British Constitutions both derive, though, as will appear later, in somewhat different ways, from Locke's *Second Treatise on Civil Government;* the third Reich was avowedly a Hegelian State; and the U.S.S.R. is officially a Marxist or Marxist-Leninist regime. It is, therefore, reasonable to expect that some knowledge of these doctrines and, in particular, of their inconsistencies will throw quite a lot of light on the actual operation of the States which claim to exemplify them in the real world.

THE STATE AS AN ORGANISM

ARISTOTLE: 384–322 B.C.

Aristotle inherited from Plato, his teacher, a firm belief that the City-State, as realized by the Greeks, was genuinely organic in character. This agreement did not commit him to approval in detail of Plato's ideal community. He was, indeed, extremely critical of it. But the nerve of this criticism is that the Platonic theory is inadequate because it does not sufficiently appreciate the implications of a thoroughgoing organic view.

The Platonic ideal was that of a State in which the governing class (including the army) was rigidly separated from the mass of the citizens by upbringing, occupation, and social barriers. Within this governing class solidarity was to be ensured by the abolition of what Plato considered the fundamental grounds of human discord, namely, private property and the family. This policy, which has sometimes been confused with that of modern Communism, was rejected by Aristotle on the ground that an organism is essentially a union of unlike and not of identical elements. A class of identical citizens would either not be an organism at all, or would be a very low-grade and formless type of being. Mere multiplication of parts produces a cancer—not a healthy growth. Aristotle's ideal was that of the maximum of differentiation which could be achieved within a single unified whole. But this differentiation was none the less, as we shall see, to be completely determined and dominated by the whole. "The State is by nature clearly prior to the family and to the individual, since the whole is of necessity prior to the parts." [1]

It is this theme which the *Politics* elaborates in detail, and in spite of the fact that Aristotle was concerned only with the highly specialized instances of human community provided by the Greek City-State, his conclusions are still of value both in themselves and because of the light they throw on the work of later theorists. This second point is of importance and deserves some explanation. Throughout the Middle Ages the works of Aristotle, including the *Politics,* were accepted by the Christian Church as practically inspired. Aristotle was not just a philosopher: he was the Philosopher; he was regarded as having expounded once and for all the whole truth about reality in so far as this could be achieved by human reason without the special light given by the Christian revelation. It was an important part of the achievement of the Reformation to challenge this view, and consequently advanced writers in the seventeenth century found themselves committed to a professional opposition to anything which Aristotle had ever written. As Hobbes put it, "I believe that scarce anything can be more absurdly said in natural Philosophy, than that which is now called Aristotle's *Metaphysiques:* nor more repugnant to Government, than much of what he hath said in his *Politiques;* nor more ignorantly, than a great part of his *Ethiques.*" But two thousand years of Aristotelian supremacy could not be easily disposed of as this and many similar denunciations would suggest. A view which had for so long been the agreed starting point for all serious inquiry could be criticized,

---

[1] *Politics,* 1253, a. trans. Jowett.
[2] HOBBES, *Leviathan,* p. 522, Clarendon Press, 1909.

but it could not possibly be ignored. Even criticism could proceed only by borrowing the despised logic and metaphysics which Aristotle himself had invented, since, for the time being at least, no serious alternatives were available. Hence writers on political theory are often most Aristotelian when they are least aware of it. The whole structure of thought and language in Western Europe has produced and still produces a powerful force in his favor.

The aim of the *Politics,* like that of the *Ethics,* was primarily practical. Aristotle was not content to formulate an ideal and to admit, as Plato had done, that perhaps, after all, it was too perfect for human beings to realize and must therefore remain as an exhibit in Heaven to be contemplated only by the true philosopher. Aristotle, too, had his ideal; but he set his research department to work at the analysis of the existing constitutions of 158 actual City-States. This detailed study of comparative political institutions leads to an interesting result. Aristotle remains convinced that all his specimens are of the same kind: they are all instances of a single type of organism. But their differences are none the less profound, and some account has to be given of them. There are monarchies, tyrannies, democracies, and so on. Some of them are successes, in the sense that they are stable and relatively long-lived. Others are failures, destroyed either by external aggression or, more frequently, by internal revolution. Now Aristotle saw clearly, as Plato had failed to do, that different collections of human beings may well be suited by different types of political organization. It is not self-evident nor even probable that the best results will be obtained by clamping a ready-made constitution on every City-State, irrespective of its historical, economic and cultural conditions. But, as soon as this is accepted, the political philosopher becomes not merely a theorist but, to use an analogy of which Aristotle was extremely fond, a doctor. He must keep the ideal of a perfectly healthy State in mind; but he must also realize that something less than perfect health is all that most of his patients can expect. His primary job is to keep them alive, and to do this he must cure their obvious maladies. Hence Aristotle aims at keeping his organisms going, however diseased and defective they may be when compared with the ideal State; and therefore we find that his object is not to promote revolution, but rather to teach even tyrants to be efficient tyrants.

At first sight this seems rather odd. It is, however, a perfectly natural development of the organic hypothesis, provided that one important qualification is accepted. The philosopher, as Aristotle clearly recognizes, must himself be able to stand outside the State and to take a dispassionate and critical view of it. It is not clear that this is a legitimate requirement, though the analogy of the doctor suggests that it may be. At any rate the notion of a semidivine lawgiver, like Lycurgus at Sparta, was one so familiar to Greek thought that its acceptance presented no immediate difficulty. But the problem of fitting the organic philosopher into his own picture is one which presents a major theoretical problem to be faced sooner or later. Aristotle, though he recognized its existence, was not seriously troubled by it. He was content to consider democratic States (in the very limited form in which Greek life provided them) and States based on force simply as more or less imperfect forms of the organic State. For him, the difference was merely institutional or administrative, not moral in character. It was the great merit of political thinkers from Hobbes to Marx that they questioned and to a great extent overthrew this Aristotelian assumption.

The sections of Aristotle's *Politics* which constitute a kind of "Political What's What" for the City-State of the fourth century B.C. still have considerable interest. But, in spite of their shrewdness, they have inevitably dated and are largely unintelligible without the help of an exhaustive knowledge of Greek civilization. The general theory, on the other hand, with which we are here concerned, remains one of the best statements of the organic view and its implications. It involves four main contentions, each of which requires explanation.

1. *The Idea of Nature*

Nature is defined as meaning both what a thing (or a person) actually is, and what it is capable of becoming, or what it ought to be.[3] I shall call these "nature A" and "nature B." If we are to understand Aristotle at all, we must realize that for him the existence of the distinction involved neither confusion nor ambiguity but was the core of his whole philosophy and, in particular, of his political theory. The point which he requires to establish is familiar enough. It has been well put, I think by Mr. G. K. Chesterton, in the following way: If a man is about to do something disgraceful, it is reasonable to say to him "be a man." By this, we do not mean "Do anything you would like to do," but rather "Do what you ought to do." On the other hand, if a crocodile is about to eat a missionary, it is of no use appealing to it in similar terms and exhorting it to be a crocodile. It *is* being a crocodile and can realize itself no other way. It would be a bad crocodile if it behaved differently. Human beings may at least be expected to have slightly different standards from those of crocodiles. It is therefore intelligible to hold that their activity in torturing one another in concentration camps is contrary to their nature B. This seems straightforward enough when it is stated, but it must be admitted that the usage sometimes leads to considerable obscurity. It is natural A to break a promise when keeping it is likely to be unpleasant or expensive, for we know

---

[3] "Nature," in its strict and primary sense, is to Aristotle the essence of things which have in themselves as such a source or impulse of change and cessation from change; and the "nature," in the strict sense, of these natural things is the form which their changing actualizes.

MURE, *Aristotle*, p. 71.

that people often do break promises in these circumstances. But it is also natural B to keep promises even when it does not pay to do so. In other words it is a worthy or decent thing to do. This distinction is often forgotten, and much confusion results. We can usually escape trouble by asking whether the opposite of "natural" in a particular context is "wicked" or "artificial" or merely "unusual." Aristotle, however, is perfectly justified in ignoring this ambiguity since he wishes to emphasize that in his view human beings and indeed creation as a whole inevitably attempt to rise from nature A to nature B; and it is because the organic State alone makes this development possible for men that it can justly be called prior to the individual.

2. *The State Is Prior to the Individual*

["The proof that the State is a creation of nature and prior to the individual is that the individual, when isolated, is not self-sufficing; and therefore he is like a part in relation to the whole."]⁴ Man's nature A is not to be self-sufficient, but helpless and incomplete. "He may be compared to an unguarded piece in the game of draughts." [5] The State makes good this deficiency, and that is why man is by nature B a political animal. "For what each thing is when fully developed, we call its nature, whether we are talking of a man, a horse, or a family." [6] In other words, the State is a precondition of man's achieving his rational end and is therefore logically prior to him. As it stands, this is simply a more careful statement of the general organic hypothesis that Society is superior to and more real than the individuals who compose it. But it is to be noted that, for Aristotle, this is strictly a matter of definition; there is no empirical evidence for saying either that the whole

---

4 *Politics*, 1253, a.
5 *Politics*, loc. cit.
6 *Politics*, 1252, b.

is necessarily superior to the part or that increase in self-sufficiency is natural B for man. Indeed, the whole doctrine of a dual "nature" rests only on a common and accepted usage which lends it plausibility and suggests that there are facts which correspond to it. Nobody is likely to dispute that some forms of association, such as the family and the herd, are natural A. They are not unusual. But it is equally clear that Aristotle is going well beyond the obvious facts in assuming that all or any forms of association are natural B, or good.

3. *Slavery*

It follows from what has been said above that, if the "peculiar institution" of slavery had not already existed in Greek civilization, Aristotle would have been compelled either to invent it or to admit that his political theory, though valid in a rational world, had no relevance to the actual condition of men in this life. The State is a natural organism, its justification lies in its capacity to fulfil the nature B of *all* the human beings, that is, of any creature which is neither a beast nor a god.[7] This would be simply impossible if all men were equally capable of development up to the highest level. For in the nature of the case, they cannot all be rulers.[8] It is an evasion of the issue to suggest that in a democracy all may rule in turn. Unless the proportion of the total inhabitants who are qualified as citizens is small in relation to the whole, this is not a practical proposition. If the theory is to work, it is essential that there should be human beings whose nature B is realized not by ruling but by being ruled. Now to be so constituted as never to give but always to carry out instructions, is to be not an agent but an instrument. And an instrument is a means by which an agent effects his purposes. Thus "he who is by nature not his own but another's, and yet a man, is by nature

---

[7] *Politics*, 1253, a.
[8] *Cf.* W. S. GILBERT, *The Gondoliers.*

a slave." [9] I can see no alternative to this conclusion on a consistent organic theory, and Aristotle was well placed in that he was in a position to formulate it without causing scandal or giving offense. Many of his successors have been less happily situated. The only point at which he may reasonably be held to have overstated the case is his insistence on the actual ownership of one man by another. This is really unnecessary. Provided one section of the community exercises complete control, and provided this control is exercised not in virtue of superior force or fraud (as Marx thought it was) but in virtue of an inborn and insuperable limitation in the capacity of the majority to function as free agents, Aristotle's conclusion is well founded. Physical proprietorship is only a technicality. "He who can be and therefore is another's, and he who participates in reason enough to apprehend, but not to have, reason, is a slave by nature." [10]

This disposes of the problem of slavery on the theoretical level. If the organic State is to work, there must be slaves, either *de jure* or *de facto*. As the State is natural A, it must further be assumed that natural B slaves exist. The practical problem for the legislator is to order his particular State in such a way that the menial jobs are done by the servile people, so that every individual is actually given an opportunity to realize his nature B. A State which fails to achieve this is unnatural, that is, diseased, and it is for the politician to restore it to health. This can normally be achieved by competent administration, and, except in extreme cases, Aristotle holds that this rather than a change in the law is the proper method to adopt. Generally speaking, his considered view is that laws are sacred and that any change in an existing constitution, however theoretically defective that constitution may be, is probably a mistake. "Sometimes and in certain cases laws may

[9] *Politics,* 1254, a.
[10] *Politics,* 1254, b.

be changed; but . . . great caution would seem to be required. For the habit of lightly changing laws is an evil, and, when the advantage is small, some errors, both of lawgivers and rulers, had better be left; the citizen will not gain so much by the change as he will lose by the habit of disobedience. . . . For the law has no power to command obedience except that of habit, which can only be given by time, so that readiness to change from old to new laws enfeebles the power of the law." [11] This passage and the conviction which it expresses lead naturally to some consideration of Aristotle's fourth fundamental doctrine.

4. *The Rule of Law*

A completely consistent organic theory is bound to maintain that laws are simply rules which the State, as an individual, adopts for the promotion of its own interest. They can no more bind or constrain it than rules of prudence, voluntarily adopted, can bind the individual man. I may, on grounds of hygiene or economy, make it a rule never to smoke before 6 p.m. But if I choose to break this rule on occasion or to abandon it altogether, I have a perfect right to do so. Indeed, as soon as I am convinced that the argument in favor of it no longer holds or that it is reversed, I ought to revise the rule.

In the same way the State, just because of its nature, can make laws for its members, but for itself they are no more than rules whose validity is limited to their capacity to promote the real or seeming interest of the whole body.

This was not Aristotle's conclusion. His State, though natural, organic and superior to the individual, should itself be subject to a law which it does not make but finds, namely the rule of reason. "He who bids the law rule, may be deemed to bid God and reason alone rule, but he who bids man rule adds an element of the beast; for desire is a wild beast, and passion

[11] *Politics*, 1269, a.

perverts the minds of rulers, even when they are the best of men. The law is reason unaffected by desire." [12] Aristotle, in fact, wants his State to be controlled by law, that is, to be prevented by its constitution from behaving in an arbitrary way toward its own members. Rousseau later cherished the same idea, and it will be considered in connection with his doctrine of the General Will. For the moment, it is sufficient to observe that it constitutes a serious inconsistency in Aristotle's main theory and the consequences of it emerge at intervals throughout the *Politics*. He can never really escape from the difficulty that, if there is a law discoverable by reason and binding *on* States, the philosopher or lawgiver who knows this law is really superior to and cannot logically be bound by the (imperfect) laws of the State in which he happens to be. "The whole is naturally superior to the part, and he who has this preeminence is in the relation of a whole to a part." [13] The good man, in fact, is not identical with the good citizen after all: yet it is necessary to the organic hypothesis that he should be. But: "Legislation is necessarily concerned only with those who are equal in birth and power; for men of preeminent virtue there is no law—they are themselves a law. Any one would be ridiculous who attempted to make laws for them." [14]

Aristotelian organic theory is thus subject to two serious qualifications. The first is that, although the State is by definition superior to the individual, Aristotle will not in practice entrust it with full legislative authority. The second, that, although slavery as an implication of the organism is accepted, the identification of the good man with the good citizen is incomplete. The philosopher slips out of the State and remains a law unto himself.

[12] *Politics*, 1287, a.
[13] *Politics*, 1288, a.
[14] *Politics*, 1284.

ROUSSEAU: 1712–1788

Aristotle and Rousseau appear to be poles apart. There seems little or nothing in common between the morning star of the French Revolution who inspired the principles of 1789 and the stanch conservative who dominated the thought of the ancient and medieval world. Nor is it easy to think that Aristotle would have had much use for Rousseau's sentimental yearning to return to a primitive state of nature and to shake off the conventions without which political life becomes an impossibility. In spite of this, the difference between the two writers, though important, is on the surface. For the central doctrine which Aristotle expressed in his conception of nature is reformulated without important modification in Rousseau's theory of the General Will.

The General Will is what is willed by a community as a whole. It is a common will for a common interest, and, as such, it is different from and may be opposed to the particular interests of individuals. When this opposition arises, the individual has an obligation to obey the General Will, since it and not the inclination to promote his own personal well-being is strictly his own real will. The resemblance between this notion and Aristotle's two senses of "nature" is too clear to need further emphasis; and Rousseau himself was perfectly aware of the organic implications of his position, though he does not seem to have noticed its Aristotelian associations. His own unambiguous statement of the position is at the beginning of his *Discourse on Political Economy:* "The body politic, taken individually, may be considered as an organized, living body, resembling that of man. . . . The life of both bodies is the self common to the whole, the reciprocal sensibility and internal correspondence of all the parts. . . . The body politic, therefore, is also a moral being possessed of a will; and this General Will, which tends always to the preservation and welfare of the whole and of every part, and is the source of laws, constitutes for all the members of the State, in their relations to one another, and to it, the rule of what is just or unjust.[15] . . . But each individual, as a man, may have a particular will contrary or dissimilar to the general will which he has as a citizen. His particular interest may speak to him quite differently from the common interest; his absolute and naturally independent existence may make him look on what he owes to the common cause, as a gratuitous contribution. . . ." [16]

Having admitted this conflict as a fact, Rousseau deals with it very summarily. The General Will is, by his definition, always right. It is the common will of the people. Hence it follows that "whoever refuses to obey the General Will shall be compelled to do so by the whole body. This means nothing less than that he will be forced to be free; for this is the condition which, by giving each citizen to his country, secures him against all *personal* dependence." [17]

This quotation not merely states clearly the strange idea that the General Will confers freedom on individuals by constraining them: it explains the grounds on which Rousseau maintained it. The General Will is my own real will. Hence, in obeying it, I realize my own real nature,[18] and am truly free, even though this entails my consenting to my own execution. The important point to notice is that what I consent to is the operation of a general law. There is nothing personal about it, and that is why it should cause me no resentment. This sounds peculiar, but is not by any means unintelligible. Rousseau, like Aristotle, disapproved of arbitrary rule. The laws of Geneva, under which he was brought up and which

[15] Everyman Edition, ROUSSEAU's *Social Contract* and *Discourses*. Translated by G. D. H. Cole, p. 253.
[16] *Social Contract*, Chap. VII, *ibid.*, p. 18.
[17] *Ibid.* My italics.
[18] Aristotle's "nature B."

he considered wholly admirable, were strict, but they were
predictable. Their operation was in accordance with reason
and not with the fancy or whim of an individual. They were
not arbitrary or tyrannical. Rousseau's ideal was that life in
society should approximate as closely as possible to what he
conceived to be a "natural" condition of existence under
knowable laws of nature. The laws of the State should, in
theory, be fixed and unalterable like the law of gravitation.
If they are this, they may be held to enlarge and not to restrict
freedom, since they can be taken into account and turned to
advantage as gravitation can be, in the planning of a rational
life. Dependence on things is not servitude; dependence on
human beings is. The thought which this doctrine expressed
was similar to, if not identical with, that of Aristotle in his
attachment to the rule of law since, for Aristotle too, as we
have seen, law was "reason unaffected by desire." Rousseau,
however, had been far more thoroughgoing and consistent
than Aristotle in his attribution of supreme legislative power
to the General Will, that is, to the decisions of the sovereign
body of the entire community. "If the State is a moral person
whose life is in the union of its members, and if the most important of its cares is the care for its own preservation, it must
have a universal and compelling force, in order to move and
dispose each part as may be most advantageous to the whole.
As nature gives each man absolute power over all his members also . . ." [19] It is, therefore, not surprising to find that
it cannot be in any way restricted by its own laws. The General
Will remains always sovereign. Hence the right of the State
to modify its own constitution must remain unquestioned.
"The voice of the people is, in fact, the voice of God." [20]

Now this is all very well and is strictly in accordance with

---

[19] *Social Contract*, Chap. IV, *op. cit.*, p. 27.
[20] *Ibid.*, p. 254.

the organic hypothesis. Sooner or later, however, the problem which Aristotle shelved by the device of the semidivine legislator has to be faced. Whether we like it or not, we have to admit that any actual legislating body is liable to enact laws which do not contribute to the general well-being of the people. The question is, When I am convinced that this has happened, what ought I to do about it? At first sight there are only two alternatives, and both of them are exceedingly unpalatable:

1. I may argue that on this occasion I am right and the people are wrong. But if this is admitted by the State, it is clear that I should be unjustly punished for disobedience to the law and the whole edifice of the General Will would collapse immediately.

2. The right of the individual to exercise his private judgment must be firmly denied and the identity of the good man with the good citizen must be strenuously maintained. This means that any law enacted by the State ought to be obeyed, even if the reason of the individual condemns it as disastrous or wicked.

Rousseau was not prepared to accept either of these doctrines. The first is inconsistent with any organic theory, and is ruled out. Hence something has to be done to square the second with the Protestant conscience. There is nothing for it but to argue that the General Will, because it is always right, will never encroach on the individual's freedom beyond what is necessary in the public interest. Hence, if a particular legislature does so encroach, we can only assert that it is here expressing not the General Will but a particular interest, and is, therefore, not a realization of freedom but a denial of it. "The General Will is always right and tends to the public advantage; but it does not follow that the deliberations of the people are always equally correct. Our will is always for our own good, but we do not always see what that is; the people is never corrupted, but it is often deceived, and

on such occasions only does it *seem* to will what is bad." [21]
The trouble about this is that Rousseau, in making the General Will always rational and, therefore, always deserving of
obedience, at once lays himself open to the charge that, in
practice, nobody can know what the General Will on any
question is. It cannot be the unanimous decision of all the
members, since such unanimity never happens. To say that
there ought to be agreement or that there would be in a rational community gets us nowhere. I am called on to do what
the law commands, and not what I or anybody else considers
that it ought to command.

There is really nothing to be done about this. It is essential
to any organic theory that somebody should speak for the
"body politic," and whether this spokesman is a monarch, a
legislator or an assembly, he must assume infallibility, at least
until he changes his mind. Rousseau, in fact, considered the
Aristotelian compromise and rejected it in principle. He fully
admitted the importance of the inspired legislator, and it is
interesting to notice that Lycurgus and Calvin are his outstanding examples.[22] But even so, such a legislator for Rousseau is a proposer of laws and not a lawgiver. "He who draws
up the laws has, or should have, no right of legislation, and the
people cannot, even if it wishes, deprive itself of this incommu-
nicable right." [23]

Since it is agreed that a public assembly will not always vote
as the legislator conceives that it should do, we reach the astonishing conclusion: "This is what has, in all ages, compelled
the fathers of nations to have recourse to divine intervention
and credit the gods with their own wisdom, in order that the
peoples, submitting to the laws of the State as to those of nature, and recognizing the same power in the formation of the

[21] *Social Contract,* Chap. III, *op. cit.,* p. 25. My italics.
[22] *Ibid.,* p. 36.
[23] *Ibid.*

city as in that of man, might freely obey, and bear with docility the yoke of the public happiness." [24] Which was precisely the idea of Hitler's plebiscites.

It may well be asked how Rosseau, even though he was not a model of logical consistency, came to maintain this kind of view without in any way abandoning his claim to be considered the champion of the rights of man. The answer lies in the part of his doctrine which we have so far neglected. The social contract, as the name of Rousseau's most widely known work implies, is comparable in importance to the general will. The latter with all its organic implications is literally born or created as the result of a contract between individuals. The contract is an agreement of each with all whereby every individual submits himself irrevocably to the general will of society as a whole and thus for the first time comes to exist, as we have already seen, in a dual capacity. As an individual he continues to exercise a particular will for his own advantage, but as a member of society, that is, as an ingredient in the newly formed General Will, he necessarily wills the common good. "In place of the individual personality of each contracting party, this act of association creates a *moral and collective body,* composed of as many members as the assembly contains votes, and receiving *from this act* its unity, its common identity, its life and its will." [25]

There is something true and important in this view. Any sound theory must account for the acknowledged fact that we do distinguish between our public and our private wills. What I should like as an individual and what I deliberately choose as a member of an institution are frequently different and incompatible things. But although this often reiterated and rather obvious truth may be a ground for supposing that the organic theory is something more solid than a

[24] *Ibid.*
[25] *Social Contract,* Chap. VI, *op. cit.,* p. 15. My italics.

philosopher's dream, it does little or nothing to get us out of the difficulty with which Rousseau is concerned. Although my institutional will is in some sense a fact, this does not prove that it is morally superior to my private will. It is even less clear that my institutional will as a citizen is morally superior to my institutional will as a freemason or a trade unionist. To say, as Rousseau does in this connection, that "the most general will is always the most just also" [26] is to beg the question. An instance may make this clear. What is to happen, we may ask, when the State at a general meeting approves a measure like Hitler's anti-Semitic Nuremberg laws? The vast majority of the German people honestly believed that this legislation was in the interests of the people as a whole. A small minority disagreed. How, in such a case, is anybody to know whether he or his opponents represent the true General Will as distinct from a private preference or prejudice? There is no rational method of settling the question, since a majority is no more likely to be right than a minority. Hence, as before, one of two conclusions is bound to follow: *One*—I retain my right of private judgment, in which case the social contract is proved to be a sham. And if, as is probable, the majority claims to "force me to be free" in a concentration camp, I can rightly argue that this is simply a display of force on their part and that since "no man has a natural authority over his fellow, and force creates no right," [27] I am being very hardly used; or *Two*—I leave my right of private judgment behind forever when I make the contract, in which case I accept without question the majority decision. This will enable me to stay on the right side of the barbed wire, but it may well seem nonsense (and wicked nonsense) for Rousseau to pretend that, in these circumstances, I still obey myself alone and remain as free as before.

[26] *Ibid.*, p. 254.
[27] *Social Contract*, Chap. IV, *op. cit.*, p. 9.

The compromise or inconsistency whereby Rousseau attempts to make the organic theory acceptable to those who believe in the importance of the individual thus breaks down. If the General Will is supreme, the contract which is supposed to bring it into existence is superfluous: what it cannot claim in its own right, it will never get by means of a contract. All that the alleged contractual basis achieves is to ensure for Rousseau the worst of both worlds. He retains just too much private conscience to be satisfied with a genuine organic State, but not enough to claim for the individual the right to oppose majority decisions, unless he can prove, which is impossible, that he and not the majority is the true expression of the General Will for the common good. Logically considered, it is not a happy conclusion. But Rousseau's personal persecution complex was so well developed that he enjoyed feeling extremely virtuous and heavily laden with sin at the same time. His famous controversy with David Hume demonstrates this very clearly.

It should be noted here that an alternative method of escaping from the dilemma of General Will versus private judgment is theoretically possible. It might be maintained, as some English Puritans tried to do, that every individual can discover the General Will if only he tries hard enough to do so. The only conflict possible would then be between his own real or General Will (known as such) and his interested desires (called by Rousseau the "will of all"). It is logically possible for this to happen, but it requires little practical experience to discover that a hypothesis which assumes that it always happens will not get us very far. As Oliver Cromwell discovered so often, even the abnormally high-minded, after protracted prayer, usually fail to achieve an agreed view as to what ought to be done about anything which is of first-rate importance.

Hegel: 1770–1831

The philosophical system of Hegel, like that of Aristotle 2,000 years earlier, is a kind of watershed in European thought. This is not the place in which to elaborate the resemblance, but one aspect of it in particular needs to be noted if Hegel's political philosophy is to be given its due. Hegelianism is, and is intended to be, a consistent whole, and this whole is organic. No aspect of it is quite intelligible except when considered as an element in the complete system. This holds equally of the work of Aristotle. The notions of form, matter, and nature which the *Politics* takes for granted, can be only imperfectly understood without a close study of Aristotelian metaphysics. In Hegel's philosophy the problem is even more pressing because the elements of his system are more completely subordinated to his central idea than were those of Aristotle. Now it is certainly true of both writers that, however much we may disagree with them, we cannot fail to take account of what they said. Hegel dominated European thought for a century, and did so not merely by collecting adherents but by stimulating violent opposition. Opposition is always related to and colored by that which it opposes. This is itself an important Hegelian doctrine and one which it is easier to accept than to understand. What it entails is a firm belief that opposition is never blank negation. It is significant only when different and conflicting answers are given to a single question. Take the case of the State. If I assert "The State is a whole which completely includes and dominates its members," you may reply "No, it isn't that at all." But this denial has meaning only in so far as you give it some substance and assert, for instance, that the State is a device created by individuals for a special purpose.

It is Hegel's contention that this movement by negation is found in all rational development, but that it is not the whole of that development. When opposition is formulated on these lines, it is the function of reason to solve the difficulty presented, since it is inconsistent with the nature of reason that it should accept a contradiction as final. To do this is to admit that the world is not completely rational, which, to Hegel, is an intolerable suggestion. But it is not obvious that any solution is possible since the original statement and the denial of it (in Hegelian language, the thesis and the antithesis) are strictly incompatible with each other, and since each of them, however carefully it is examined, is found to express an important truth. In these circumstances reconciliation can be effected only when it is realized that neither thesis nor antithesis is complete in itself. Both fail because both are to some extent partial or abstract. They can be accepted only in so far as both of them are seen to be elements in a wider (organic) whole. This final moment is known as the synthesis, which includes within itself the thesis and the antithesis. It is not in any sense a compromise between them. Both are present completely in the result but both have nevertheless been transcended and absorbed by it.

Reverting to the instance of the State, we should have to say that it is not merely organic but superorganic. It somehow, when properly considered, includes in itself both the claim of the individual to freedom and the claim of society as a whole to his complete subordination. Both views are thus correct. What is shown to be unreal is the conflict between them. And this is precisely what Hegel does claim to show. This whole theory of development by thesis, antithesis, and synthesis, or (as Hegel frequently describes it) by assertion, negation, and negation of negation, constitutes the essence of the Hegelian dialectical method. It is not easy to understand and certainly cannot be grasped (as Marx, for instance, supposed that it could be) by considering a few simple instances of its application. All that can be done on these lines is to produce a curious and false theory of the nature of the physical universe. What is vital to Hegel's complete view is precisely what is cut out of it when it is deliberately turned upside down by dialectical materialism, namely, the fundamental assumption that the universe as a whole is rational and that there can be no problem which is ultimately insoluble. There is no other justification for the doctrine that the opposition between thesis and antithesis must give rise to a higher synthesis. If this inherent rationality is admitted as a self-evident fact, then it certainly follows that, as Hegel puts it, the real *is* the rational and the rational *is* the real: and it is on this assumption only that the Hegelian view of the universe in general and of the State in particular will bear examination.

I have given this very brief indication of the general character of Hegel's dialectic only as a warning that there is a great deal of philosophical theory behind his doctrine of the State and the summary statement of his view which is all that will be attempted here is necessarily incomplete. But since it is fatal for any study of political theory to neglect his view there is no alternative to attempting a summary of it.

The Philosophy of Right

"The problem is to find a form of association which will defend and protect with the whole common force the person and goods of each associate, and in which each, while uniting himself with all, may still obey himself alone, and remain as free as before." [28]

We have already considered the method by which Rousseau tried to deal with his own problem. But it is none the less useful to restate it, since it is from Rousseau's attempted answer and in particular from his account of the general will that

---

[28] ROUSSEAU, *Social Contract*, Chap. VI, *op. cit.*, p. 14.

Hegel's political theory originates. The least difficult approach to Hegel is through Rousseau.

The first point to notice is that, on two fundamental issues, Hegel was convinced that Rousseau had been entirely right in principle though he had failed to develop his own view properly. He was right, in the first place, in his insistence that the State did not restrict human freedom, but expanded it. He was right, too, in holding that the State did this because it expressed a common or General Will, which, when properly considered, was seen to be at the same time the real will of the citizens.

These are not the only points of agreement. Hegel also held that the basic form of human society is the family, and that the State must somehow include the whole sphere of contractual relations between citizens within itself.

There is thus no lack of common ground between Rousseau and Hegel, and it is not at first sight easy to see exactly what it is that separates them. In the simplest terms the answer is "The French Revolution." Rousseau by no means entirely accepted the implications of his own doctrine of the General Will. He continued to believe that man possessed inalienable natural rights and that it was the function of the State to defend and protect these with the whole common force. The State came into existence as the result of a social contract with this end in view. It was on this aspect of Rousseau's doctrine that the theorists of the French (and also those of the American) Revolution concentrated. Hegel disapproved very strongly of the French Revolution, and saw clearly that Rousseau's "abstract" theory of the rights of man was the philosophical basis of it. Hence he wrote: "The definition of right which I have quoted involves that way of looking at the matter, especially popular since Rousseau, according to which what is fundamental, substantive, and primary, is supposed to be the

will of a single person in his own private self-will, not the absolute or rational will. . . . This view is devoid of any specu-
lative thinking and is repudiated by the philosophic concept. And the phenomena which it has produced both in
men's heads and in the world are of a frightfulness parallel
only to the superficiality of the thoughts on which they are
based." [29]

The purpose of Hegel is to demonstrate that the State en-
sures all the legitimate claims of human freedom and at the
same time to deny to the individual all right to challenge its
authority. This he does by restating Rousseau's theory in his
own terms.

The family is the starting point. Here we find human society
in its simplest form as a primitive kind of unity. The members,
so Hegel contends (and there is some factual evidence to support him here), actually regard the whole, that is the family,
as real and themselves as merely aspects or accidents of it.
There is immediate recognition of the right conferred by
status and no claim to rights by the individual. This condition, though belonging primarily to the family in the narrower sense, can equally be detected in larger associations in
which a patriarchal or even a feudal organization is maintained. It is the thesis of the positive moment with which we
begin. The antithesis or negation is provided by what Hegel
describes as bourgeois society, better known today under its
Marxist name of "capitalism." What is here "negated" is the
primitive unity of society. We find instead of it a multitude of
independent persons held together only by purely external ties
of contract. The State is thus reduced to the level of a limited-
liability company, and the door is thrown open to revolution.
"When these abstract conclusions came into power, they af-
forded for the first time in human history the prodigious spec-
tacle of the overthrow of the constitution of a great actual

29 HEGEL's *Philosophy of Right*. Translated by Prof. T. M. Knox, p. 33.

State and its complete reconstruction *ab initio* on the basis of pure thought alone." [30]

Family society may thus be described as unity without differences, bourgeois society as a collection of particulars without unity. How is this conflict to be overcome? What is the synthesis which can get over the contradiction and preserve what is valuable in the claims of both sides?

Here we have again Rousseau's problem of reconciling the will of all with the general will, but the Hegelian solution is very different. Simply to count votes and hope that in the process interested or, as Hegel would call them, abstract views will be found to cancel one another out and leave the General Will as a residue is completely unsatisfactory. By accepting it we should simply underwrite "abstract particularity" and in principle abandon the generality of the General Will altogether. It would no longer be general but would become one among a number of competing particular wills.

What we have to do is to conceive the State neither as an organism in the simple sense nor as a mechanism composed of independent parts, but as something superior to both these. It is the family raised to a higher power, a superorganism in which each of the elements consciously identifies himself with the whole and wills its interest because that interest is indistinguishable from his own.

It is easy to object that Hegel is here simply cutting the knot and confusing what ought to be with what actually is. The whole problem arises, it will be said, simply because individuals do not will in this kind of way. To say that they ought to do so may be true, but it is hardly an important contribution to political theory. But this objection is not as fatal as it sounds, since it ignores Hegel's primary assumption that the real and the rational are identical. If it is rational for me to identify my will with the General Will, then it follows that my real will

[30] *Ibid.*, p. 157.

is so identified. My impulse to oppose the General Will is automatically considered as abstract, partial, and essentially unreal. Hence I lose nothing and achieve my freedom when my apparent will is suppressed by the General Will.

The State is real, and the function of philosophy is not to criticize but to understand it. "This book, then, containing as it does the science of the State, is to be nothing other than the endeavor to apprehend and portray the State as something inherently rational. As a work of philosophy it must be poles apart from an attempt to construct a State as it ought to be. The instruction which it may contain cannot consist in teaching the State what it ought to be: it can only show how the State, the universe of the ethical, is to be understood." [31]

It will be rightly inferred that Hegel was not disposed to accept half-measures or compromises where the rights of the State were involved. He conceived it as being not merely real and superorganic, but as the highest form of reality; in fact, as God. "In considering freedom, the starting point must be, not individuality, the single consciousness, but only the essence of self-consciousness; for whether man knows it or not, this essence is externally realized as a self-subsistent power in which individuals are only moments. The march of God in the world, that is what the State is." [32]

It is important to remember that in this and similar passages Hegel is not talking about an abstraction. He really means the actual State as it exists here and now. Prussia, naturally, was primarily in his mind; but he was far from denying that other States, though less fully developed, possessed the same essential characteristics. From this it follows that there can be no judge between States. They are ultimate, and when they disagree there is nothing for it but that they should fight it out. This is a good and not a bad thing, since

[31] *Ibid.*, p. 11.
[32] *Ibid.*, p. 279.

war puts the individual in his proper place. "War is the state
of affairs which deals in earnest with the vanity of temporal
goods and concerns—a vanity at other times a common theme
for edifying sermonizing. . . . War has the higher significance that by its agency . . . the ethical health of peoples is
preserved in their indifference to the stabilization of finite
institutions; just as the blowing of the wind preserves the
sea from the foulness which would be the result of a prolonged calm, so also corruption in nations would be the product of prolonged, let alone 'perpetual,' peace." [33] It is also
quite natural, on this view, to hold that undeveloped peoples,
that is those not organized in divine States, have no rights
whatever. "The civilized nation is conscious that the rights
of barbarians are unequal to its own and treats their auton-
omy as only a formality." [34]

Hegel was perfectly sincere in all this. He was not, as has
sometimes been suggested, putting on an act to please the
Prussian authorities. He might, as some of his followers in
England and other countries have done, have toned down
the picture and obscured the obviously dictatorial and aggressive nature of the State as he conceived it. But he was under
no temptation to do this, either because of his own tempera-
ment or because of the prevailing atmosphere of his time and
country. So the theory is there, and is there without disguise
or apology. For Hegel it involved no absurdity and the individual, who was permitted by the State to make his own decisions in matters, such as the choice of a vocation, which were
important to him but irrelevant to the well-being of the
State, was receiving all in the way of personal freedom that
a reasonable man could demand. "Reason itself requires us to
recognize that contingency, contradiction, and show have a

[33] *Ibid.*, p. 210.
   Hegel presumably assumed that the Germans in future would always win
their wars.
[34] *Ibid.*, p. 219.

sphere and a right of their own, restricted though it be, and it is irrational to strive to resolve and rectify contradictions within that sphere." [35]

We may well ask exactly what is to be made of this repulsive doctrine, but there is a further general point to be considered before we do so. It is not immediately clear whether what we are offered by Hegel is a historical account of the development of mankind or rather a logical analysis of the structure of a particular State or States at the beginning of the nineteenth century. In fact it is both. Hegel has simply taken over and elaborated the Aristotelian conception of nature, which we have already considered, and applied it to the evolution of the State. It is thus perfectly possible for him to hold (a) that the earliest forms of human society really are patriarchal and that bourgeois societies and constitutional States come into existence at a later period in history; (b) that all three types may be found in existence at the same time; (c) that the later types contain in themselves the earlier, and that in them what was only potentially present in the former is now realized and made actual. But it makes no sense for him to say that the earlier ought to be other than they are. States are judged only by "world history," that is by their capacity to survive and to crush their rivals in successful wars.

Finally it must be observed that the organic State, as conceived by Hegel, is neither arbitrary nor tyrannical by his standards. It is a monarchy, but the monarch himself is the expression and mouthpiece of the State. He does not govern it from without but acts strictly in accordance with the constitution. The rule of law is thus guaranteed. The people get their rights as prescribed by the constitution. But this definitely does not mean that the constitution exists to protect rights which existed before it was formulated. "It is absolutely

[35] *Ibid.*, p. 137.

essential that the constitution should not be regarded as something made, even though it has come into being in time. It must be treated rather as something existent in and by itself, as divine, therefore, and constant, and so exalted above the sphere of things that are made." [36] The constitution, in fact, provides the structure which simple society lacks. It is what makes the State into a differentiated unity in which all that is real and valuable, both in the family and in bourgeois society, is transcended and preserved.

Hegel and Later Political Theorists

Hegel's philosophy involves four main assumptions. These have already emerged in the foregoing discussion, but it may be useful to repeat them here:

1. The rational is the real. Taken strictly, this would imply that pure thought without any reference to immediate experience can discover the entire truth about the universe. This is not true, and Hegel himself shows it to be false in practice. None of his works would be convincing except to a being whose experience was generally of the same type as his own. But the consequence which does follow from it, and which he accepts, is that politics is a rational and not an empirical inquiry. It enables him to ignore particular historical and psychological facts and to talk in general terms about the State, society, the individual, etc., without any further inquiry as to whether reality provides any instances to which his definitions can be applied.

2. Any whole is more important and therefore more real or concrete than are the elements of which it is composed.

3. Among wholes, the more differentiated is more real than the less differentiated.

4. The State, which is a whole composed of self-conscious self-determining agents differentiated by a rational constitutional system, is the highest reality which exists. It may therefore properly be called divine.

36 Ibid., p. 178.

None of these assumptions can be treated as absurd, but none of them are self-evident. And political philosophers since Hegel can generally be classified in terms of the Hegelian assumptions which they reject.

Thus the type of democratic theory developed by the English philosophical radicals in the early nineteenth century in effect accepts 1 and denies the remainder. It consequently accepts as final what Hegel regarded as the imperfect form of bourgeois society held together only by contract. Other writers who are attracted by the organic theory in principle but reject Hegel's particular development of it, accept 1, 2 and 3 but deny 4. In other words they hold that something other than the State, *e.g.* the Church, is the association which exhibits the highest form of organic connection.

Marx claims to reject all four assumptions. This claim is not borne out by his performance. In fact he accepts 1 and thinks of a world-wide society of rational beings in much the same way as the English radicals did. He differs from them as to the practical possibility of achieving the ideal by peaceful means. Both he and his successors tend gradually to reintroduce 2, 3 and even 4 under new names.

All these are more or less consciously rationalist approaches, that is they all accept 1. But this is not necessary. It is perfectly possible to maintain that the whole problem of the nature of the State and its relation to the individual is one which can be studied only by empirical methods, and that we cannot ignore or even treat as relatively unimportant the particular facts brought to light by history, anthropology, psychology, and other sociological studies. It must, however, be admitted that the influence of Hegel is strong even on many who hold this view. There is an undoubted tendency, when 1 has been denied, to accept uncritically 2 and 3. Even 1 is liable to slip back again unnoticed in the implicit assumption that because it can be shown that things are like this, it follows that this is how they ought to be.

This is not necessarily a serious matter. What is much more important is that in their anxiety to repudiate Hegelian rationalism many sociological writers have tended unduly to depreciate the part played by reason in human affairs, and have talked as if force, and force alone, was deserving of serious consideration. And, partly at least as a reaction against this extreme anti-intellectualist view, writers who disapprove of the wholesale employment of force have tended more and more to the opposite pole and are found maintaining that force is always and necessarily a bad thing. We thus get the odd view that the proper answer to fascism is pacifism, perhaps the most expensive fallacy which Hegel unintentionally bequeathed to Western civilization. But, whatever we may think of his moral sentiments, Hegel was remarkably faithful to his organic theory. The purist might argue that, in his zeal for protecting all existing institutions, he slightly exaggerated the importance of constitutional law at the expense of the omnipotence of the State. But this amounts to very little. He did not give much away.

THE STATE AS A MACHINE

A. THE STATE BASED ON FORCE

We come now to those political philosophers who have defined the State not as the natural expression of the whole of an evolving society but as the means by which a comparatively small number of people impose their will on a more or less reluctant majority. The State ceases to be coextensive with society and becomes more closely identified with what, in ordinary language, is called "the ruling class." Force or coercion, which for organic theory is merely an acci-

dent resulting from the imperfect knowledge or defective wills
of the members, now becomes the essence of the whole matter. This change of outlook is not always immediately obvious.
It is possible to conceal it, at least in part, by the supplementary assumption that the citizens for some curious reason have
agreed to accept despotic government. They may be held to
have voluntarily signed away their freedom and to have con-
tracted to obey. On this view it is argued that the creation,
though not the operation, of the State based on force involves
consent by the governed. This refinement, however, is not
inevitable and many writers, especially in the nineteenth and
twentieth centuries, dispense with it and define the State in
terms of force without qualification. The philosophy of
Hobbes exemplifies the contract form of the force theory; that
of Marx expounds the doctrine of undiluted force. The important practical distinction between these theories lies in
this: For Hobbes and for those who think like him, the State
(identified, as I have said, with the rulers) has at least some
claim to obedience in addition to its possession of overwhelming might. This claim rests on a promise, or rather on a rational
decision, which is supposed to have been made before the force
came into existence and by which the exercise of that force is
authorized. For Marxists, who reject the doctrine of contract,
the State has no authority or moral backing whatever. In practice, Hobbes is the prophet of reaction. His dictatorship is
avowedly designed to sanctify the permanence of existing institutions, especially that of property, and is therefore a dictatorship of the right. Marx, on the other hand, stands for revolution. For him existing institutions rest on force and on
nothing but force, and they have, therefore, no right or claim
to survival. He agrees with Hobbes that dictatorship exists and,
further, that no government except a dictatorship is at present
psychologically possible. His aim is to replace by force the
dictatorship of the right by a dictatorship of the left. It is

therefore not surprising that the theories of Hobbes and Marx, in spite of important minor differences, are essentially alike.

The differences are clear enough:

1. Hobbes favors an absolute monarchy: Marx aims at a dictatorship of the working class.

2. Hobbes deplores revolution against any *de facto* regime, provided only that it is capable of maintaining order and guaranteeing defense against foreign attack: Marx is a revolutionary.

3. Hobbes claims that government is based on a rational belief of the governed that it is to their interest to submit to it; Marx regards it as the deliberate oppression of the weak by the strong.

But on the vital point at issue they are in complete agreement. Both hold consistently that in human affairs force not law is what decides. "The laws have been contrived by our enemies . . . in the interests of the wealthy and propertied classes. We, who possess nothing, can only be bound by the law as long as we are too weak to set it at naught." [37]

"The Lawes of Nature (as Justice, Equity, Modesty, Mercy and in summe doing to others as we would be done to), of themselves, without the terror of some Power, to cause them to be observed, are contrary to our natural Passions, that carry us to Partiality, Pride, Revenge, and the like. And Covenants without the Sword, are but words, and of no strength to secure a man at all." [38]

These quotations, with numberless others which could be cited from the works of Hobbes, of Marx, and of their followers, express the belief on which the entire view is based. They are liable to be misunderstood, and, even more, to be misrepresented. They do not mean or imply that might is right, or even that justice can usefully be defined as "the interest of the stronger." Even less do they maintain, or need to maintain, that force and right are necessarily opposed to each

[37] Communist Manifesto. Edited by Ryazanoff, p. 311.
[38] HOBBES, *Leviathan*, p. 128.

other. The assertion that God is on the side of the big battalions means, not that wrong is always triumphant, but simply that right, in the absence of adequate force to support it, is certain to lose.

It is no great matter whether this conviction is described as cynical or as realistic. If the view about human nature which it takes for granted is correct, it is true. Otherwise it is not. And this is a matter which can be settled only by analysis of facts; there is no theoretical solution to the problem. There are, however, two points which deserve notice at this stage, because, if they are neglected, the logical weight of the theory is likely to be missed.

In the first place it must be recognized that many people, as a result, so these theorists would urge, of habit and tradition, like to believe that their own exercise of force is on the side of right. The whole culture of Western Europe leans strongly in this direction. Hence the frequency with which might prevails over right is often masked by legalistic fictions. Marx, naturally, maintains that the alleged social contract on which Hobbes claims to rely is just another of these. And, secondly, it must be emphasized that the force which is in question is not merely potential but immediately mobilizable. If we merely count the former, it is certain that no one man or small minority could dominate a large community for any length of time. But this cannot properly be used as it has sometimes been used (and Hobbes cannot be acquitted of thinking along these lines) to show that acquiescence is always accompanied by consent or even approval. It may be. But, in practice, especially under modern conditions, quite a small organized armed force can maintain itself and continue to rule for an indefinite time if it is ruthless in "purging" potential opposition before it is organized.

Properly stated, then, the theory amounts to this: It is admittedly wicked to ill-treat human beings, or to exploit them in the interests of a privileged minority. Human nature, however, is such that this is bound to happen, and we have no alternative but to make the best we can of the situation as we find it. For the organic theory, people do not merely want to be better than they are; they have a real tendency to become so unless thwarted by circumstances. The General Will and the good State are not utopian dreams but existing facts. For the force theory, they are mere utopias. Human beings are now defined as purely selfish agents who have no obligation, except to act in such a way as to increase their individual well-being. In Rousseau's language, the will of all is supreme; the General Will is an idealist fiction, and from this it follows that nothing but a deficiency of might prevents everyone from behaving tyrannically toward his neighbors.

It is at this point that Hobbes and Marx part company on a question of fact. Hobbes maintains that a monarchy or a ruling class, although it is wholly selfish in its motives, will not normally oppress its subjects, since it has no true interest in doing so. The wise slave-owner does not gratuitously ill-treat his slaves, because they become weak and inefficient if he does. Marx, on the contrary, considered that it did pay the capitalist to exploit his workers to the limit, just because they were not his slaves; and that the process of exploitation would necessarily be continued and accentuated until the workers were sufficiently organized to take advantage of a temporary or permanent weakening of the bourgeois or capitalist position. This might happen in the event of an unsuccessful war and most certainly would occur sooner or later as a result of changes in economic methods of production. When it did, there would be a successful revolution, if the workers were quick to take their chance. The capitalists would be expropriated, and the proletariat would become in its turn the ruling and *exploiting* class. This difference in outlook is, at least to some extent, the result of historical circumstances.

Hobbes' view was the more plausible before the industrial revolution, but Marx was intelligible enough at the time of the Communist Manifesto (1848).

THOMAS HOBBES: 1588–1679

"Fear and I were twins." When Hobbes said this he stated the simple truth. Whether he was justified in blaming the coincidence of the Spanish Armada with his birth for his abnormal sensitiveness is less certain and is of no importance. What matters is that he was an easily frightened man; and since, like most philosophers, he took it for granted that the vast majority of mankind were very much like himself in character, it is not difficult to understand the twist which this weakness gave to his whole political philosophy. Many have held that desire to dominate others is the strongest of human motives, but most of them have wanted such dominion in order to get something. Hobbes wanted it in order to avoid something. His strongest motive is always the wish to avoid pain; and, above all, to avoid violent death. Hence he is naturally preoccupied with possibilities of disaster which only strength and prudence may avert; and prudence itself, though necessary, has its disadvantages. "For as *Prometheus,* which interpreted is, *the prudent man,* was bound to the hill Caucasus, a place of large prospect, where an Eagle, feeding on his liver, devoured in the day as much as was repayred in the night. So that man, which looks too far before him, in the case of future time, hath his heart all the day long gnawed on by feare of death, poverty, or other calamity; and has no repose, nor pause of his anxiety, but in sleep." [39]

The outlook for man was therefore not a happy one. But it was not altogether hopeless. Hobbes believed that men were ultimately ruled by their passions and that their passions were poor guides to conduct. He knew that they had reason too, and

[39] *Leviathan,* p. 82.

reason, though it could not directly control the passions, could frequently enable us to circumvent them and so to avert calamity. Rational desire is always, in his view, directed to the promotion of the individual's private interest; and, if he acts in accordance with this desire, he is being moral. From this it follows that promises and religious scruples should never be relied upon by a rational man, since they are impotent to restrain the passions. "The bonds of words are too weak to bridle men's ambitions, avarice, anger, and other Passions, without the feare of some coercive Power." [40]

But although Hobbes was inevitably skeptical as to the efficacy of the moral law or the law of nature, as he preferred to call it, he was as convinced as anybody of its "manifest authority." "Princes succeed one another; and one Judge passeth, another commeth; nay Heaven and Earth shall passe; but not one tittle of the Law of Nature shall passe; for it is the Eternal Law of God." [41] Hobbes may have been a hypocrite when he wrote this and many parallel passages. Marx would certainly have said that he was one. "Law, morality, and religion have become for him [the proletarian] so many bourgeois prejudices, behind which bourgeois interests lurk in ambush." [42] But this is simply to beg the question as far as the view is concerned. What is perfectly clear is that Hobbes was, at least ostensibly, prevented by his respect for morality from basing his State on naked force, though his conception of human beings and their effective motives made it extremely difficult for him to do anything else.

His solution of the difficulty was this. In the absence of organized society, men exist in a state of nature. This does not mean a State in which they are controlled by reason or moral law. Quite the contrary is the case; for since, in the absence

<hr>

40 *Ibid.*, p. 105.
41 *Ibid.*, p. 213.
42 *Communist Manifesto*, p. 40.

of civil government, there is no constraint to regulate their impulses, each is moved by his own fears and not by a calculation of what his true interest requires. No doubt men intend, even under these conditions, to act reasonably and to keep their promises; they may even do so when they have nothing to lose. But there is no security. "No Arts; no Letters; no Society; and, which is worst of all, continual feare, and danger of violent death: And the life of man, solitary, poore, nasty, brutish and short." [43]

This would be an unsatisfactory condition for any collection of human beings. But for men as Hobbes conceived them in his own image, it was simply frightful, and they must clearly get out of it at any cost. They therefore agree with one another to set up a monarch with complete coercive might to rule over them and thereby produce artificially a situation in which their fear of breaking the law is made normally to exceed all other fears. It is a strange doctrine, but not completely incredible. After all, some dipsomaniacs do agree in a cool hour to their own imprisonment, and I suppose that a party of them, if they had their cool hour at the same time, might not unreasonably agree to devote their joint fortunes to the establishment of a home from which they would have no right subsequently to claim release without the approval of the superintendent whom they had themselves appointed. However, we need not labor this point, since Hobbes himself claims that his contract is based on logical analysis rather than on historical fact. What he maintains is that, if men already in society would consider what their position would be if all civil constraint were removed, they would find that this state of nature or something very like it would probably be their fate. Civil society may fairly be described as a permanent contracting out of the state of nature.

Evidently this kind of contract is entirely different from

[43] *Leviathan*, p. 97.

what Rousseau, for instance, subsequently had in mind. Rousseau's men arranged their State in order to enlarge their freedom and remained collectively sovereign and absolute after they had done so. Their problem was to know what was right. When they did know, they were more than likely to act reasonably and realize their real, as distinct from their apparent, wills. The trouble with Hobbes' men was that, while they generally knew what the law of reason or self-interest required of them, they also knew that they would seldom act in accordance with their knowledge. Their wills were not bad but hopelessly weak. Since, then, they fully realized that they would never resist temptation in any form, they arranged for a monarch to whom they voluntarily and finally surrendered their right of choice.

Their contract was not a contract in the ordinary sense at all. It was a desperate attempt to ensure that they would pursue the course which reason assured them that their interest impelled them to pursue and from which they knew that their passions would deflect them unless the strongest passion of all, namely, fear, were mobilized to keep them to it.

The upshot is that the monarch is entrusted once for all not merely with force but also with a semblance of right. He is not himself a party to the original contract; he makes no promises, but is the beneficiary of the contract which the citizens make with one another. And his dominion is completely unrestricted because, unless it is so, there is no adequate security against the collapse of the commonwealth and a return to the state of nature which is the worst of all possible states. Civil law becomes what the monarch wills. If he is a competent monarch, it will tend to coincide with the law of nature; but, whether it does or not, it is law because the monarch wills it and for no other reason.

"These dictates of Reason (the law of Nature), men used to call by the name of Lawes; but improperly: for they are but conclusions, or Theoremes concerning what conduceth to the conservation and defence of themselves [*i.e.*, the citizens]; whereas Law, properly, is the word of him that by right hath command over others." [44] And again: "The office of the Sovereign (be it Monarch, or an Assembly), consisteth in the end, for which he was trusted with the Sovereign Power, namely the procuration of the *Safety of the People;* to which he is obliged by the Law of Nature, and to render an account thereof to God, the author of that Law, and to none but him." [45]

The State is thus frankly and necessarily coercive in its operation, and its laws express simply the will of the ruler, who, like any other man, is actuated by desire for his own security above everything else. Hobbes claims none the less that its laws ought to be obeyed. The material grounds for such obedience are apparent, since the monarch has overwhelming force at his disposal and, in the interests of his safety, he will kill me if I refuse it. But if I suppose that my disobedience will go undetected, it is still unreasonable for me to break the law. It may be a bad law. But I ought still to recognize that by flouting it I am challenging the whole principle of government which on reflection I am bound to approve, since it alone protects me from something far worse than any inconveniences which the support of it can involve. "The estate of Man can never be without some incommodity or other; and the greatest, that in any forme of Government can possibly happen to the people in general, is scarce sensible, in respect of the miseries, and horrible calamities, that accompany a Civill Warre." [46]

If we ask, Is there no "ought" beyond this? Is it not maintained that the State ought to be obeyed because it conduces

---

[44] *Ibid.,* p. 123. This rather weakens our belief in Hobbes' sincerity in his remarks on the Law of God quoted above.

[45] *Ibid.,* p. 258.

[46] *Ibid.,* p. 141.

to the realization of a moral purpose? The answer to both questions is in the negative. Hobbes recognizes no effective moral purpose other than the promotion of security, and, in so far as he demonstrates that security can never be promoted except by obedience to the monarch, he has given such obedience all the moral sanction it can have. He does, indeed, invoke the approval of God on his contentions: "The present ought alwaies to be preferred, maintained and accounted best: because it is against both the Law of Nature, and the Divine positive Law, to do anything tending to the subversion thereof." [47] But this adds nothing, since the Monarch is the sole interpreter of both these laws and it may fairly be assumed that he will not interpret them in any sense hostile to his own position; and it is not merely his right, but his duty for the preservation of the safety of the realm (on which his own safety depends), to suppress ruthlessly all heterodox opinions. The clergy, for instance, are merely his nominees and their views must be his: "It is from the Civill Sovereign, that all other Pastors derive their right of Teaching, Preaching and other functions pertaining to that office: and they are but his Ministers." [48]

If we now consider Hobbes' position, it is hard to deny that it hangs together very well. If it is agreed, as it must be, since we are here concerned with consistency and not with truth, that the mass of men are as Hobbes defines them, then his conclusions on government are inescapable, and we need not quarrel with his argument that any established order had better be supported simply because it is an established order. What this amounts to is that the vast majority of men are so constituted that they would genuinely suffer less by enduring any dictatorship, however outrageous, than by risking their lives in an attempt to overthrow it; their contract, as we have

[47] *Ibid.*, p. 429.
[48] *Ibid.*, p. 422.

already noted, is not a contract, but a statement about their interests, whose truth they are bound to recognize when they think about it calmly but which they are liable to forget or to ignore when blinded by passion or momentary enthusiasm.

Hobbes would be even more consistent than he is if he avoided the temptation to admire actions based on a theory of conduct different from and irreconcilable with his own. He is not really entitled to describe the monarch's conduct as either virtuous or vicious. The monarch is as little subject as anybody else to control by the law of God or nature. Indeed he is not subject to it at all. Toward his subjects he has no obligation in the ordinary sense, and, if he fails to exploit them, he does so merely because he thinks this a wise policy, and he deserves no special commendation for it; nor, in Hobbes' view, can he reasonably be called wicked if he takes a different line in the promotion of his personal well-being. If Hobbes is right, he is incompetent. But that is all.

Far more surprising is the tribute which Hobbes pays to courage in his discussion of justice. "That which gives to humane Actions the relish of Justice," he remarks, "is a certaine Noblenesse or Galantnesse of courage (rarely found) by which a man scorns to be beholding for the contentment of his life, to fraud or breach of promise." [49] As well, surely, that it is "rarely found"; no competent Hobbesian monarch could have very much patience with it. Still, Hobbes does pay his tribute to virtue, and it would be hard to deny that his formulation of the force theory gains in plausibility from his lapse. To put it shortly, what Hobbes wanted was a quiet life. If his view of human nature was correct, the only political theory which could give him a quiet life was the force theory, and he therefore embraced it. But he never gave up, as logically he should have done, his belief that other things besides security were somehow important. He was not cut out to be a

[49] *Ibid.*, p. 114.

crusader, but he never quite believed in his own amoral doctrines.

KARL MARX: 1818–1883

Marx has been compared with a Hebrew prophet, and the comparison is apt. Denunciation is the keynote of the *Communist Manifesto* and of *Capital*. It is not mere denunciation. Marx might have adapted Rousseau and written "The workers are born free, and everywhere they are exploited. I understand both the origin of this exploitation and the only method by which it can be stopped." What he wanted to do above all else was to spread his own religious conviction that Western civilization was rotten to the core. And, in the end, he succeeded. Much of his economic theory was unsound, and many of his political prophecies were wildly wrong: but his theory gave intellectual support to many who were already shamefaced about the effects of nineteenth-century capitalism, and enabled them at least to hope that men were not inexorably bound by the iron laws of classical economics.

It is, however, a grave mistake to think of him simply as a sort of revivalist preacher denouncing the hypocrisy and vices of the ruling class. He was that, but he was a great deal more besides. His followers claim that he inaugurated the scientific study of political as well as of economic theory, and, although this claim is often misunderstood and usually misstated, there is a good deal of substance in it.

The essence of Marx is his contention that theory and practice are inseparable from each other. This does not mean, as Hegel and his successors would have it, that they are different sides of a single activity. To say this is to assert precisely that superiority of mind over things which Marx was perpetually concerned to deny, and which, in the end, he rejected so utterly as to compromise his own genuine view. It is quite easy to suppose from a casual reading of selected passages (and many isolated texts can be cited in support of the supposition), that Marx was a materialist in the extreme sense of the term, and is logically committed to maintaining that all human action is a mere reflection of the behavior of physical bodies: in other words, that there is no human action at all. This is a mistake. His doctrine is that there is theory, which is a genuine product of mind, and there is practice, which is the putting into operation in the material world of conclusions reached by theorizing. These are perfectly distinguishable activities, and it is possible for either to take place almost, though not completely, without reference to the other. Pure mathematics or mathematical logic is almost wholly theoretical, and some conscious action is very close to mere behavior. Sensible action, however, is action deliberately adapted to the physical conditions prevailing at the time at which it occurs. Foolish action is action based on a theory which does not accord with the facts. Hence, as the factual situation changes, there can be no fixed and unalterable rules for directing action. What is sensible in 1850 may well be foolish in 1950, because the situation has altered in the meantime. This sounds reasonable; but it marks a great change in approach to the problem of political philosophy from that of the writers we have considered so far. [For all of these, and in particular Aristotle and Hobbes, proceed by elaborating a theory and then proceeding to a series of applications of it. The theory is evolved with little reference to concrete facts, and if later it appears that facts are reluctant to accept it, so much the worse for them.] The point is not merely that these writers worked in this way but that they meant to do so. Marx, as we shall see, was not by any means faithful to his belief that this method was fatally defective. But he did at least believe that it was. And it is fair to say that the theories which he failed to question were not as obviously inadequate when he wrote as they became later on.

The consequence of this approach is that there are two sides to Marx, and it is important to distinguish them from each other. They are, (*a*) the economic theory set out in the *First Volume of Capital* and in the *Critique of Political Economy;* (*b*) the analysis and criticism of actual economic and political situations, of which the best known are probably those dealing with the Paris Commune of 1871. These two sides are not related to one another in the same way as are the theories and applications of earlier writers. Where politics is concerned, the Marxist "theory" is inextricably bound up with conclusions, based on genuine research into the published data, of the way in which wealth and power were actually distributed under the special conditions provided by the economic organization of Western Europe between 1800 and 1850. Marx does not offer any political theory as a system of timeless, necessary truth, and his view makes sense only when it is considered in its context. That context is the economic exploitation revealed in Engels' *Condition of the Working Class in England* and in the later volumes of *Capital*. These are not widely read, but they are the true basis for the whole theory of history developed in the *Communist Manifesto*.

Thus no part of Marx can be appreciated, or even understood, without reference to the rest. Marxism is a method, not a theory, and Marx, as he himself said, was not really a Marxist.[50]

Hobbes had thought of the existing State as a system of government which ought to be maintained, because, however oppressive it was, it did, at least, ward off the return to the state of nature. Marx thought of it as something which ought not to be tolerated, however efficient it might be, because it in-

---

[50] *Cf. History of the C.P.S.U.(B), 1942*, p. 356. "The Marxist-Leninist theory is not dogma but a guide to action."

volved the exploitation of workers by capitalists. Hence the aim, and the sole aim, of the Marxist method was to produce successful revolutions by the industrial workers.

The method itself is easy enough to state in general terms, but to apply it we need a great deal more than a system of abstract definitions. We must have before us a detailed analysis of the particular situation of a specified country at a given time; and this analysis is concerned with the actual location of political and economic strength. Until we know who controls the financial organization and the machine guns, we cannot say whether effective political action is possible or not; and to guess that it is possible is not to know how best to set about it. Marx was a revolutionary, but he had as little patience as Lenin and Stalin with heroic risings which had no prospect of success.

To gain this knowledge is a laborious process. It requires a detailed acquaintance with facts which the average man has neither the time nor the opportunity to acquire. It is also a specialist's job which requires training and hard work. Marxist slogans are no substitute for these, though it is both easy and popular to suppose that they are.

The only consistency of which the method admits lies in its revolutionary purpose. "Philosophers have attempted to interpret the world: what matters, however, is to change it." [51] Those who expect and look for some other consistency are doomed to disappointment and are liable to think that Marxism is merely a collection of phrases designed to account for the absence of any coherent political policy. But there is not the slightest reason why a Marxist should, as a matter of policy, support any one type of capitalist regime against any other type. He is under no obligation whatever to back liberalism against fascism, or *vice versa.*

This line of approach to political problems is entirely at

[51] MARX, *Theses on Feuerbach,* xi.

variance with the accepted principles of liberal democracy, both in Britain and in the United States. But, however little we may approve of it, it is of the utmost importance not to disregard or to misunderstand it. A genuine Marxist is inconsistent only if he does something which, in the opinion of the party leaders, tends to prevent or delay the coming of a successful revolution. Where no revolutionary situation exists, he normally favors liberal measures, since these are likely to strengthen the position of the workers and so to assist in the eventual deployment of revolutionary force. But when there is already the possibility of revolution, the opposite policy may well be called for in order to stimulate hostility to the existing regime. Marxism and "open diplomacy" do not go together.

Thus Marxists in capitalist countries, who opposed the last war until 1941 when Russia (the successful revolution) was attacked, may well have been mistaken in their analysis of the situation: but they were perfectly consistent.

We now have to consider the revolutionary aim itself. In origin it arose, no doubt, from sheer indignation at the operation of capitalism. But this indignation was not a Marxist monopoly. It was expressed by such very un-Marxist authors as Dickens and Disraeli. Indeed, it was the common ground of humane writers and thinkers of the early Victorian age. What distinguished Marx from his contemporaries was the account which he offered of the cause of the prevalent misery of the working classes in all capitalist countries, and his conviction that it could be cured not by philanthropy but only by revolutionary action.

To get at the cause, we must reconsider the course of human history and regard it not as a chronicle of the wars of monarchs but as the gradual development of social organization. It was assumed by Marx (in accordance with the customary oversimplification of the age) that the only operative motive in human nature is a desire to promote the material well-being of the agent; [52] and it was accepted that, as soon as men escape from their primitive state (which is politically uninteresting), they are distinguishable into rulers and ruled. It is naturally no part of Marx's policy to justify the position of existing rulers, and he is able to discard at once the devices by which earlier writers had tried to do so. Rulers are rulers, not in virtue of natural superiority, divine right, or consent, express or tacit, of the ruled, but simply because, as a result of luck or good management, they have found a chance to benefit themselves at the expense of their fellows.

This is one side of the picture. The other, from Marx's point of view, is enormously more important. For, while the emergence of one particular group of people rather than another as the exploiters of a particular nation at a particular time is largely a matter of historical accident, the existence of *exploiters of a certain type* in any given epoch is not accidental but it is governed by discoverable laws. What settles it is the control of the means of production, and in any society the class which exercises effective ownership over these will necessarily dominate the remainder. Classes, therefore, are neither "natural" in Aristotle's sense nor divinely ordained. They are essential economic divisions which become political only as a result of material causes. What happens is this: The indispensable means of production, that is the material basis of it, are labor, land and capital (which, for this purpose, is defined as meaning real capital such as mines, factories, ships, etc., and not money). These vary in relative importance at different stages in human development, and these variations are inevitable. They do not depend on human wishes or plans. Broadly speaking, when the most important factor in production is agriculture, the landowners in any country are bound to form the ruling class; when it is factories and other capital

[52] See below, p. 265.

capable of being operated by unskilled labor, the capitalists; and when it is skilled labor, the urban proletariat.

Now it is certain that the ruling class will always exploit the remainder of the population, and, since the skilled workers in the cities are nowhere a majority even of the lower income groups, this analysis suggests that the peasants, in particular, are bound to be exploited by somebody until the end of time. That is why collective farms are important. They convert the peasant into an urbanized worker and thereby produce a solid interest of workers and peasants against landlords and capitalists. This is a detail, though not an unimportant one. What really matters is that investigation reveals the existence of a peculiar form of State appropriate to each of these three levels of development. The State, it will be remembered, is for Marx "nothing more than a committee for the administration of the consolidated affairs of the bourgeois class as a whole." [53]

It is, therefore, not surprising to learn that, as the conditions of production change, the existing State ceases to meet the requirements of the new exploiting class. The feudal State, based on status, was not an effective instrument for the use of the capitalists. It was, therefore, eliminated and replaced by the capitalist State based on contract, that is on the freedom of the laborer to dispose of his own labor in the open market. In Marx's language, "The Bourgeoisie has degraded personal dignity to the level of exchange value; and in place of the countless, dearly bought chartered freedoms, it has set up one solitary, unscrupulous freedom—freedom of trade. In a word, it has replaced exploitation veiled in religious and political illusions by exploitation that is open, unashamed, direct and brutal." [54]

But this replacement of one type of exploiting committee by another, though it is inevitable, does not happen auto-

[53] *Communist Manifesto,* p. 28.
[54] *Ibid.,* p. 28.

matically at the moment when economic conditions justify it. There may be a revolutionary situation, but actual revolution may be postponed, since the new ruling class is not yet organized while the old one still controls the armed forces. In the end, the old type of State collapses and the new one comes into being bringing with it the appropriate moral and political beliefs and, what is even more important, the property relations suitable to the interest of the now dominant class.

"It is not the consciousness of men that determines their existence, but, on the contrary, it is their social existence that determines their consciousness. At a certain stage of their development the material productive resources of society come into contradiction with the existing productive relationships, or, what is but the legal expression of these, with the property relations within which they had moved before. From forms of the development of the productive forces, these relationships are transformed into their fetters. Then an epoch of social revolution opens. With the change in the economic foundation the whole vast superstructure is more or less rapidly transformed. In considering such revolutions it is necessary always to distinguish between the material revolution in the economic conditions of production, which can be determined with scientific accuracy, and the juridical, political, religious, æsthetic, or philosophic—in a word, ideological forms wherein men become conscious of this conflict and fight it out. . . . A revolutionary epoch cannot be judged from its own consciousness." [55]

On this general theory of history depends the Marxist contention that the State is not something fixed and unalterable. Its character depends on the level of economic development and the distribution of power between classes in a particular community at a particular time. All that can be stated as an abstract truth is that, as the conditions of production change,

[55] *Handbook of Marxism,* p. 372.

feudalism gives way to capitalism and capitalism gives way to socialism. This tells us little or nothing without a detailed study of actual societies.

A further consequence of Marxism is that a communist State is impossible. It is a contradiction in terms, since communism (as contrasted with socialism) means a society in which there are no classes. Where there is no ruling class there is no exploitation. But the revolution by which capitalism is abolished does not produce this state of affairs. It gives rise only to a new State which, like its predecessors, is a dictatorship. This workers' socialist State is identical in theory with feudal and capitalist States in that it again is merely an instrument by which one class in society exploits the remainder.

The ultimate communist organization of society in which this final form of State has itself disappeared or, as Engels puts it, "withered away," is not much considered by Marxist writers. The impression given of it is that it resembles fairly closely the ideal, though not the practice, of liberal democracy. It is conceived as simply an administrative device with little or no coercive power. But as it cannot come into existence until not merely bourgeois institutions but bourgeois ideology have been entirely eliminated by the proletarian dictatorship, that is, until average human psychology has been radically altered, it is generally agreed that any detailed discussion of it would be premature or "utopian" at the present time.

Marx, as we have seen, regarded his doctrine, not as a statement of eternal political truth, but as a method of investigation into the practicability of revolutions based on analysis of ascertainable facts of history and economics. He also held that revolutions were bound to happen, since they were the necessary product of the impact of material conditions on human nature in the mass. Everything thus depends on his initial assumption that human conduct is predictable in accordance with known laws. Now, whether this view is correct or not, it is clear that, if Marx is right, his ground for indignation at the activities of capitalist exploiters is very weak. Unless it can be argued that exploitation is the result of deliberately willed actions, there is nothing wicked about it; and it is hard to avoid the conclusion that, if the materialist interpretation of history is true, capitalism and landowners can no more help exploiting their workers than they can help eating and drinking. All alike are conditions of survival, and on a consistent self-interest theory of action there is nothing in them to give rise to moral fervor. They just happen, and there is really nothing more to be said about them. But it is essential to Marx that we *should* be indignant about exploitation, since, unless we are, the fundamental Marxist aim of producing revolutions against capitalism cannot be justified.

It is not enough for Marx to prove that revolution is inevitable. Death is inevitable, but we find nothing unreasonable in attempting to postpone it for as long as possible. In the same way, the dictatorship of the proletariat and communism might, logically at any rate, be inevitable and bad. The solid ground for maintaining that they are good and ought to be furthered at any cost is the firm belief of Marx, the prophet, as distinct from Marx, the materialist historian, in the supreme value and importance of the happiness of individual human beings. This belief is presupposed by Marxism, as it is by liberal-democratic theory, though it cannot be reconciled with a faith in history as a necessary process; and from this point of view, it must be insisted that the pseudo-Hegelian "dialectic" in which Marx and his successors clothe their historical determinism makes no difference whatever to the result. If it is true that exploitation is a crime against humanity, and if Marx was talking sense when he wrote "The journal [the Communist Journal of 1847] is to champion a holy and righteous cause, the cause of justice against injustice, the cause of the oppressed against the oppressors. We stand for truth against superstition and falsehood," [56] then the materialist theory of history is not what it claims to be. Unless, further, we regard the materialist theory as a mere statement of tendencies as distinct from a natural law, we cannot attach any meaning to the view that a revolutionary situation may not actually issue in revolution unless someone, like Lenin, takes the proper steps to see that it does so. If revolutions are inevitable, they have no heroes.

To avoid basing their case for revolution on a moral view about the dignity of man, Marxists sometimes found it not on the wickedness but on the alleged incompetence of capitalism as a method of production. This is clearly preferable from a materialist point of view, though it robs Marx's denunciations of their force. The trouble is that it is difficult if not impossible to make out a convincing case on these lines. It is easy enough to show that individual capitalists are often exceedingly incompetent. After all, they are supposed to be human, and even communists, as Marx and Lenin were painfully aware, are liable to error. This is a very different matter from demonstrating that the capitalist *class* is bound to make mistakes on the wholesale scale which is needed in order to bring about the economic catastrophe which Marxism postulates. Indeed, capitalists in modern times have to be doubly stupid, since the Marxists have patiently explained to them the blunders which they must not make if they wish to retain their power. If historical determinism were a genuine law and not merely the statement of a tendency, this would not matter; but if that were so, knowledge would be equally useless to the communist.

In fact, however, Marx, the prophet, was probably closer to the mark than Marx, the scientific historian. "When the moral consciousness of the masses declares this, that, or the other economic phenomenon to be wrong, as happened at one

---

[56] RYAZANOFF, *Communist Manifesto*, p. 288.

time in the case of slavery and at another in the case of serf-dom, *this means that* the phenomenon in question has already outlived its time, that new economic conditions have arisen, thanks to which the old ones *have become intolerable and must be swept away.*" [57] This is not very good materialism, but it is sound sense. People are much more likely to abolish or aban-don capitalism because they think they ought to do so than they are to be constrained by its internal contradictions.

Marxism, in fact, involves a major theoretical inconsistency. The method may be sound and the aim, at the date when it was propounded, morally justified. But this does not alter the fact that the faith in humanity which Marx's revolutionary purpose postulates is one which his economic materialism emphatically refutes. As a critic has said, "If the origin and validity of non-economic factors lie simply in their being 'the ideal reflection of social relations,' then they are not causes but effects, and every claim of ideas to determine history is denied." [58] The influence exerted by *Capital* and the *Com-munist Manifesto* is itself a refutation of this view.

Marx espoused the theory that force based on economic in-terest is the key to all human behavior because he saw clearly that vested abuses would never be overcome by ideals and aspirations alone. But he could not follow that theory to the bitter end without sacrificing the moral indignation which had first inspired him to adopt it. He rightly held on to his belief in the importance of human individuals in spite of the inabil-ity of the force hypothesis to accommodate it.

THE STATE AS A MACHINE (CONTINUED)

B. THE DEMOCRATIC STATE

I propose to call the political hypothesis which remains for consideration the liberal-democratic theory of the State. As

[57] ENGELS, quoted by RYAZANOFF, *Communist Manifesto*, p. 172. My italics.
[58] KARL MUHS, *Anti-Marx*, p. 33.

this name, though it seems to me less liable to objection than any alternative, is nevertheless open to criticism, it requires a little explanation. Both "liberal" and "democratic" in the current language of political controversy are agreed to be good or complimentary words. "Democratic," in particular, is included in the U.S.S.R. vocabulary as well as in that of the Western powers as a term of approval, not of abuse. "Liberal" is less popular, but in Britain and the United States it is, on the whole, an adjective which implies praise rather than blame. It is, therefore, perfectly possible to embark on prolonged and sometimes passionate discussions as to whether one form of government is "really" more democratic than another. Little good can come of such debates, since it will usually be found that "democratic" is taken by both parties to mean nothing more precise than "beneficial"; and, since there is no agreement as to what "beneficial" means, "democratic" remains equally empty of any particular significance. But it is important for political theory that it should have a definite meaning since, whether we approve or not, it will continue to be employed because of its strong emotional appeal, if for no other reason. This being the case, the theories put forward by John Locke and his successors have, on historical grounds, a better claim to it than anybody else's; but we cannot safely ignore the many changes through which it has passed on the long journey from Pericles to Stalin, and I think that the addition of "liberal" to it is of some advantage as a reminder that other claimants exist. But as "liberal-democratic" is rather cumbersome, I shall generally use either "liberal" or "democratic" as synonyms for it.

The essential point about the liberal-democratic theory is that it defines the State as a system of government resting on consent. This, as it stands, does not differentiate it from the theories we have already considered. Any form of general-will theory claims to rest on the consent of the entire community (including that of avowed and active dissenters), and even a State admittedly based on force may easily be consented to (in the sense of being passively accepted) by most or all of its members. Clearly, then, the consent which democratic theory postulates is something more positive than simple acquiescence in an accomplished fact, and it may be argued that "consent" is too negative a term to use in this context. Ideally this is correct, but here again it would be unwise to attempt a divorce between history and practice on grounds of logical appropriateness; and the association which has grown up in two and a half centuries between the phrases "government by consent" and "government by the people" (as distinct from "government for the people") is quite strong enough to outweigh what is, strictly considered, a defect of terminology. But it must be admitted that this association depends rather too much on Anglo-American usage. It is not at all safe to rely on it in other languages.

Turning now from linguistic points to the substance of the democratic hypothesis, we must recall that its essential characteristic consists in the overriding importance which it attaches to the individual. It is this which clearly and finally distinguishes it both from the organic theory as a whole and from the idea of the State as simply the wielder of supreme force. We have already noticed in anticipation what the chief difficulty confronting any such view is bound to be. To put it shortly, we may say that the democratic theory, considered simply as a theory, cannot possibly be self-supporting; and this is a special problem which the other theories do not have to face. It is true that their exponents have usually found themselves constrained to break with or go beyond their fundamental doctrines in order to accommodate themselves to widely held views about the value and moral claims of the individual. But it was perfectly possible for them to avoid doing so. It is extremely simple to produce a consistent organic or force theory; the difficulty is to persuade any considerable number of people in the traditionally democratic countries to believe in it. Very few of the champions of these hypotheses appear to be quite happy about them when their implications are forced into the open. The efforts of T. H. Green and, to a lesser extent, of Bosanquet, to compel the beliefs of Victorian liberalism to agree with Hegelian political theory deserve careful study from this point of view; and Thrasymachus, in the first book of Plato's *Republic,* gives a good demonstration of the awkward position of a consistent force theorist when he submits himself to cross-examination. Thrasymachus is never refuted. He is made to look rather silly and, not unnaturally, gets rather cross. His trouble is not that his theory is inconsistent but that it involves consequences which he had not anticipated. It is not very hard for Plato to trap him into admissions which he cannot reconcile with the view he is claiming to support.

Democratic theory (which, incidentally, is dismissed by Plato in two pages [59]) is equally liable to this sort of trouble. In addition it has to face a major problem of quite a different kind. It claims to rest the authority of the State on consent, and by consent it means not passive acceptance but active, voluntary cooperation by all the members. Yet nothing can alter the fact that membership of the State is not a voluntary act at all. Hence, quite apart from any practical difficulties, it looks at first sight as if the democratic theory is bound to be imperfect. As we have already observed, if authority presupposes consent by the governed, then any genuinely voluntary institution, whether it is a church or a bowling club, has a stronger claim on the loyalty of its members than any State can possibly have,[60] and so we look like being forced back on the dilemma between either accepting the organic theory to justify author-

[59] *Rep.* 420 and 421.
[60] See above, pp. 59 and 60.

ity or renouncing all claim to authority and admitting that there is nothing for it but more or less thinly disguised force. That is the way in which Plato saw the problem, and, although we may well decide that he missed something out, it would be hazardous to assume that what he missed was perfectly obvious. He was not a careless thinker.

If, therefore, the democratic hypothesis is to survive, even as a theory, it needs to insist that the State is not an end in itself but simply a means. It has to claim that the ends which the State is invented to protect and to further are superior in importance to all other ends, so that its authority rests on them and not on anything inherent in itself. The State ought to be obeyed, not because of what it is, but because of what it does. This amounts to saying that liberal political theory depends upon a moral or religious faith in the absolute value of men, or at any rate of some men: and it is best to recognize this implication at the outset since otherwise the view is bound to be hesitant and unconvincing.

This statement of faith would not be universally accepted. It is certain to be challenged by those who hold that the essence of liberal-democratic theory is to be found not so much in the supreme importance of the individual as in its insistence on the rule of law. I do not agree with this formulation and shall explain in greater detail the reason for my disagreement later on. For the moment I will only say that belief in the rule of law, if it is put forward as an alternative and not simply as an important supplement to belief in the moral value of the individual, seems to me to be quite useless as the basis of a political theory. It sounds good and makes a useful slogan, but it has no substance. Laws do not govern, neither do they protect or further anything whatever. When we say that they do, what we mean is that they are rules which we invent to assist us in furthering or protecting something which we hold to be valuable on other grounds. Admittedly the words "The Constitution" have achieved quite a high degree of mystical sanctity in the United States; but this is only a trick. The Constitution is a collection of rules. Respect for it can be logically grounded on the belief that, if people keep those rules, the life, liberty, and happiness of individuals will be protected. Apart from this belief, the rules would have no sanctity and no importance. It should be noted that in this country the words "habeas corpus" and "Magna Charta" evoke the same sort of response for the same reason.

There is a real difficulty about the moral basis of democratic theory which probably explains the reluctance of many of its advocates to be quite honest about it. It is this: Most people, certainly most of those who have sufficient individuality to approve in general terms of the liberal view, have what may be called reserved subjects where moral questions are concerned. They support in theory government by the people, but they also maintain one or more "sacred cows" which are, by definition, inviolable and immune from democratic interference. These "sacred cows" are very varied. The rights of trade unions, the supremacy of the white race, the Established Church and antivaccination are all liable to be included among them by different people. Indeed, any cause whatever is capable of being regarded in this light. I am not at this stage saying anything for or against "sacred cows" as such, even though some of them are surprisingly hard to distinguish from skeletons in cupboards. The point about them is that their existence makes the formulation of liberal-democratic theory exceedingly awkward. It is all very well to say that the State has authority because it upholds and protects essential rights. But, unless there is general agreement as to which rights are essential, this may not get us very far: and it is certainly true that many who sincerely believe in the validity of a democratic theory of some kind are most reluctant to accept it in a form which would logically entitle any government to interfere with those particular "sacred cows" for which they have an especial regard.

We may put it in this way: The moral view which democratic theory in its simplest and most persuasive form implies is liable to conflict with other moral and religious beliefs; and when it does so, the latter must give way. If we seriously mean that the claim of all men to make their wills, that is, their actual, not their "real" wills, effective, is of paramount importance, then we cannot reasonably claim that some spheres should be shielded as a matter of principle from the consequences of popular decisions.

On the other hand, we cannot deny that any State, in so far as it can justly claim to be supported by the active wills of its members, rests on consent *because* it respects and defends what they regard as their particular rights.

How, then, can its authority be theoretically vindicated against those of other societies whose membership is at least equally voluntary and whose moral basis cannot be proved inferior?

The assumption of universal and immutable moral values which the State is invented to preserve is a good theoretical basis for justifying the authority of the State in general. But it looks as if nothing short of a World-State can extract much loyalty from it, and that only at a heavy cost in loyalty to other forms of association. But it is not easy to maintain the authority of other forms of association without reducing that of the State to vanishing point.

This problem emerges quite clearly in the actual history of the democratic theory over the past 300 years.

On the one side, we find what may be called universal liberalism based on the belief that all human beings, irrespective of race, sex, color, and creed, have an absolute and inalienable right to be treated as ends in themselves. No one of them

ought ever to be regarded simply as an instrument to promote the good of somebody else. This, if pressed to extremes,
would imply that they ought not to be controlled, even in
their own interests, in any way whatever. We have here the
ground for internationalism as a political creed. It may be advocated on quite different grounds—for instance, on those of
general economic advancement. That, however, is another
matter, and there is little or no connection between the two
arguments, though they are often systematically confused
with one another. This form of liberalism, which inevitably
reduces the State in theory to an administrative convenience,
has a greater appeal in the United States than it has in England,
but it is powerful, at least as a theory, wherever liberal democracy is a live political force.

On the other side is a more restricted liberal hypothesis
resting on the assumption that, in any particular society, individuals have specifiable rights and claims relative to one
another which it is the function of their particular State to
preserve. The particular State is not equally bound in theory,
and may not even be bound at all, to recognize and defend
equal rights for all human beings irrespective of the State to
which they belong. The practical difference between these
points of view is clear. On the first, England was morally
bound to disregard British interests in defense of Abyssinia in
1935, irrespective of whether other members of the League
supported her or not; on the second, she had no such obligation, and what was needed was a view not about morals but
about political and economic interests.

Now it must already be obvious that the second position
is more difficult to establish than the first, unless we fall back
on a pure force theory which is not here in question. But
although it is harder in theory to believe in the rights of
Englishmen that it is to believe in the rights of man,
it is a good deal easier in practice to support the former

than the latter; and I do not think it is unfairly cynical to say that a good many writers attempt unsuccessfully to found their case on the rights of man when what it really requires is something quite different which they are not anxious to make public. They would do much better to publish it, since it is perfectly respectable and, as pure political theory, though it is harder to state, is neither less intelligible nor less consistent than the universal liberal view with which it is contrasted. Whatever the authors of the Declaration of Independence asserted to the contrary, the inalienable rights of men as such to life, liberty, and the pursuit of happiness are neither self-evident nor demonstrable. They are not self-evident since many sane men, who understand what they mean at least as clearly as those who assert them, hold that they are not well founded: whereas no one outside a lunatic asylum denies that $2 + 2 = 4$. And the only demonstration which can be offered of their truth is that it is to the material advantage of everyone to recognize them, which, as Marx has rightly argued, is simply false.

So we may conclude that neither universal nor limited liberal democracy can produce a complete theory of the State except in relation to an express or implied system of morals. And the moral theory which would support the one would inevitably refute the other.

Since it is clear that liberal-democratic theory is necessarily complicated, it may well seem that I am doing it something less than justice by considering the work of only one of its supporters, namely, John Locke. This limitation is not due merely to a desire for brevity, though that is a not unimportant consideration. There are two other reasons. To begin with, it must always be remembered that democratic theory depends on moral philosophy and does not include it as a by-product (as organic theory is bound to do) or exclude it altogether, which is what a force theory, consistently developed, is destined to achieve. This being the case, it is not surprising to find that the views of moralists are at least as important as those of political theorists in the development of democratic theory, and it is with this aspect of the case that Chapter 5 must deal. The second point is that democratic theory has not been altogether fortunate in its professional exponents. They have tended, in my opinion quite rightly, to put forward some sort of limited liberalism as their political theory; but they have also frequently attempted to base this doctrine either (a) on the maxim that human beings ought always to be treated as ends; or (b) on the assumption that the State is organic in character and is naturally prior to the individual. But, as we have already observed, these principles are radically inconsistent both with each other and with the theory which they are supposed to support. On these lines we get to nothing but the completely negative and empty doctrine which conceives the State as being a "hindrance to hindrances of the good life," which, in the end, says precisely nothing about it. Indeed, it is fair to say that far more light is thrown on democratic theory by the words of statesmen who have tried to give it practical expression than by its philosophical supporters. Abraham Lincoln, to take one example only, was in practice, though not in theory, a strictly limited liberal-democrat, and was not ashamed of it. He considered slavery to be theoretically indefensible, but was perfectly prepared to acquiesce in its existence if he were convinced that, by so doing, he would contribute most to the preservation of the Union. President Wilson, by contrast, knew little and cared less whether the preservation of any political unit was a good thing or not. He believed in a natural right of self-determination and could not see the force of any argument which ran counter to it. It is to the principles implicit in the writings and speeches of these and many other genuinely democratic statesmen that we have to go in order to obtain any real insight into the alternatives between which democratic theory has to choose. And they do not lend themselves to any brief and tidy statement.

Locke's theory, too, has had such a great and obvious influence on actual constitutional developments on both sides of the Atlantic that it is not possible, even if it were desirable, to overlook them. The sections which follow are therefore nothing like as narrowly confined to Locke as their predecessors have been to the authors whose views they have attempted to formulate.

John Locke: 1632–1704

By 1689, when Locke produced his *Letter concerning Toleration,* followed almost immediately by the *Two Treatises of Government,* the great majority of his countrymen were thoroughly sick of ideologies, both political and religious. England had not suffered anything like the disorganization and material destruction which many continental countries had endured as a result of them; but quite enough had happened to make men ask whether these upheavals were really necessary, and to be very ready to agree with Locke when he insisted that they were not. The revolution of 1688 was not at all a heroic business, and, if it had been, Locke would have been the worst possible person to defend it. He had no use for heroics or for any other kind of "enthusiasm." What he wanted was a workable compromise, and he saw no theoretical reason why this should not be achieved. Not that he was at all a contemptible person. He wanted liberty, as he understood it, very much and would have made considerable sacrifices to obtain it. But he was perfectly certain that extremism and hysteria were not efficient methods of achieving that purpose, and consequently he rejected them. "Give me liberty or give me death" would not have made any appeal to him. Locke, like the revolution of which he so strongly approved, was sensible rather than glorious; and both of them have stood the test of time uncommonly well.

Locke's whole outlook on politics is incomparably more modern than is that of the other great political theorists of the seventeenth and eighteenth centuries. Hobbes or Rousseau would be completely lost in any political discussion at the present day: Locke would not find much difficulty in understanding what it was about.

None the less it must be admitted that his theory has far more loose ends than Hobbes or even Rousseau would have considered permissible. This is not because he was an indifferent thinker; he was a very acute one. But it was his deliberate policy to avoid following his argument to the bitter end unless the matter in hand required him to do so. For him, thinking, like any other activity, must be justified by results, and he saw nothing to commend in "the useless employment of idle or overcurious brains, which amuse themselves about things out of which they can by no means draw any real benefit." [61] In a word, Locke was, and desired to be, the philosopher of the ordinary man. As he put it, "The commonwealth of learning is not at this time without master-builders, whose mighty designs, in advancing the sciences, will leave lasting monuments to the admiration of posterity; but everyone must not hope to be a Boyle or a Sydenham; and in an age that produces such masters as the great Huygenius and the incomparable Mr. Newton, with some others of that strain, it is ambition enough to be employed as an under-laborer in clearing the ground a little, and removing some of the rubbish that lies in the way of knowledge." [62]

From this general attitude toward men and the world, it naturally follows that Locke's conception of the character of his fellow differs widely from those held by most political

[61] KING's *Life of Locke*, Vol. I, p. 164.
[62] LOCKE, *Essay, Epistle to the Reader*.

thinkers. Locke's men are recognizable Englishmen. They are acquisitive and anxious to promote their own interests; but they are also fair-minded and open to conviction by argument and discussion.

Consequently, Locke's "State of Nature" or idea of how men would tend to behave in the absence of civil government has nothing in common with the bear-garden which Hobbes had envisaged. For "The State of Nature has a Law of Nature to govern it, which obliges everyone: and Reason, which is that Law, teaches all Mankind, who will but consult it, that being all equal and independent, no one ought to harm another in his Life, Liberty, or Possessions." [63] This law of nature, again unlike the one contemplated by Hobbes, is no mere aspiration. It is operative. For "Truth and keeping of Faith, belongs to men as men and not as Members of Society." [64] In spite of this the State of Nature is an inconvenient condition in which to exist, for, although men are fundamentally decent and respectable, they have their weaknesses. Not only do they sometimes misbehave, but they are often in real and unavoidable doubt as to what their rights are. It is agreed that all rights are concerned with property, and property is interpreted in the widest possible sense, "that is, his Life, Liberty and Estate." Indeed, it seemed obvious to Locke, and he did not puzzle himself as to why it was obvious, that every man had an absolute and unquestionable right (a) over his own body (subject to a religious ban on suicide); and (b) over anything with which he had "mixed his labor," provided always that he could make good use of it. "Nothing was made by God for man to spoil or destroy," but "as much as anyone can make use of to any Advantage of Life before it spoils, so much he may, by his labor, fix a property in." [65]

[63] *Second Treatise of Civil Government,* § 6.
[64] *Ibid.,* § 15.
[65] *Ibid.,* § 31.

These are excellent principles, but they are too general to exclude differences of opinion even between entirely honest men. It would be difficult and indeed impossible to specify in advance the point at which one man's freedom infringes another man's legitimate property, and the complicated nature of production, even in the seventeenth century, made it impossible to say at a glance what was the contribution of different agents to the making of a joint product. "It would be a strange catalogue of things that industry provided and made use of about every loaf of bread before it came to our use if we could trace them; iron, wood, leather, bark, timber, stone, bricks, coals, lime, cloth, dyeing, drugs, pitch, tar, masts, ropes, and all the materials made use of in the ship that brought any of the commodities made use of by any of the workmen, to any part of the work, all of which it would be almost impossible, at least too long, to reckon up." [66]

There is thus a need for an arbitrator between man and man who will settle doubtful and disputed issues. At this point, however, we are bound to notice that unanimous agreement as to the justice of these decisions will hardly ever be obtained. If it were, no arbitration would be needed. Consequently the original and essential social compact is nothing more nor less than a general agreement to accept majority decisions as binding. Until this is done, no progress can be made in eliminating the disagreements to which the State of Nature is necessarily subject. This original compact is intended to be no more than plain common sense. There is nothing mystical or difficult about it, no organic State and no General Will distinct from and superior to the actual wills of the people who agree. They are responsible moral agents who know what a promise is and who recognize an obligation to keep it. They also understand the elementary truth that, if we want, as we are bound to do, decisions on which action can be taken, we must accept and

[66] *Ibid.*, § 43.

abide by the condition without which such decisions simply cannot be made, namely, majority rule. The majority need not be a bare majority. It may be two-thirds or any other agreed fraction; and it may be a majority of representatives and not of the people as a whole. These are matters of importance, and must be decided on the merits of the particular case. What is far more important is that some definite procedure should be agreed for settling when a proposal has received majority approval. Provided this is done, the definition of what constitutes a majority is relatively a triviality. It is the acceptance of majority rule in principle that is the foundation of all legitimate government.

This theory of what constitutes the beginning of a new State has been given practical expression in the formation of the revived League of Nations. The critical discussions at Dumbarton Oaks and at Yalta were mainly concerned with the "procedural" question "What is going to constitute a majority on the new Security Council?" and until this was agreed, no progress could be made. As soon as it was settled, it became possible to lay down, at least in outline, the Constitution of the proposed organization. It may reasonably be doubted whether Stalin saw it in quite that light, or even saw any sense in it at all.[67]

However this may be, Locke held that, as soon as the majority principle was generally agreed, a constitutional State could be formed by majority decision. But that State is in no way absolute. It is a trustee, or rather a body of trustees appointed to safeguard specified rights which are, or should be, clearly laid down in the deed of trust, which is the Constitution. Its activity is strictly limited to carrying out the terms of the trust. Within them it has wide discretionary powers; outside them it has none whatever.

[67] The attitude adopted by the Russian Delegation toward majority decisions of the Security Council has confirmed this view

This doctrine leads easily enough to the establishment of some body, such as the Supreme Court of the United States, which can decide in cases of uncertainty whether the State Legislature has, in fact, acted unconstitutionally, that is outside the terms of the trust deed, or not. Locke himself did not anticipate this and might well have disapproved of it as pressing his principle too far. As we have seen, he was by no means prepared to admit that anything which would make his theory logically watertight was for that reason alone to be accepted as politically desirable. He was, however, perfectly clear that, whenever it was obvious to the average citizen, after due consideration, that the State had broken the trust, either by infringing the written constitution or by acting contrary to the Law of Nature (which the trust supplements but cannot override), then it is not merely the right but the plain duty of all honest men to restrain it or to remove it. "For all Power given with Trust for the attaining of an End, being limited by that End, whenever that End is manifestly neglected or opposed, the Trust must necessarily be forfeited, and the Power devolve into the Hands of those that gave it, who shall place it anew where they shall think best for their Safety and Security." [68]

Locke, of course, did not follow Hobbes in supposing that revolution entailed anarchy. For him, it was just a change of management which might well be for the better. Thus an important part of the case made by the American colonists was that they had no representatives in the British Government; that, therefore, they had not consented to its decisions, and, consequently, that taxes imposed on them were contrary to the Law of Nature and so, illegitimate. Hence resistance was a manifest duty.[69]

Whatever may be thought of Locke's trusteeship theory as a

[68] *Ibid.*, § 149.
[69] *Cf.* LOCKE, § 140.

theory, it is impossible to deny that his beliefs about the origin of States are closer to the facts than are those of many of his opponents. There is plenty of evidence for maintaining that prepolitical society, whether or not we call it the State of Nature, was not and is not invariably a state of unrestricted war of every man against every man; and that governments do generally spring from the practical need for more or less uniform administrative practice rather than from special divine ordination or human predatory tendencies. Security against perpetual aggressions seems to be a later and more sophisticated requirement.

This, however, has little to do with the question "What does government amount to now?" and from this point of view nobody could seriously hold that Locke's insistence on consent was anything but insanely optimistic about human nature, if it was intended as a general truth. But there is no good reason for supposing that he did mean this. His concern was to expound the theory on which, in his opinion, British constitutional practice ought to be based, and, while he would probably have held that other nations would be well advised to adopt that theory and to imitate that practice, he gave no thought to the problems which such an assertion would involve. It is therefore rather unfair to saddle him with responsibility for the expansion of his view which has been developed by his successors.

This is not the only point at which Locke's theory has been so improved and developed since his time that it has yielded results which he did not foresee and of which it is unlikely that he would have approved. Philosophically, he is himself to blame for this, since he ought to have worked out even more fully than he did the limitations which his own empiricism imposed on *a priori* theorizing. But this is not to the point. All that we are here interested in is the actual consequences which have ensued on what may fairly be described as a too determined application of principles which, in general terms, he certainly supported.

Evidently the foundation of his whole case is that men are quite reasonably moral and respectable if they are left alone and that the main object of government is to help them when required. The State, it must be repeated, is a trustee: it should not become a busybody. Rulers, however, since they are human, are only too likely to become a vested interest unless steps are taken to prevent them from doing so; and it is therefore expedient to prevent too much strength from being concentrated in the hands of any one person or body. In particular, men are notoriously bad judges in their own cases; indeed, this is the ultimate reason why civil society exists at all. Hence, it is advisable that the person or body which makes rules should not also be entrusted with the obligation to enforce them. In other words, legislative and executive authorities should be distinct from each other.

This, as Locke states it, is a sensible piece of practical advice. But it has been developed by French theory and American practice into a portentous doctrine of the Separation of Powers for which the union of legislative with executive authority, regarded by Locke as politically inconvenient, becomes morally abominable; and, in addition, the judicial power, to which Locke had paid no special attention, is carefully distinguished and separated from the other two.

The aim of Locke had been to provide a device to prevent his State from being overwhelmingly strong. The consequence of a rigid application of the Separation of Powers is to make it exceedingly weak and hesitant. This may be a good thing. We may want our trustees to be so restricted by the terms of their appointment that concerted and vigorous action by them becomes almost an impossible aspiration. It is not, however, essential to Locke's democratic theory that we should do this. For him, it is a matter of expediency, not a moral or political principle, and, like so many of his other points, it is made with an eye to the special conditions prevailing in England at the time when he wrote. For the Executive was the King and the Legislature was Parliament; and, in Locke's view, it was demonstrably undesirable that either of these should be supreme at the expense of the other. In particular, it was important that the King should not be able to maintain a standing army. More than this, there should not *be* a standing army at the disposal of the government to enable it to over-awe its own people: and the best method of preventing this was a reasonable splitting up of power between different parts of the State which, in the prevailing circumstances, would guarantee that the desired result would be attained.

The development which Locke's view of the position of laws in the State has undergone is even more striking than is the evolution of the theory of the Separation of Powers. It in-volves the substitution of The Law for the laws, and the notion of a Rule of Law as a sort of mystical idea at which democratic government is supposed to aim. The position of Locke is clear enough. He certainly did maintain that no State can exist without laws and that good laws are in truth a means of de-fending and enlarging individual liberties. "Those who are united into one Body, and have a common established Law and Judicature to appeal to, with authority to decide Con-troversies between them, and punish offenders, are in Civill Society one with another; But those who have no such common Appeal, I mean on Earth, are still in a State of Nature, each being, where there is no other, Judge for himself and Execu-tioner; which is, as I have before showed it, the perfect State of Nature." [70] Furthermore, "Law in its true notion is not so much the Limitation as the Direction of a free and intelligent Agent to his proper Interest, and prescribes no further than is for the general Good of those under the Law. . . . The end

[70] *Ibid.*, § 87.

of Law is not to abolish and restrain but to preserve and enlarge Freedom. For in all States of created Beings capable of
Laws, where there is no Law, there is no Freedom." [71]

All of this is extremely important. What Locke is maintaining is that freedom is ensured only when governments govern
in accordance with known laws enacted by properly constituted majorities. Nobody ought to be "subject to the incon-
stant, uncertain, unknown, arbitrary will of another man." [72]
In this sense, and in this sense only, did he hold that laws
are an essential condition of civil liberty. Governments are
appointed to govern: and it is for the people from time to time
to settle how much of that governing should be determined
by law and how much should be left to the discretion of the
governors, or, as he calls it, to the prerogative, which is
"nothing but the Power of doing public Good without a
Rule." [73] Thus nobody could extract any definite view from
Locke as to the limits which government by Orders in Council
could not exceed without infringing democratic principles,
because there could be no such limits. It is all a matter of
whether power held on trust is wisely used in a particular case
or not. Thus, from the opposite point of view, "They have a
very wrong notion of government who say that the people
have encroached upon the prerogative when they have got any
part of it to be defined by positive laws. . . . For the end of
government being the good of the community, whatsoever al-
terations are made in it tending to that end cannot be an
encroachment on anybody." [74]

This would seem to be an unpromising foundation on which
to erect any sort of theory to the effect that, in a democratic
State, The Law is somehow sovereign and enjoys a peculiar
kind of sanctity because it is The Law. But it is not difficult

[71] *Ibid.*, § 57.
[72] *Ibid.*, § 22.
[73] *Ibid.*, § 166.
[74] *Ibid.*, p. 164.

to see the line of thought which leads to such a conclusion and to recognize that, while it is no part of Locke's own theory, it springs quite naturally from the practical working of that theory. It is undeniable that Locke's State has a tendency to produce rule by lawyers. The State is a trustee having moral authority to enforce its decisions only within the limits laid down by the Constitution. Hence, it must in the end rest with the Courts to decide whether its laws and executive acts are within the powers entrusted to it. The position in Britain is different from that in the United States, since the former has no Constitution laid down as such, and Parliament cannot, therefore, legislate unconstitutionally. But executive action can be illegal, and it is for the Courts to say when it is. Rule by lawyers is consequently less pronounced in Britain than it is in the United States. Since, however, it is bound to be a prominent feature in any State of which Locke's theory holds good, and since this implies, in a quite intelligible sense, that the Courts have power to limit the activities of the Executive and, in the United States, of the Legislative as well, the emergence of Constitution worship on both sides of the Atlantic is not so strange a phenomenon as it appears at first sight to be. What such worship tends to overlook is that any Constitution can be changed. I do not mean, changed by Constitutional Amendment, since the rules for doing this are contained in the Constitution itself and are therefore a part of it, but by a political revolution which, on Locke's theory, is itself a recognized political act. It is not recommended as a habit, but if any Constitution, however voluntarily accepted and legally administered, were in the opinion of a majority of the people to stand in the way of their interests, they would, on Locke's theory, be perfectly entitled and even obliged to ignore it if its inherent rigidity prevented its immediate alteration to fit their requirements. The Americans were not really bound, though many of them no doubt thought they were, to hold a

Presidential election in 1944. There was no legal means by which they could avoid doing so. But that is another matter. It is perhaps worth noticing, though it is not very relevant at this point in the discussion, that belief in the Rule of Law in some more exalted sense than Locke would have attached to that phrase, tends to generate a quite exaggerated faith in the capacity of legislation, provided that it is constitutional, to produce results, even if it does not correspond with the general view as to what is sensible. The betting laws of Britain and Prohibition in the United States, not to mention the League of Nations, are cases in point.

CONCLUSION

It should by now be clear that Locke was not formulating a theory about the State by the same method as the other writers we have considered. The organic theorists more or less openly say "Suppose that the State is like this, and let us then calculate the position of the individual." Force theories, on the other hand, say "Suppose that individuals behave in accordance with quite simple laws and have no moral scruples; let us then calculate the conditions under which they will exist in society." Locke is much more diffident about his prospects than this, though, on the surface, he may not always appear to be so. The fact is that, while he profoundly mistrusted the capacity of rationalist theorizing to tell us anything valuable about reality, he remained, as far as exposition was concerned, very much the child of his age. Hence, catchwords like "the Social Compact," "the Law of Nature," "Sovereignty," and so on, abound in his work and make it difficult for us to realize how practical and empiricist his approach to political theory was. In fact, the way in which he poses his question is something like this: "I am going to assume that people in general agree pretty well with what experience shows myself and my immediate associates to be, that is, reasonably acquisitive, reasonably honest, and extremely anxious to arrange their own lives without unnecessary interference from the State. The problem is to find the kind of State which such people will be willing to obey." This produces the consent theory. But the whole structure rests on the assumption that all individuals have a generally agreed moral code and that, for the most part, they act up to it. This is a wide assumption and one naturally looks to what Locke has to say about morals for some justification of it. But here, as far as his official view is concerned, the results are very disappointing, for Locke is nowhere more completely caught by the rationalism from which he was trying to escape. Moral knowledge, he says, is as capable of real certainty as mathematics. "The idea of a Supreme Being, infinite in power, goodness, and wisdom, whose workmanship we are, and on whom we depend; and the idea of ourselves, as understanding, rational beings, being such as are clear in us, would, I suppose, if duly considered and pursued, afford such foundations of our duty and rules of action as might place *morality amongst the sciences capable of demonstration."* [75] Fortunately he did not pursue this line very far, and the instances he gives to illustrate it are not encouraging. A far better account of what he must really have thought is contained in a private letter of a later date. "With the reading of history, I think the study of morality should be joined; I mean not the ethics of the Schools fitted to dispute, but such as Tully in his Offices [76] . . . and above all, what the New Testament teaches, wherein a man may learn to live, which is the business of ethics, and not how to define and dispute about names of virtues and vices. True politics I look on as a part of moral philosophy, which is nothing but the art of conducting men right in society, and supporting a community amongst its neighbors." [77] This more useful view is

[75] *Essay Concerning Human Understanding,* Bk. IV, Chap. 3.
[76] CICERO, *De Officiis.*
[77] *Life of Locke,* Vol. I, p. 9.

amplified and developed in an excellent paper on "Scrupu-
losity," [78] of which the burden is that "God allows us in the
ordinary actions of our lives great latitude," since "if we were
never to do but what is absolutely the best, all our lives would
go away in deliberation and distraction, and we should never
come to action." It is important to notice these hints of an
empiricist approach to moral problems, since, if they are followed up (and Locke admittedly never did follow them up),
they lead to the reflection that the universalization of his observations on the moral standards of himself and his friends
may not have been as justifiable as he and many others like
him have assumed that it is. For if, without gross falsification
of fact, we could assume that Locke was typical, not merely
of the English (which would be going pretty far), but of human beings all over the world, then we could legitimately
conclude that the consent State on British or American lines
would be advantageous to all men, without reference to their
traditions, education, and character. Possibly Locke, if pressed,
would have held this view. In his rationalist vein he would
have found it hard to avoid, but his good sense, as it so often
did, would probably have saved him from disaster.

But, whether he would have done so or not, it is only too
clear that many of his democratic successors have taken the
plunge, sometimes with dire results. It is, indeed, an attractive
idea that nations should become arbitrary units for administrative convenience in the "federation of the world," and
much American and British political speculation assumes it.
Thus President Wilson honestly believed until he got to Paris
that he was facing a situation which was at any rate no worse
than what confronted Washington at Philadelphia and that his
task was to get fundamentally rational and right-minded States
to agree on some machinery for settling their disputes. Hence
he came to believe that all the other statesmen at Versailles

[78] *Ibid.*, pp. 204–212.

were exceedingly wicked men and thought seriously of appealing to their supposedly more virtuous peoples over their heads.

But it is not essential to take this line. The idea of an eternal and immutable moral law common to all rational beings is certainly the simplest and tidiest on which the democratic State can be based. But it is not the only possible foundation. It is feasible, though not necessarily correct, to suppose (a) that in any actual society there tends to be a more or less agreed standard of moral behavior; (b) that in some countries, though not in all, this is of the kind which Locke assumes; (c) that in other countries it is radically different; and, therefore, (d) that the theory of the State based on consent can have only limited and not universal application.

This may seem unduly complicated and unduly pessimistic, but it does seem to be the working hypothesis of most actual democracies, at least for most of the time. The United States, indeed, have not so far had it forced too bluntly on them because they have on the whole clung to isolation from the affairs of politically backward peoples outside their own country; and, to some extent, they have clung to isolation in order to avoid being faced with that kind of difficulty. Hence, what would otherwise be a surprisingly large proportion of the American population still maintains as an article of faith the possibility of exporting democracy indiscriminately, and will not be happy until this belief is either accepted by other nations or proved beyond a shadow of a doubt to be fallacious. Possibly experience in China may help in this respect.

The results of this long chapter may now be summed up as follows: We have considered the particular forms in which the three main hypotheses, stated abstractly in Chapter 2, have been put forward by a number of leading authorities, and found that none of these statements are precisely in accord with the pure theories concerned. The case of Locke is peculiar, partly because his cautious approach and limited claims make it unfair to attribute any very rigid doctrine to him and partly because in the nature of the case no democratic political theory can be stated or criticized without a fuller investigation of its moral basis than has so far been attempted.

The next question to be considered is whether any actual States exemplify the theories or not. There are three obvious possibilities:

1. It may appear that all existing States are genuinely of one of the types. The alternative theories would then be of no importance.

2. No State may satisfy any of the theories. In which case we should have to look for a better theory.

3. Some States may satisfy each of the theories.

These possibilities are not exhaustive. It may be that from different points of view or for different purposes two or three different theories may fit the same State, even though, as has already been pointed out, the theories are inconsistent with one another. This is not a nonsensical suggestion. The corpuscular and wave theories of light are mutually inconsistent and yet are both applicable for different purposes.

At this point a caution is necessary. It may easily seem that the democratic theory in one of its forms is obviously right and the alternatives obviously wrong. This should not be too hastily accepted. Admittedly the theories of Locke and his successors seem to conform to facts much more closely than do those of Marx or Hegel. But it is unwise and dangerous to forget that the facts with which in normal peacetime most of us are directly acquainted are only a small and specially selected sample. Whether they are a fair sample or not, and whether even they themselves are as full a confirmation of Locke's hypothesis as they appear to be is what we must now investigate.

CHAPTER 4

States in Theory and in Practice

When we say this is a man, that a horse: this justice,
that cruelty: this a watch, that a jack: what do we
else but rank things under different specific names,
as agreeing to those abstract ideas, of which we have
made those names the signs?—LOCKE.

"ENGLAND IS a democratic State; the U.S.S.R. is a Marxist State; Germany is (or was) a Hegelian State." Each of these assertions seems simple enough. All of them have been propounded quite often, and all of them have, from time to time, been contradicted. So, one would suppose, there should not be very much difficulty in saying what they mean. Superficially, this is the case. If we are asked, what is the meaning of "England is a democracy?" we may perhaps reply that the government of the country is carried out by representatives of the people, elected by ballot on a practically universal suffrage; that these representatives are in power only for a maximum period of five years, and, should they fail to discharge their trust to the satisfaction of the electors, they will be dismissed and replaced by others in much less time than that. In short, the government of England can reasonably be described as government, not merely for the people, but also by the people, in so far as it is possible to achieve this for forty-odd millions of inhabitants. We need not for the moment inquire whether a similar account could have been offered equally easily of the governments of Russia or Germany, say in 1939; for it will immediately be said that the description of England which I have given, even if it were far more detailed and precise than I have made it, would not go to the root of the matter at all. The essence of democracy, it will be pointed out, does not consist in electoral or legislative machinery but in something far more profound and difficult to state.

I have already made it clear that I agree with this criticism. The types of organization found in different societies cannot rightly be regarded as more than an indication, and by no means an entirely reliable one, of the political theories which most of their members habitually accept. But here again we are in a difficulty, for it may be argued that the mass of people are likely to be deceived in a matter of this kind. You do not make any proposition true by believing it to be true. And, although a lot of individuals may say and honestly believe that their State is a "device of government" based on the consent of the governed, it may in reality be nothing of the kind. If it is true that all States are organic, or are just exhibitions of force, then anyone who says that his particular State is somehow different must be either deluded or a liar.

This is an awkward point and, to a certain extent, it has to be conceded. Any theory can be made to accommodate the facts provided that its advocates will accept an adequate number of unverifiable subordinate theories to help it out. The lunatic who believes that he is God, or Napoleon, or a teapot, need never fall into contradiction, though he needs rather a lot of subsidiary hypotheses to buttress his central doctrine.

This does not mean that all theories are equally acceptable to those who are not lunatics, and, as far as political theories are concerned, what we need to know in order to judge between them may be stated thus: Can it be sensibly maintained, without the introduction of unverifiable subordinate theories, that any one of the main political theories is either a true account of the nature of all existing States or a universally accepted ideal to which existing States more or less closely approximate? It must be admitted at once that a disputant who supports his political theory on rationalist grounds and does not mind bringing in subordinate hypotheses may well deny that this question is worth asking. In any case, he may say, it cannot possibly be answered by an appeal to experience, and no inquiry into what people believe about the State has any bearing on the answer to it.

There are two arguments which such an objector may profitably employ, and both of them require some attention here.

In the first place it is possible, as I mentioned above, to admit that nearly all Englishmen believe their personal liberties to be extremely important, but to maintain that this belief is simply mistaken. There is no logical answer to this assertion, for the mistake, if it is a mistake, is not one of reasoning. Belief in the importance of the individual springs from a special kind of moral sentiment and does not admit of confirmation or refutation by argument. However convinced we may be that the man who believes that Bach is superior to swing music (or *vice versa*) is mistaken, we cannot prove this either to him or to anybody else. What is called for is conversion, which is not a logical process. Hence there is a case for maintaining, as I propose to do, that if all men genuinely believe the individual to be supremely important and the State to be something which individuals invent for their own purposes, this is good evidence of the applicability of the democratic hypothesis. In the absence of a revelation, it is the best evidence we can have: and the same holds good, *mutatis mutandis,* of the competing political theories.

This brings us to the second objection. It may be argued that, whether the individual is supremely important or not, there can be no convincing grounds for maintaining even that most Englishmen believe him to be so. Such a statement, it will be said, could rest on nothing but guesswork or on wishful thinking in support of democratic political theory. We must therefore ask what kind of evidence there is for the view that this or any other belief is genuinely held by most people. After all, they may be lying or pretending, and it seems rather bold to claim any high degree of certainty about something so difficult to establish as other people's beliefs must necessarily be. This certainly has some force, but I doubt whether it is as formidable an objection as it looks. Suppose I say "X believes that prison reform is vitally important," and that I am asked how I know this. Broadly speaking, there are three complementary answers I can give: (1) He says so. This is not enough, since he may be lying or deceived about his own state of mind. (2) His behavior supports his statement. He does, in fact, devote much of his time and money to supporting the case for prison reform. This is better. But a slight acquaintance with the "debunking" school of biographers will show that it is not enough. Seemingly benevolent behavior may spring from almost unprintable motives. (3) Direct acquaintance with him convinces me of his sincerity. In other words, I know enough about his character to be certain that the proposition "He believes in prison reform" makes sense, whereas the theory that he is greedy for domination or a sadist or the victim of an Oedipus complex, does not.

Now it may be admitted that evidence of this kind is not logically perfect. However strong it may be, the possibility of a false conclusion cannot be excluded. As against this, we may surely retort "Is there any conceivable evidence which could be more convincing?" Of course if you know that no human being can attach importance to anything except his own material advancement, it follows at once that "X believes prison reform to be vitally important" is false. But how do you know it? Surely on the strength of exactly the same kind of evidence, unless it is a mere guess unsupported by facts.

To pursue this further here would again take us too far afield. I hope I have said enough to show (a) that we can have good though not logically perfect reasons for making statements about other people's beliefs; and (*b*) that such evidence cannot rightly be discarded because some theories, for whose validity no evidence is produced, lead to results which are inconsistent with it.

If this is admitted of individuals, it would seem unreasonable to deny that it is in principle capable of application to communities. The practical difficulties are far from being negligible, but it should at least not be nonsense to say that the U.S.S.R. is (or is not) a Marxist State, assuming that we mean by this to say something about the state of mind of its citizens and not merely about its official political structure.

It is evident that we should make the job very much more simple if we could assume with confidence that the same answer to our question will necessarily hold good for all communities, irrespective of time and place and without reference to the culture and level of economic development attained by the people who make them up. Such an assumption would be unwarranted. We find it easy to save ourselves the trouble of investigation by catch phrases like "Human nature doesn't change," and it would clearly be the case that, if human nature were uniform, human societies would also differ from one another only in detail and not in principle. But although this idea of the essential identity of human beings is strongly held, it is not established fact. Men may be equal and therefore in some sense identical in the sight of God; but it is surely not obvious that they are identical in any other respect. Equally, it is not certain that differences between men, and therefore between their States, are differences merely of degree. Stoic and, later, Christian thought often inclined to the view that they were; but the thinkers of classical Greece were not confident about this. Quite apart from distinctions of status within a single State, which are implied by the organic theory itself, there are texts both in Plato and in Aristotle which clearly suggest that the difference between Greeks and barbarians (that is, non-Greeks) was regarded as fundamental.

We must therefore be prepared to find that none of the suggested theories will apply satisfactorily to all States, or even to all contemporary States, since the assumption on which the contrary view rests has itself no firm foundation in experience. It is the product of Greek metaphysics and of the Christian religion, not of political philosophy.

If we decline to accept the idea of human uniformity as our starting point, we appear to be faced with an undertaking of appalling extent. For it would seem that we are committed to finding out about all the States there are and have ever been, at all stages in their development and decay. And, further, it has already been admitted that we can never firmly establish a view as against any opponent who is determined to defend his own theory to the bitter end. As Marxists in particular have discovered (though they are not the only users of this method of controversy), much can be done by insisting that hardly any State is what it seems to be, and hardly any individual believes what he says he believes. To take the second of these points first, we can avoid being bluffed into too simple conclusions only if we have an extensive acquaintance with the habits and characteristics of the community which is under discussion. Any particular assertion about it can usually be shaken, or at least made to look a little doubtful, by the application of any alternative political theory with appropriate supporting hypotheses to make it fit. But there does come a point at which this process no longer looks plausible. You can maintain, if you want to, that the British Labor Party is bent on acting as the faithful ally of the British capitalist class. If anyone points out that members of the Labor Party deny this charge, you simply reply that they are untruthful. If it is said that their behavior does not support that view, you contend that their behavior is deliberately intended to mislead. And so on. There is no end to the game, but a moment does at length arrive when the reasonable man is bound to echo the Duke of Wellington and say "If you believe that, you will believe anything."

The first difficulty is more serious. We may rightly argue that it is not necessary to examine every cat and dog which exists, or ever has existed in the world, in order to be able to distinguish cats from dogs. But to some extent this evades the issue. We do want very badly to know the way in which particular States are likely to behave, and, even more, the extent to which it is reasonable to hope that their behavior can be influenced by argument; and the answer we give to this question depends to a considerable extent on our view as to which of the political theories corresponds to the facts. It would be idle to reason with a Marxist State, but a democratic State would be more likely to respond to persuasion than to a display of naked force. This consideration sets at least a provisional limit to our inquiry. The more States we know about the better, and I will go so far as to maintain that some knowledge of the history and political organization of a few States is essential to any understanding of political theory. To understand it thoroughly, an exhaustive inquiry into political history and institutions is indispensable, and it may even be that nothing short of some direct personal acquaintance with the working of institutions in selected States is adequate. I cannot myself lay claim to any of this equipment, and therefore must admit that my treatment of this part of the subject is both tentative and dogmatic. The temptation to omit it altogether is strong. But I feel that it is better to make the attempt and to fail than to take the line of least resistance. The need for some link-up beween political theory and practical political thinking seems to me to be sufficiently important to make even a defective account at this point worth having. It may at least stimulate some more competent authority than I can claim to be to make a more successful effort.

The four States which I shall deal with are Germany, Russia, the United States, and Great Britain. This is a somewhat arbitrary selection, but the grounds for it are fairly evident. Germany, though she has for the moment ceased to exist as an operative political force, is and will remain a major preoccupation. Russia and the United States are the only surviving great Powers. Great Britain, though not in the same class as far as material resources are concerned, is easily the next Power in importance and is so different from other second-class Powers as frequently [1] to be included in the first class by a pardonable mistake. In any case I, and presumably most readers of this book, find her position one of absorbing interest. Other States which many people will inevitably consider deserving of inclusion are omitted, because I do not think that the peculiarities of their outlook and behavior differ sufficiently from those of the greater organic and democratic States to justify fuller treatment. The fact that I know very little about them is also a contributing factor.

STATES BASED ON FORCE

I shall first consider the force theory and shall take the Marxist form of it as typical. My reason for considering it before the organic and democratic theories is simply this: There are no States based solely on force, and therefore no States corresponding to the Marxist hypothesis. This is a sweeping statement which does not admit of conclusive proof, but I will try to make clear the grounds which appear to me to justify it. The problem is simple enough to formulate. We have merely to ask whether all or most people behave as they

---

[1] But not always, as the loan negotiations with the United States have demonstrated.

would behave if the fundamental propositions of Marxism were true or were generally believed to be true: and the case for maintaining that people do not behave in this way seems to me conclusive.

By way of preliminary, it must be emphasized that, although Marxism as a political hypothesis does not fit the facts, this in no way detracts from the value of Marxism as a method of analyzing political situations. Some explanation of this statement will show both the strength and the weakness of Marxism itself and of other similar theories.

At first sight it might seem that in denying the existence of any State corresponding to the Marxist theory we must be asserting that the Marxist view about human nature and the Marxist theory of economic causation are hopelessly wrong. And if they are, we should surely not expect that any analysis based on them could be very helpful in forecasting and planning political moves. This is going much too far. The Marxist theory is inadequate to the facts, not because of what it puts in, but because of what it leaves out. To put it differently, Marx transforms genuine, important and easily observable tendencies into hard and fast necessities; and, since the tendencies are real and verifiable, his readers, like himself, are apt to accept them as the whole of reality and arbitrarily to interpret all conflicting phenomena as just misunderstood instances of them. It is an obvious truth that hardly anybody who has economic superiority likes surrendering it to somebody else. There is a strong tendency for people who have dominion to cling to it. Hence it is sensible enough to assume for planning purposes that any economic group which finds its position threatened will try to ward off the threat. There is nothing very profound about this, though it is liable to be overlooked by optimists who suppose that economic restrictions can be imposed on any strong group without danger that they will be countered by force. But it is too easy to generalize this into an alleged "law" and to hold that no economic group will in any circumstances relinquish any of its empire without defending it to the last by propaganda, intrigue and, finally, violence. Marxist "laws" are not always as easy to see through as this. But all of them will be found on examination to have the same characteristic: They start from an evident and well-marked experience (which is all to the good) and infer from it a universal and necessary law which is never wholly true and often seriously incomplete. Now, it was important, at the time at which Marx wrote, that somebody should emphasize as strongly as possible the fatal flaw in many of the "enlightened" theories of the eighteenth and early nineteenth centuries. Reason is not enough; and one atomic bomb is worth a lot of good intellectual arguments as a means of persuading your adversary to see the justice of your cause. But Marx, in his theory if not in his practice, seriously overstated this most important truth. For if his view about economic necessitation is accepted, there is and can be no appeal to anything except force, and this contention understates the power of reason as badly as earlier views had overstated it. Engels ultimately admitted this weakness in classical Marxism, but without at all clearly recognizing what his admission implied. He wrote: "Marx and I are partly responsible for the fact that at times our disciples have laid more weight upon the economic factor than belongs to it. We were compelled to emphasize its central character in opposition to our opponents who denied it, and there wasn't always time, place, and occasion to do justice to the other factors in the reciprocal interactions of the historical process. But just as soon as it was a matter of the presentation of an historical chapter, that is to say, of practical application, things became quite different; there no error was possible. Unfortunately, it is only too frequent that a person believes he has completely understood a new theory when he has taken over its fundamental ideas—and even then in an incorrect form. And from this reproach I cannot spare many of the recent 'Marxists.' " The whole of this letter, which is dated 1890 and is quoted in full by Sidney Hook,[2] is an elaborate attempt to have it both ways, to accept the incompleteness of the Marxist hypothesis and to pass this off as a matter of no great moment.

It would be unfair to make too much of an isolated passage. But this letter is equivalent to a statement that classical Marxism is only a partial and not a complete theory of human social relations. Reason is not enough: but force is not enough either, and what Marxism does, though Engels naturally would have repudiated the suggestion, is to describe a pathological symptom which is always present but seldom dominant in a reasonably healthy society, and to suppose that the behavior of society depends on it and on nothing else. Hence Marxist analysis, though it is often a valuable guide and never worthless, is also never entirely adequate. It tends to be most valuable when States, whether organic or democratic, are internally disordered and therefore ripe for a revolution of some kind; which, from the point of view of practical communist agitation, is a valuable asset. But its application to normal cases (like that of Freudian psychoanalysis, which is in a very comparable position) is liable to produce fantastic results unless careful steps are taken to ensure that the situation analyzed is one to which this method of treatment is adapted. There are, or may be, groups in any society which *will* react on Marxist lines to the slightest suggestion that their strength should be reduced. But not all groups are like that: and it requires judgment, not merely blind faith, to decide which are which. We must consider this matter rather more closely and ask what are the characteristics which any Marxist State would have and whether it can be maintained that those characteristics have actually been in evidence to any noticeable extent.

2 *Toward the Understanding of Karl Marx,* pp. 275–278.

The basis of all Marxist theory is the class struggle defined in terms of the methods of economic production current in any given time and place. Further, it is assumed that for at least a century and a half this struggle in all advanced industrial countries has lain between the working class, who have nothing but their labor to sell, and the bourgeoisie or capitalists, who own the means of production. There cannot be more than two classes of decisive practical importance in any State at any one time, since the dialectic [3] does not allow for three-cornered fights, and there cannot be cooperation between the classes since their opposition is what makes the dialectic process work. Now it will not do to say that all this is either nonsense or Hegelian trappings which Marx accepted in order to sell his theory to the intellectuals, though he himself never took it seriously. The Marxist State, we must remember, is a committee for managing the affairs of the ruling class, so, unless there is a ruling class defined in terms of economic production, there is no Marxist State either. Marxism would then cease to be by definition a force theory, and, although it might be all the better for that, it would be of no special interest to us here.

Now Marxist classes are by definition international. There is community of interest between the workers of the world and between the capitalists of the world: But there can never be community of interest between workers and capitalists in any one country.

Unfortunately for this theory, it has been abundantly demonstrated that for practical purposes international class solidarity, in the sense defined by Marx, is largely a myth. The Third International, though it asserted its beliefs strongly and persistently, was as helpless in 1939 as the Second International had been in 1914. There are admittedly one or two contrary instances which can be produced. Some British dockers really

---

[3] See above, pp. 86–87.

did refuse to load ships with stores for the armies of inter-vention against the U.S.S.R. in 1919; and there was a lot of agitation in democratic countries about the Spanish Civil War. But when full weight is given to these and kindred manifesta-tions, they do not amount to much and are enormously out-weighed by innumerable cases in which no international soli-darity whatever has been visible. It has every appearance of being a luxury, not a necessity, and its importance in times of real international crisis has always been negligible. It can be argued that the workers are hoodwinked by imperialist propaganda, by the Churches, and so on. This might just have been plausible in 1848; none but the most credulous could swallow it in 1939. Marxist doctrines, though generally dis-couraged by the authorities, were perfectly accessible in all capitalist countries between the wars.

The case for saying that international capitalist solidarity is a fact has rather more to support it, but nothing like enough to verify the Marxist theory. There are three main arguments in its favor:

1. The existence and the continued expansion of international cartels of all kinds lend color to the belief in an international conspiracy of capitalists to exploit the working class. Now it is true that cartels have a strong tendency to restrict production by vari-ous means in order to increase profits, and this is a bad thing from the point of view of everybody except themselves. But it is quite as strongly deplored by fellow capitalists as it is by wage-earners; and in any given country it can more reasonably be attacked as un-patriotic than as a contribution to international exploitation. There is an element of force in it, but this can easily be over-estimated.

2. Capitalists have a common interest in starting wars because this is the only way in which they can maintain the rate of profit without which capitalism will not work. In the absence of imperi-alist wars, sold to the workers by plausible bourgeois propaganda,

the communist revolution would inevitably arrive very quickly. As against this it is unfortunately only too obvious that capitalists throughout the last peace were archappeasers. If there really was a capitalist conspiracy on an international level to produce a war against Russia or anybody else, it certainly was managed in a most peculiar way.

3. Finally, there is the very topical argument that capitalists in German-occupied territory tended to be collaborators, that is to support the bourgeois fascist regime of Hitler against the interests of their own people rather than work for an allied victory in alliance with the U.S.S.R. It is pretty certainly true that they did this, though much of the evidence is of doubtful authenticity. But it gets us nowhere, since there were capitalists on both sides and it has never been suggested that collaboration began only when the U.S.S.R. was invaded or that the Communist Party did much to organize resistance movements before that date. If the Marxist hypothesis were valid, the bourgeoisie in occupied Europe ought all to have changed sides in June, 1941, since, prior to that date, Russia, to put it mildly, was not strongly pro-Ally.[4]

What emerges from all this is the important truth that few rich men favor communism and that some of them consider a national defeat in war less likely to impoverish them than social upheaval at home. Further, it is true that rich men, just because they are rich, do tend to have social and economic connections outside their own countries and are naturally sympathetic toward one another's difficulties on their various home fronts. This is clearly a tendency of which account must be taken for many purposes. But it is a very long way from constituting the kind of international capitalist solidarity which Marxism requires. It is not even true to say that most capitalists put class before country. The issue in real life is never as simple as that, and a plausible case can usually be made out for holding that there is no real incompatibility be-

---

[4] Yet we now have it on authority of Stalin that the war was a war against Fascism from the start and not merely after Russia was invaded.

tween the two. Collaboration is a particularly slippery subject since, as Hobbes remarked, "If a man consider that they who submit, assist the enemy with but a part of their Estates, whereas they that refuse, assist him with the whole, there is no reason to call their Submission or Composition an Assistance; but rather a Detriment to the Enemy." [5] In other words, collaboration plus sabotage may be a more effective opposition than open defiance. Of course, this sort of defense can be used to cover anything; and similar more or less specious arguments can be used about cartels and war-mongering. My point, however, is simply to show that the case for international class war as a fact has never been made out, and I do not think that the evidence in favor of its existence is impressive.

International solidarity between men of learning in all departments has for many centuries been a tangible reality to an extent which neither labor nor capitalists approach. It is not a class organization, and admittedly is not very operative in times of crisis, though even then it is not entirely ineffective. The explanation is that nearly all research workers need to know their colleagues in other countries in order to make the most effective use of their own efforts. Some capitalists are similarly placed; but the rank and file of labor movements, whatever their intellectuals may want, are not internationally minded. Marx and Lenin, like many of their followers, were queer fish. They were themselves uprooted emigrees, neither contented nor popular in the numerous countries which gave them shelter. Thus they had no fatherland themselves, and realized that their hope of promoting revolutions depended on their ability to persuade the working class to have none. They failed.

If then we are to admit that the Marxist force theory, with all its ramifications, never covers all the facts, can we give

[5] *Leviathan*, p. 549.

any indication of the conditions under which the Marxist method of analysis in terms of power is likely to be helpful rather than misleading as a means of prediction and planning? I think we can. Marxism is and claims to be a statement of what would happen if the economic interests of the individual (interpreted in a very simple materialist sense) were the sole motives operative in generating action; and it is not very difficult to discover the practical conditions under which this theory is likely to approximate to the facts. Marxism will give quite accurate predictions in a democratic society which is in rather a bad way, since such societies provide the maximum of material grounds for general discontent combined with the minimum restriction on agitation. It has less validity for any sort of organic State and practically none for any society whose members believe that it is threatened with extermination in war.

It may well be said that this account is unfair to Marxism in two ways. In the first place it could be argued that I have confused community of interest with community of feeling, but that it is the former and not the latter on which the theory relies; and, in the second place, it may seem that I have concentrated unfairly on the Marxist view and have neglected other forms of the force theory which are at least equally open to criticism. Both these points deserve consideration. As regards the first, a consistent Marxist would certainly hold that the failure of class solidarity to make itself felt in practice is theoretically unimportant. His view is that class *interest* is a hard, economic fact. Individuals, for various reasons, may fail to recognize it, and their behavior may show that they ignore it. But it will operate none the less just as gravity does, whether or not anybody knows about it or takes account of it; and we ignore it at our peril. Marx and Lenin were therefore scientifically correct in holding that the workers have no fatherland. The workers who disbelieve them are flying in the face of destiny and allowing a sentimental prejudice to obscure the truth.

The weakness of this defense is that it is completely rationalist and nonempirical. Classes, in the Marxist sense, are defined in terms of economic exploitation, and exploitation is the necessary consequence of a psychological assumption. But the fact that workers and capitalists do *not* feel any noticeable degree of international solidarity as groups is strong evidence that there is something wrong with the Marxist system of definitions. Unless and until the workers and the bourgeoisie display a genuine will to practical international collaboration, there is no solid reason for claiming that they exist as real classes at all. They are abstractions to which no actual groups of people correspond. It might also be argued with some force that, if anything real did correspond to them, it would be more like a Hegelian organic State (called a class) than Marxism could readily accept.

To turn to the second point, I have concentrated on Marxism not because it is incompetent but because it is easily the most efficient and logical form of the force theory. It has evolved a highly complicated system of subordinate hypotheses to account for the obvious fact that its original predictions have not worked out correctly, but it has none the less clung to its initial assumptions, namely class war and the force State based on egoistic psychology. My objection to it is that the multiplication of hypotheses which it demands has long exceeded the limits of plausibility. Marxism can show (what nobody has ever doubted) that all States contain gangsters and that some gangsters become rulers; but not that all rulers must act as gangsters if they are to survive as rulers.

The same conclusion, however, follows much more quickly and simply if other forms of the force theory are taken as examples. The Hobbesian theory is quite incapable of accommodating political events in England even within fifty years of its being produced. For we must always remember that force theories are not telling us about what ought to happen but about what, if they are correct, must inevitably happen. They ask to be judged on their capacity to predict; and the judgment has never been favorable except in highly restricted and artificial fields. This will not stop force theories from being produced and from deceiving the unwary; and they have no better friends than those religious and ethical extremists who seek to prove by rationalist methods that they are utterly false.

ORGANIC STATES

What are the beliefs and behavior we should look for in the members of a State which will satisfy the organic theory? Since the basic assumption of any such theory is that the State is more real and, therefore, more worthy of respect than the individual, the fundamental requirement is that the life and happiness of the individual should be regarded as relatively unimportant. As F. H. Bradley has put it, "The man who in any degree has made this [the organic] point of view his own, becomes more and more reconciled to the world and to life, and the theories of 'advanced thinkers' [mechanistic theorists] come to him more and more as the thinnest and most miserable abstractions. . . . He sees the true account of the State (which holds it to be neither force nor convention, but the moral organism, the real identity of might and right), unknown or 'refuted,' laughed at and despised, but he sees the State every day in its practice refute every other doctrine, and do with the moral approval of all what the explicit theory of hardly anyone will morally justify. He sees instincts are better than so-called 'principles.' He sees in the hour of need what are called 'rights' laughed at, 'freedom,' the liberty to do what one pleases, trampled on, the claims of the individual trampled under foot, and theories burst like cobwebs. And he sees, as of old, the heart of a nation rise high and beat in the breast of each one of her citizens, till her safety and her honour are dearer to each than life, till to those who live her shame and sorrow, if such is allotted, outweigh their loss, and death seems a little thing to those who go for her to a common and nameless grave." [6]

This belief in the claims of the State must be generally held and not merely the perquisite of a few isolated thinkers, in any State which is to be a serious candidate for inclusion in the organic category. It implies a corresponding attitude toward authority in general and to the head of the State in particular. This may not be a necessity for the philosopher who is supposed to be able to recognize the State as being a Real Will immediately present in himself and in all his fellow citizens. But most people do not feel like that. They need something more concrete and accessible to express what abstract thought must formulate in this terminology. I have no experience of this kind myself, so I may well be mistaken, but I should suppose that anyone who not merely thinks but feels himself to be one with his fellows in a mystical body called the State would normally expect that body to have a recognizable head: and that head would be the subject of more or less religious veneration. No doubt the elite who knew their Hegel might do better, but it would be unwise to assume that, in any actual State,[7] these are likely to be very numerous.

It might seem from this that the existence of any dictator or absolute monarch would be convincing evidence that the majority of his subjects accepted in a more or less confused form an organic theory of the State. But this would be an ex-

6 BRADLEY, *Ethical Studies,* p. 184.

7 The organically minded Greeks, on the whole, managed without dictators, though they had goddesses. The fact that most of their City-States, and especially Athens, were republics has led many later writers to suppose, wrongly, that they were also democracies. This, in turn, has given rise to the far more dangerous delusion that organic theory and democratic practice are closely connected with one another.

aggeration. Dictators may be temporary accidents reluctantly accepted and tolerated only for fear of getting something worse, or even from sheer inability to reject them. I am not disputing that force can do a lot, especially in the short run. What we are concerned with here, however, is the kind of mentality which likes dictators and which can only with difficulty and without enthusiasm contemplate a world in which they do not happen.

These points amount only to a slightly amplified statement of the tests which are briefly formulated above. If we want to know whether a State satisfies the organic theory, we have to ask (*a*) do most of the inhabitants habitually say that they feel about the State in this way, (*b*) do they habitually behave as if they did, (*c*) is their general character consistent with such a habit of mind? It seems clear to me that at any rate one great Power and one temporarily obscured great Power go a long way toward satisfying the conditions.

Russia

Before we embark on this and the following sections, it is as well to recognize clearly what they do and what they do not purport to show. What is contended is that some actual States do exhibit those general characteristics which the organic and democratic political theories respectively assert that the State must have. Furthermore, from this point of view it is maintained that, for a considerable period of time at any rate, Russia and Germany, not to mention Japan and an unspecified number of less important States, have fulfilled the conditions required by the organic theory. Obviously this statement needs to be carefully scrutinized if serious misunderstanding is to be avoided. It was a commonplace of political argument in the nineteen thirties to claim that there was no important difference between the Russia of Stalin and the Germany of Hitler, or, alternatively, that there was nothing whatever in common between these regimes. Neither of these statements will bear serious examination. It will shortly be apparent that, while there was a difference, and a very important one, between them, it was not a difference of political theory. There is no reason why an organic State should be "right" rather than "left," or why it should be tolerant rather than intolerant about many points to which, as individuals, we are bound to attach a great deal of weight. On the other hand, there are some respects in which opposition to the will of the community, which means in practice to the decisions of the government, cannot be tolerated by any organic State but must be by any State which accords with democratic theory. Hence there are four attitudes which I may adopt toward any State. (1) I may approve of the theory which it exemplifies but object to the way in which, within the limits of that theory, it is organized. For instance, I might agree with the democratic political theory of the United States but hold that the special method of checks and balances adopted within that theory is a bad one. (2) Or I may loathe the theory but approve the practical operation of it in some departments. Thus, many people bitterly disapproved of the organic nature of prewar Germany but felt that England had a good deal to learn from Hitler's methods of solving the unemployment problem. (3 and 4) Or I may loathe or approve both the theory and its expression in a particular State. Hence, such statements as "All organic States are fascist," or "godless," or "efficiently organized," can be proved only by experience, since these are peculiarities which have no *necessary* connection with organic or democratic political theory.

Turning now to the special question of Russia, there seems no reasonable ground for questioning the essentially organic nature either of the Czarist State or of the Socialist State which has succeeded it. As regards the first of these points, little argument is necessary. The complete and absolute supremacy of the State (within which the Orthodox Church may for these purposes be included) over the individual was, and remained to the end, official czarist political theory. This authority was personified in the autocratic ruler himself. In practice it was subject to inevitable limitations by custom and the power of the ruling class; but in principle it was unrestricted. Constitutional forms, in so far as they existed at all, were grants by the Czar, that is to say they were privileges and not rights. And if the Czar did not approve of the use his subjects made of them, they could be and were promptly withdrawn. The individual had thus no rights at all. Serfdom was not abolished until 1861, and the position of the Russian peasantry thereafter was not greatly changed. Admittedly the State was not a perfect organism. Plenty of Czars were assassinated, and, if we may trust the picture presented by the great Russian novelists, the peasantry was more clearly conscious of the Church than of the State as the embodiment of Russia. Nor would it be true to say that this condition of things was universally accepted as right and reasonable. But if we distinguish between objections to the theory and resentment against particular hardships and oppressions, the former are not very impressive.

It may well be said that all this and a good deal more is certainly true of czarist Russia. But czarist Russia was shaken in 1905 and was swept away forever by the Revolution of 1917, and therefore it has now nothing but antiquarian interest. What Lenin did was to abolish the czarist State, which was a feudal system slowly turning itself into a Western capitalist regime, and to substitute for it a Marxist dictatorship of the proletariat, that is a State based on force, as an interim measure, prior to the establishment of a classless society. That is what is supposed to have happened. Lenin's intention may well have been that it should happen. But there are convincing reasons against believing that it has actually done so. On general grounds of probability alone, we should surely require overwhelming evidence that the entire political outlook of a vast and backward nation had undergone such a spectacular change in so short a space of time. Even if we take the abolition of serfdom quite seriously, we have only a period of about fifty years of industrial development at our disposal. It is true that during that time, capitalist methods of production were introduced on quite a large scale in St. Petersburg and other great cities in western Russia. But this process, although in Marxist theory and in fact it tends to stimulate the expansion of liberal in contrast with organic political beliefs, and to that extent to render the organic State less universally acceptable, does not work miracles. Lenin, at any rate, considered Russia a very poor subject for a communist revolution. When, however, in 1917, a revolution, which could hardly have been less Marxist than it was, either in origin or in motive, actually broke out, he succeeded in gaining control of it and, with almost incredible skill and leadership, managed to give it at least the outward semblance of a genuine Marxist product. Nor is there any ground for doubting that, at that stage, Lenin himself together with the emigree Bolshevist leaders, Trotsky, Kamenev, Zinoviev and their fellows, honestly hoped that a world revolution would ensue on this beginning and that, after a relatively short period of working-class dictatorship to liquidate counterrevolution, a world society very like that advocated by radical democratic theory would come to birth. The State (*i.e.* the proletarian dictatorship) would, as Engels had predicted, wither away.

It would be idle now to ask whether Lenin ever came to recognize that this belief had no connection whatever with Russian realities. From 1919 until 1921 (for his effective career ended then) he was far too occupied in keeping his revolution in existence to have much opportunity for reflecting upon its future course. But, sooner or later, reflection was bound to occur, and, when it did, it revealed a cleavage of

opinion which split the Bolshevist Party for more than ten
years and was settled only by the banishment or execution of
Trotsky and the orthodox Marxists. The issue was essentially
very simple. Officially the point of theory involved was whether
communism could be successfully inaugurated by one country
surrounded by a hostile capitalist world, or whether, as Marx
had supposed, world revolution based on world-wide class
antagonism was the only possible aim for scientific socialism.
On this level it was possible to argue against the Trotskyites
that Russia was really a continent rather than a country and
therefore need not be overcome by capitalist opposition which
her unlimited resources in men and materials would enable
her triumphantly to defeat. This was quite a good debating
point, but it left the main issue untouched. The true question
was whether in Soviet planning national or international aims
were to have priority. And what Stalin and his supporters
knew perfectly well was that this was not really a question at
all. Nothing much had happened to the general Russian outlook on life between 1919 and the moment at which Stalin
effectively succeeded Lenin. There had been a succession of
calamities. But Russian peasants were quite accustomed to
calamities. There had also been a change of government and
a change in economic and political organization. State capitalism was replacing the mixture of free capitalism and control by landowners which had operated before 1914. But, as
far as political theory was concerned there was still Holy
Mother Russia, there was still an autocratic Czar who em-
bodied her, and there was still the kind of dictatorial regime
which was generally accepted as being not merely inevitable,
but right. The Russian worker very sensibly took little or no
interest in the wants of a distant and abstract international
proletariat, but was prepared, as he always had been, to endure
a life of hardship on the instruction of his accepted rulers.
Bolsheviks who returned from abroad never reconciled them-

selves to this hard fact. Stalin, on the other hand, with his colleagues who had remained in Russia and had a knowledge derived from experience of the kind of State in which they were living, never had any real doubt about it. That is why they were bound to win. In retrospect, this seems quite obvious, but it was not equally so at the time. Trotsky and his associates were by no means the only people who sincerely believed that if the oppressed and exploited throughout the world were given a chance to find out the facts, they would without doubt hail their deliverers and march together into a world-wide classless society. But it never looked like happening; and it was Russian stubbornness, not foreign intervention and class enemies, that compelled the reversion from militant communism to slightly modified czarist political theory. It was the only theory which fitted the Russian reality, and practice had to accommodate itself as best it could. The funeral ceremonies of Lenin [8] alone were enough to show how utterly foreign Marxism was to the Russian atmosphere. Democracy, it is only fair to say, is equally repugnant. The funeral of Mr. Roosevelt made an interesting and significant contrast to that of Lenin, and one may feel tolerably confident that Mr. Churchill will never be embalmed and exhibited to an endless stream of pilgrims in an imposing mausoleum in Parliament Square. This is not merely a matter of taste. It exemplifies in a small but striking way the fundamental difference between organic and democratic States.

It has indeed been clear for a long time now that Russia is not a Marxist State and has no intention of becoming one. Her interest in world revolution as such is negligible, though her interest in revolutions in other peoples' countries as a means to an end remains considerable. The end, however, is not the dictatorship of the workers of the world. It is the eco-

[8] *Cf.* WALTER DURANTY, *U.S.S.R.*, p. 94.

nomic progress and security of the Russian Empire.[9] Nevertheless, the language of Marxism has been preserved almost intact. Kulaks and middle peasants who objected to collective
farms were solemnly described as class enemies; so were ordinary traitors who were detected and executed in the purges
of the nineteen-thirties. They were actually removed for
preferring private or foreign interests to those which the State,
through its head, had laid down as its own.

More recently, it must be admitted, the camouflage has
deteriorated a great deal. Differences in remuneration for
quality and intensity of work performed might conceivably
be swallowed by a strict Marxist as an inevitable though temporary expedient. But differences in status could not be. There
may be no great harm in paying generals and admirals more
than common soldiers and sailors, but, as far as I know, every
officer in the Red Army has at least one personal servant and,
what is more significant, regards any suggestions that he should
look after himself in any way not simply as a bore but as an
insult to his status as an officer. This is neither Marxist nor
democratic. It is just the old caste system which is so closely
identified with organic political theory. One further point
deserves notice. During the recent war, Russian soldiers sacrificed themselves in vast numbers with the same staggering
indifference to death for which they were conspicuous in 1914–
1917. But their battle cry was not "Proletarians of all the world,
unite!" It was "Death to the Fascist *invaders of our Country.*"
The Internationale and the Comintern are no longer essential
to the U.S.S.R.

It can be said that these are just wartime phenomena and
that too much weight should not be attached to them. On the

[9] At the moment (March, 1946) an attempt is being made to revive Marxist
slogans and to replace Peter the Great and Suvorov by Marx and Engels. It
may be doubted whether this should be regarded as a serious move to substitute a Marxist for an organic State. If it is, it is unlikely to get very far.

other side of the balance we must certainly set the new Constitution of the U.S.S.R., adopted in 1936 by no less than 96.8 per cent of the ninety-four million electors eligible to vote. Certainly this document has more in common with the thought of modern liberalism than with that of Hegel. "All citizens of the U.S.S.R. are guaranteed the right to work, the right to rest and leisure, the right to education, the right to maintenance in old age and in case of sickness or disability." And again, "In order to strengthen Socialist society, the Constitution guarantees freedom of speech, press, assembly, and meeting, the right to unite in public organizations, inviolability of person, inviolability of domicile and privacy of correspondence, the right of asylum for foreign citizens persecuted for defending the interests of the working people or for their scientific activities, or for their struggle for national liberation." [10]

No democrat could ask for more than that as a constitutional safeguard for the things he holds to be of first-rate importance, and unquestionably the new Constitution as a whole is appropriate to a liberal-democratic and not to an organic State. But we have yet to see whether, under peace conditions which have never obtained in Russia since it was adopted, liberty to oppose the policy of the Communist Party will amount to anything. It is not, I fancy, too cynical to expect that the Russians will continue to be "educated" on the best Hegelian principles, and that the overwhelming majority of them will not resent it.

It is legitimate to expect that, whatever the constitutional trimmings for the moment may be, Stalin will continue to govern the Russians on approximately the same lines as his predecessors on the throne of the Czars have always done. Neither he nor they could work any different system. This does not imply that the *purpose* of the Stalin regime is identical with that of the Romanovs. It is true that both have as their

10 *History of the C.P.S.U.(B)*, p. 345.

aim the security and prosperity of Russia. But they mean very different things by that phrase. In terms of Plato's view previously cited,[11] we may say that the Romanov State was a bad one because it exaggerated the importance of one class and provided excessive happiness for that class at the expense of the whole. Lenin and later Stalin have corrected this tendency. In particular, they have abolished the system of "exploitation of man by man" on which it depended. The State may exploit individuals, but nobody else may do so. And, whatever service the State may call for, it may be questioned whether exploitation is technically the correct description of it.

Although, therefore, there was a real measure of agreement between Russian and German theory as to the relative importance of the State and of the individual in the scheme of things, their applications of the theory were immeasurably different. It was true of both that the individual had no rights other than those with which the State, in the exercise of its unlimited discretion, chose to endow him. But Hitler and Stalin in the exercise of their discretion endowed very different types of people.

There is, however, one common element in organic States to which they are bound to give practical expression and which discriminates them most sharply from democracies. This is their attitude toward justice. Purges and propaganda trials are not really mysterious occurrences. In any State to which the organic hypothesis is applicable, they are more or less inevitable, though, for political reasons, there may be considerable variations in the amount of external publicity accorded them. They might also happen in a pure force State; that is, in a State in which an armed minority tyrannized over a reluctant but helpless majority. And, since Marxism encouraged the view that Russia was a State of that type, this explanation was frequently offered and accepted. It was hard to believe this even

11 See above, pp. 36–37.

before the war and, in view of the devotion to their State which millions of Russians have displayed and the total absence, as far as is known, of any attempt to overthrow the regime, it is plain nonsense now. Nor is it in the least necessary as an explanation of the facts. For the aim of a court of justice in an organic State is necessarily entirely different from that appropriate to a democracy. In the latter, opposition to the State, if it takes certain clearly specified forms, is a crime. In the former it is always a sin; and the accused as well as the accusers recognize it as a sin. The question for the court to settle, then, is not "Can this be proved in accordance with rather strict rules of evidence?" but simply "Do we believe this?" Not, "Can we demonstrate that X has broken the rules?" but simply "Is X a traitor?", that is, "Has he acted against the interests of the State?" If the court is satisfied that he has, it is immaterial whether the law has or has not actually foreseen the possibility of the special kind of act which he has perpetrated.

This attitude is diametrically opposed to the democratic idea of what justice ought to be. And it is even more unintelligible to democrats that the accused in such trials should apparently cooperate with the prosecution. So unintelligible that torture, drugs, bribes, and all sorts of other explanations have been invented to account for it. These may conceivably have been true in some instances, though I think this highly doubtful, and the evidence of all qualified observers who have been present at the big Moscow trials is quite consistently against it. It is surely much simpler to suppose that people who live in and accept a god-State are as liable as any other types of religious enthusiast to be overwhelmed by a consciousness of sin. Stalin has invented a good many things, but I hardly think he can or would claim to have been the first to produce such consciousness.

Russia, then, has at least all the obvious characteristics which an organic State might fairly be expected to show: There is nothing to be gained either by concealing this fact or by resenting it. But it is important to decide whether such a State may reasonably be expected to continue peacefully side by side with States of an entirely different type. To this question we shall return at a later stage.[12]

GERMANY

It would be generally agreed that Hitler's Third German Reich exhibited the salient characteristics of an organic State in their most aggressive and, to us, most unattractive form. State worship was not concealed or watered down as it is and has been elsewhere. It was flaunted. For years before the *coup d'état* of 1933, hardly anybody who witnessed the annual Nazi orgy at Nuremberg could fail to observe that it was a religious festival in honor of the god, Deutschland, and that this god was somehow incarnate in the person of Adolph Hitler. There was no question but that Hitler conceived himself as embodying the General Will of the collective German people. He said so, he behaved as if he was, and he was generally accepted as being what he claimed to be. Nor, in view of what happened during the war, would it be sensible to question the blind devotion to the national cause with which the Germans as a whole were inspired. By democratic standards, that cause could not have been more wrong than it was. But State worship was strong enough to enable both soldiers and civilians to carry on for years under conditions seemingly unsupportable to human beings; and German civilian morale was unbroken at the end.

It is at least equally clear that no doctrine of the natural rights of man had any place in the convictions recognized by the Third Reich. Here, as in the case of State worship, there was no question whatever of concealment or apology. The function of the Courts of Justice was openly asserted to be

12 In Ch. 6.

to serve the interest of the State: and the State could be bound by no law. Law was the will of the State formulated by the Führer. Entirely consistent with this attitude was the belief that Germans were a peculiar people, different from and superior to all other peoples. In particular they were different from and superior to the Slavs. So there was and could be no question of Poles or Russians having rights. There were, literally and not metaphorically, "lesser breeds without the law," and it may be doubted whether any moral qualms have been felt by loyal Germans at revelations of what went on in Belsen and Buchenwald.

So it is not surprising that "liberation from the Nazi yoke" has not resulted in a great crop of enthusiasm for self-government. The organic Hitler State was real. It was more real than its members, and now that the State is in abeyance, the Germans are behaving exactly as, on pure organic theory, they ought to behave. They are waiting for somebody to give them back their organic State, and, presumably in due course somebody will do so, since there is no sign that they can live without it.

Nor is this all. There is at least quite a good case for saying that this condition of mind is no invention of recent years. It has been an outstanding German characteristic for a long time. Even those who doubt whether it is really helpful to discover the black heart of modern Prussia already beating in the pages of Tacitus' *Germania* may still admit that German policy during the past century takes some explaining on any other lines.

But, however good this case looks, there are some gaps in it. It is not necessary to go back very far or even to enter into controversy as to the extent, if any, to which Luther seriously believed in the extreme value of the individual conscience. For nobody can seriously dispute that, within quite recent times, Germany has been the scene of two major liberal movements. Frankfurt (in 1848) and Weimar were both failures. Neither of them ever looked much like being anything else. But they were facts for all that, and quite a number of Germans demonstrably believed in both of them up to a point. There was also a strong German Trade Union movement in the nineteenth and twentieth centuries, and even the Reichstag, though its effective strength was small, was sometimes a trouble to the rulers of the Second Reich. In the event, the bark of the German socialists was worse than their bite. But their bark had at any rate been loud enough to make some competent observers believe that they really would vote against war credits in 1914. They did no such thing, and Lenin told them what he thought of them. But the belief that they *might* act in conflict with the god-State on a major issue was not regarded as completely outrageous. Nor were groups other than the socialists completely negligible. The "Kulturkampf" between the Bismarck regime and the Roman Catholics did amount to something. Finally, it is fair to remember (though the Germans are not at all likely to let it be forgotten) that in the last free elections before Hitler's final acquisition of power (1933) the Nazi Party acquired less than fifty per cent of the total votes polled. Hitler was, in fact, outvoted by the Communists, Social Democrats and the Catholic Center, and the Reichstag fire was needed to straighten things out.

What are we to make of all this?

The solution which is at the moment most widely favored by eminent Germans with a taste for psychoanalyzing their compatriots is what may be called the split-personality theory. Germany, we are told, has a sort of double personality.[13] There is a good Germany which is there all the time, but the bad Germany dominates it and commits all the crimes. What we need to do, then, is simply to put the good Germany in control and all will be well. This view is naturally wrapped up

---

[13] *Cf.* EMIL LUDWIG, *Germany: The Double History of a Nation.*

in a good deal of mythology and metaphor, and it is never quite clear which of two entirely different positions its exponents are trying to maintain. It might be argued that Germany is a genuinely organic society which is frequently wicked *as a whole* but which is none the less fundamentally sound at heart and can be reclaimed *as a whole* by proper treatment. Whether the treatment recommended is a long spell of penal servitude or a short dose of compulsory reeducation is unimportant. What matters is the implicit assumption that Germany is an organic whole with a single personality to be praised or blamed. The alternative, also widely publicized, is that Hitler's Reich was in truth a State based on force in which a small minority of gangsters tyrannized over the good or neutral majority through the medium of the Gestapo. On this view it was held that, when the last Gauleiter had been strangled with the entrails of the last S.S. man, a liberal-democratic State would at once emerge from the shadows and give a demonstration of what the good Germany could accomplish. This case was never very convincing, and the war and the postwar period have already finally ruled it out. Nothing democratic has yet emerged from the shadows, and there is little or no reason to suppose that anything will do so in the future.

Can we, then, make any sense of what has happened and is happening in Germany on the organic theory? I think we can, and am inclined to hold that the apologists who take this line are, in principle, correct. But I would also suggest that they see the implications of their own view. The truth would not be beneficial to Germany, since, if it were accepted, the penalty exacted would be painful, of long duration, and not open to argument. Hence it is hardly surprising that there is a strong tendency to muddle up the organic theory with the force theory. The former is plausible, but its consequences are unpleasant. The latter is entirely lacking in probability as far as Germany is concerned. But its acceptance would mean that German guilt was punished as soon as selected "war criminals" were safely executed. It is naturally hoped that the total incompatibility of the two theories with one another will escape notice under the obscurity of a lot of psychological verbiage.

But, before we can assert with confidence that Germany shows all the signs of being an organic whole and, therefore, deserves to be dealt with on that basis, we have to ask what the "good Germany" claimed by the apologists has to be said for it. There are, and at any rate for the past two hundred years there have always been, an appreciable number of Germans who have genuinely believed in the value of the individual and have therefore proved quite indigestible by the organic State. They have always been unpopular and have occasionally been persecuted by various governments; there is no evidence that they have ever found or made adherents to their view in any large numbers among the mass of the population. In the last resort, Frankfurt and Weimar both collapsed because scarcely anyone was prepared to shed anything more precious than ink in support of them when it really came to the point. Hence the liberal-minded Germans have tended, very naturally, to migrate to more congenial political climates overseas and their influence on thought has been far greater outside Germany than inside it. This process has also been progressive, and one may fairly doubt whether, after the very thorough purges conducted by the Nazis before and during the war, anything much survives in Germany today. Fundamentally this German liberal minority had something, but not much, in common with the left-wing Russian opposition which was finally eliminated by Stalin. It was internationalist and believed in the rights of man rather than in the exclusive rights of Germans; but it was not, on the whole, at all revolutionary. Indeed, the internationalism of its members was in many cases highly qualified. It is by no means true that everyone in Germany who disapproved of Hitlerism and the god-State also disliked pan-Germanism or felt brotherly love toward the Poles. Democrats are not necessarily pacifists or opposed to imperialist policies, though they have at least a tendency to disapprove of wars; and there is reason to suppose that many German liberals and social democrats accepted Hitlerism because they supported an expansionist foreign policy even though they rejected the organic State for which Hitler stood.

Apart from the liberal intellectuals, there seems no good ground for doubting that the vast majority of the German people did and still do hold themselves to be members of an organic or superorganic Nation-State conceived on strictly Hegelian lines; or, alternatively, that the political theory which Hegel formulated was and remains essentially valid of the community which he had in mind when he formulated it, namely, Prussia. Whether or not it was then true of other German States is a matter of no great moment, since, more recently, its general validity for Germany as a whole has been so firmly demonstrated.

This conclusion need not commit us to the view that all individual Germans, or even the majority of them, consistently thought that Hitler himself or his actual regime was good. Many, no doubt, especially among the generals and the Catholic Center, strongly disagreed with the Nazi party line on many important points. They acknowledged themselves more or less explicitly as members of the organic German Reich, but did not like Hitler as the expression or incarnation of that Reich. In fact their acceptance of that particular god-State was an incomplete one, and they have therefore been placed in the embarrassing intellectual position already mentioned in connection with Rousseau, namely that of experiencing guilt and self-righteousness at the same time.

They could disown Belsen but still claim that the German cause was at bottom just and righteous. Their soldiers were heroes—not murderers. But this alibi is really very thin. Many representatives of the Churches and the Wehrmacht no doubt thought that Hitler and the bosses of the Nazi party were just crooks. None the less they, and with them the nation as a whole, accepted those crooks with merely formal protests because their home and foreign policies were held to be, on the whole, advantageous. And from 1939 to 1942, when it looked as if they had backed a winner, there were no complaints.

In fact, if we exclude the genuine liberals or such of them as survive, it seems abundantly clear that Germany satisfies the conditions of the organic hypothesis to a very high degree. The "good" Germany, if it exists at all, is represented only by those who, while they have never questioned the organic character of the State, have felt some reluctance in approving of Hitler's internal policy. But they accepted it all the same as the only condition under which the ideals of Grossdeutschland could be, as they hoped, immediately realized.

If further confirmation were needed, it could be pointed out that all modifications made by Hitler of the Weimar Constitution have combined to make German institutions conform completely to organic theory. The *Gleichschaltung* of the States, the inclusion of the Wehrmacht in the party, the Labor Front and the People's Courts are all evidence for the same conclusion. Possibly they *might* have been unwelcome innovations imposed on a reluctant nation by self-appointed tyrants, but I believe that anyone who considers the known facts will in the end have to agree that all of them actually functioned far more smoothly and efficiently than they would have done had they not been extremely appropriate to the beliefs and characters of the overwhelming majority of the German people.

There is, however, a further point which deserves some mention, though it is hard to say how much importance should be attached to it. The Germans have habitually wanted to have the law on their side. The Hitler regime itself displayed remarkable touchiness about this, and unquestionably devoted much time and trouble to producing facts which would provide its political and military policies with some sort of legal foundation in the eyes of its own people. A lot of effort was expended in demonstrating that Czecho-Slovakia in 1938 and Poland in 1939 were systematically persecuting their German minorities, and in arguing that air attacks on cities were not initiated by the Luftwaffe. The second of these propaganda offensives is interesting, since it was in full blast before the German government or High Command expected that German cities would ever be seriously bombed. It was thus a moral defensive to justify German attacks on British cities. We need not inquire whether the political and military leaders of Germany were themselves deluded by their own legalistic reasonings. Possibly some of them were. But Goebbels certainly thought that the German people as a whole would be favorably impressed by them, and the evidence is that he judged correctly. It is not easy to see why convinced believers in the organic State, which is by definition above all laws, should have needed this kind of anesthetic. Presumably the answer is that the ordinary German was up against the same difficulty in practice as that which Aristotle and Hegel had both discovered in theory. He wanted his organic god-State but did not wholly approve of its lawless implications. It seems to me that this desire for legality is a better argument than is the existence of alleged "good" Germans for holding that organic theory, even in Germany, has not been accepted absolutely undiluted; and this should be remembered even when it is admitted that the effects of the dilution have been practically negligible.

DEMOCRATIC STATES

The distinctive characteristic of the democratic State is government by consent. And government by consent means more than passive acquiescence by the governed in an existing regime. It implies active participation by all citizens in the activity of government. This, however, is a situation which is easier to define than it is to recognize, since there are no very obvious marks by which active participation can in practice be distinguished from acquiescence. The difference is primarily one of outlook, and is not necessarily expressed in overt acts. This is so much the case that, in normal circumstances, we may not even find it perfectly simple to be clear about our own position in societies with which we are connected. "I belong to so-and-so, but I am not a very active member of it," is quite a common form of statement, and it is liable to be misleading. It suggests at once exactly the condition of unquestioning acceptance which we have taken as characteristic of the members of an organic society. This may easily be a false appearance. It is not democratic to be ostentatiously active about government. Provided the machine is working properly, it is much better to leave it alone than to be perpetually tinkering with it. All the same, it is clearly a problem to know how we are to discriminate between acceptance of the State simply because it is the State, which is the organic attitude, and support of the State because it is performing with reasonable efficiency the job which it is created to perform, which is what democratic loyalty requires.

The matter is further complicated by the present-day status of the word "democracy" as a slogan. To sacrifice it is now definitely a disadvantage from the point of view of popular appeal. Hence we can be reasonably certain that when a national leader foreswears "democracy," even if he describes it as "demo-plutocracy" or "decayed liberalism," he means what he says. It is by no means equally certain that those who officially adopt democracy as part of their program are interested in it except as a profitable catchword.

When Hitler abused democracy, there was no reason to disbelieve him: but it is less easy to believe Franco when he claims to support it.

We cannot, therefore, hope to identify democratic States solely by taking the criteria for organic States and inverting them. It is true that State worship and democracy are incompatible. More accurately, since the democratic State is by definition a machine, to worship it is to commit idolatry of a rather foolish type. But, although the prevalence of State worship, for instance in the Third Reich, is quite easy to establish, the absence of it in Britain or the United States is more open to question. It is always hard to prove a negative.

So we have to start at the other end and concentrate on the importance which liberal-democratic theory avowedly attaches to the individual. But here again where politics is in question, difficulties are bound to arise. We have already seen that both the theory and the practice of the organic State do, in an intelligible sense, express the general will of their members. Nothing but an extreme form of force State could completely ignore the desires and aspirations of its citizens. Now the theoretical difference between the organic and the democratic State turns on the question whether the rights of the citizens as individuals are regarded as fundamental or whether they are granted as an act of grace, revocable without notice on the fiat of the government which enunciates the general will of the community. And what we want to know is, how to decide in a particular State which of these two possibilities is realized. Obviously, there are many general indications which will help in this. We must get what we can out of political organization and institutions which, though by no means infallible, are none the less valuable guides. We must also ask about the general attitude of the citizens toward the State and its functionaries, since this is a reasonably safe guide to the extent to which State worship is seriously treated as a cult. There is, however, a far more efficient test than these, one which they can supplement but which they cannot at all replace. The common man, especially the common intellectual, may easily be apparently cynical about his organic State and so careless in his worship of it as to promote doubts as to whether it is really organic at all. Some leading Germans like Göring and Ribbentrop were not unsuccessful in producing this illusion during the last peace. But the ultimate criterion of a democratic State is bound to be the legal existence of an officially recognized opposition.

That this is the case becomes apparent if we revert for a moment to Locke's formulation of the liberal-democratic hypothesis. It is clear that the trusteeship theory will work only if the government is subject to real criticism as to its administration of the trust; and, further, that no criticism is real unless there is a permanent threat to the trustees that they may be replaced if they fail to give satisfaction. In one sense, such a threat must always be present to any ruler, since revolutions are always conceivable. But the central point of democratic theory is that such replacement should be capable of happening by constitutional means; and this implies an opposition which can turn itself into a government by acquiring whatever kind of majority is agreed to be necessary for that purpose.

A further implication, which is both essential and exceedingly difficult to express, is that both majorities and minorities should be loyal to the system. Majorities must not tyrannize and minorities must not obstruct, even though there can be no rule laid down for determining the point at which government becomes tyranny and criticism becomes obstruction. Mr. Churchill and the Conservative Party went into opposition in July, 1945. In a different political atmosphere they would have gone into exile or taken to the "maquis."

These conditions, too, must be satisfied in fact and not merely on paper. The 1936 Constitution of the U.S.S.R., as we have seen above, imposes no bar on the existence of an opposition to the C.P.S.U., but it may reasonably be doubted whether the organization of such an opposition would be a healthy undertaking. It may be, as Communist apologists would claim, that this unhealthiness arises, not from any government action, but from the settled determination of the masses to adhere to their present regime. After all, propaganda for racial equality in the southern States of the U.S.A. or the South African Union is not universally welcome. This is beside the point. A regime which extends no protection to critics of its own policy may easily have a majority (in some sense) on its side. It is not acting democratically. The theory of democracy is that anybody who considers the State to be acting wrongly has a right to say so, and that the State has an obligation to safeguard him, however little it likes his views.[14] To argue that the people do not want this is simply to maintain, what in some countries is perfectly true, that the people are fundamentally undemocratic and attach no importance to government by consent as liberal-democratic theory defines it.

To put it differently, no democratic society or government can regard absence of opposition to itself as something of which it can be proud. Such absence is evidence either of apathy or of repression; and neither of these on democratic principles is a good thing. Hitler, on the other hand, was justifiably proud of his ninety-nine per cent plebiscites; but Hitler was not setting out to be a democrat, even though he

[14] But it is no part of the duty of a democratic government to tolerate organizations whose aim is to overthrow it by methods which are not constitutional: and there is no simple criterion for deciding when opposition ceases to be legitimate and becomes conspiracy. Democracy of the British variety and rationalism do not go well together.

did infrequently assert that national socialism was the only true democracy.

THE UNITED STATES

"In America the principle of the sovereignty of the people is not either barren or concealed, as it is in some other nations; it is recognized by the customs and proclaimed by the laws; it spreads freely, and arrives without impediment at its most remote consequences. If there be a country in the world where the doctrine of the sovereignty of the people can be fairly appreciated, where it can be studied in its application to the affairs of society, and where its dangers and its advantages may be foreseen, that country is assuredly America." [15] This was true when it was published in 1835, and nothing has happened since that date to qualify it. Beyond the boundaries of the United States, however, there have been changes, and it would no longer be accurate to claim America as unique or even as preeminent in exhibiting a genuine instance of government by the people. This point is not immediately relevant. What concerns us is that the United States have for a century and a half satisfied to a notable extent the requirements of liberal-democratic political theory. We may at first be inclined to say that that is not so very surprising since they were founded in order to do just that. Everybody knows that the Constitution was intended to express and give effect to democratic principles, and there is no reason for astonishment that it should have done so with success. To argue in this way is to support a view which is too simple and which is likely to lead to trouble unless it is carefully controlled. Certainly, as De Tocqueville and many others have observed, the freedom which Americans have long enjoyed and the Constitution under which they live are inseparably connected with one another. It is easy, but fallacious, to infer from this interconnection that the Con-

[15] DE TOCQUEVILLE, *Democracy in America,* Chap. IV.

stitution, because it is a good Constitution, produces the freedom. In fact this is almost the opposite of the truth, and it is necessary to recognize that the reason why the United States correspond to the democratic hypothesis is not because their Constitution fulfils certain abstract requirements, such as the separation of powers or the assertion of the inalienable rights of man. Nothing could be more mistaken than to suppose that the Constitution was evolved as the only possible, or even as the best possible, political system for human beings as such. Its authors were extremely familiar with liberal political theory and were especially influenced by the thought of Locke and of Montesquieu. But the actual document as it was finally accepted by the States was the product of hard political bargaining and repeated compromise. The reason why it has worked is not that it is good or rational in the abstract, but that it was calculated to meet the requirements of the men who created it and of their descendants. They needed a democratic Constitution because they were democratically minded men; they did not become democratically minded because they adopted that kind of Constitution.

When this is said, however, it must at once be added that the Constitution does about as much as a Constitution can do to ensure the existence and continuance of a democratic State, and for precisely that reason it could never be operated in a State whose members were of another type. The theory of checks and balances which dominates it presupposes a willingness to compromise and cooperate without which the entire edifice would immediately collapse. The powers of the President, Congress, and the Supreme Court to thwart one another are such that any one of them, by determining to force through or to obstruct a policy without reference to opposition or minority opinion, can produce a total deadlock; and there is no machinery by which such a deadlock can constitutionally be broken. It was assumed that this situation would not arise, and it was considered more important to ensure that no department of government should function without effective criticism than to provide against a contingency which, with good will, ought always to be excluded from the realm of practical possibility.

The separation of powers, then, provided (and it is a large proviso) that it is worked in a sensible way, is at least capable of generating the kind of opposition to arbitrary government which democracy requires. This, however, is rather a technical point as far as the United States are concerned, for it is not too much to say that their whole system of administration from top to bottom assumes that opposition is a good and necessary thing. American political parties, to a greater extent than British, oppose one another as parties rather than as supporters of conflicting principles.

The underlying assumption of the Constitution is that conflicting views can always be reconciled by discussion, and, whatever the aim of its framers may have been, its effect is unquestionably to make any attempts at majority tyranny abortive. There are too many points at which a sizable minority can defeat them. The extreme difficulty of amending the Constitution itself, except where virtual agreement is achieved, is an instance of this general rule. American practice, then, as well as American constitutional principle, is extremely, some would say excessively, tender toward the rights of minorities of almost every sort. There have been and are exceptions to this toleration, but nobody can deny that, in general, it is upheld. Something, however, has to be said about the exceptions, since it is necessary to decide whether they are of such kinds and importance as to compel some modification of the view expressed above that the United States are essentially a democratic and not an organic State. It might still be that appearances were deceptive and that only such opposition was permitted as the rulers considered desirable. This suggestion is not quite as nonsensical as it sounds. There are skeletons in the American cupboard, and, although they have not the significance which is sometimes attributed to them, it would be foolish to deny that they really are skeletons. The most important of them are the color question and the treatment given to those who hold, or are supposed to hold, left-wing political views. Both involve extremely complex issues, but something must be said about them here if only to avoid the charge that their existence has been deliberately ignored.

No sane and responsible person claims that there is no color problem, or believes that its solution within the limits imposed by democratic theory is a simple matter. Nor can it be disputed that the United States, for economic, historical, and geographical reasons, are faced with it in a peculiarly pressing and intractable form. That this is so is not the fault of anybody in particular. It is due to bad luck, not to bad management, and Lincoln in his Second Inaugural overstated the moral responsibility of Americans for its existence. Our concern, however, is not with the merits of the case. It is simply to say whether the manner in which an admittedly atrocious difficulty has been handled is consistent with government by consent, or whether the treatment which colored people in America have received can be explained only by another theory. Have they been regarded as human beings having inherent rights or have they been sacrificed deliberately in order to promote the well-being of the whole community or a section of it, irrespective of their own claims and wishes?

The first and most apparent point which must strike anybody who attempts to answer this question is that colored claims have not gone by default. No case has even been more fully stated or more passionately debated. The second is that, on paper, those claims have been met. The charge, however, is that they have been met on paper only and that the intention of the Thirteenth, Fourteenth and Fifteenth Amendments

to the Constitution enacted after the Civil War has to a great
extent been rendered futile by persistent and successful sabotage on the part of the Southern States. Undeniably there is
a good deal in this charge; and it may be added that, largely
as a result of the color question, something approximating to
a one-party system of election to political office has developed
in the Solid South. Its worst effects are mitigated by primary
elections within the Democratic Party (a good instance of the
spontaneous generation of opposition in American life [16]), but
it is there all the same. But what do these facts prove? Not, I
think, that colored inferiority to whites is based on a general
acceptance of organic arguments and outlook. There are still
Americans (including Senators) who support Alexander
Stephens, Vice-President of the Confederacy, in his enuncia-
tion of "the great truth that the Negro is not equal to the
white man, that slavery—subordination to the superior race—
is his natural and normal condition." [17] But their number is
small in proportion to that of the citizens of the United States
as a whole. The theory of the *Herrenrasse,* which is good
organic theory, has no place in responsible American thought
today.

There are two fundamental difficulties which stand in the
way of any solution of the United States color problem. The
first is that, on a straightforward theory of government by consent, no solution to it is possible. As Lincoln put it: "If all
earthly power were given me, I should not know what to do as
to the existing institution. My first impulse would be to free
all the slaves and send them to Liberia, to their own native
land. But a moment's reflection would convince me that
whatever of high hope (as I think there is) there may be in this
in the long run, its sudden execution is impossible. If they were

[16] BROGAN, *The Free State,* p. 60.
[17] Cornerstone Speech, 1861, BIRLEY, *Speeches and Documents in American
History,* Vol. II, p. 238.

all landed there in a day, they would all perish in the next ten days. . . . What then? Free them all and keep them among us as underlings? Is it quite certain that this betters their condition? I think I would not hold one in slavery at any rate, yet the point is not clear enough to me to denounce people upon. What next? Free them, and make them politically and socially our equals. My own feelings will not admit of this, and if mine would, we well know that those of the great mass of the whites will not. Whether this feeling accords with justice and sound judgment is not the sole question, if indeed it is any part of it. A universal feeling, whether well or ill founded, cannot be safely disregarded. We cannot make them equals. It does seem to me that systems of gradual emancipation might be adopted, but for their tardiness in this I will not undertake to judge our brethren of the South." [18] And later in the same speech: "The doctrine of self-government is right—absolutely and eternally right—but it has no just application as here attempted. Or perhaps I should rather say that whether it has such application depends upon whether a Negro is not or is a man. If he is not a man, in that case he who is a man may as a matter of self-government do just what he pleases with him. But if the Negro is a man, is it not to that extent a total destruction of self-government to say that he too shall not govern himself? When the white man governs himself, that is self-government; but when he governs himself and also governs another man, that is more than self-government—that is despotism. If the Negro is a man, why then my ancient faith teaches me that "all men are created equal," and that there can be no moral right in connection with one man's making a slave of another." [19] Few men have ever stated a vital issue with that degree of honesty in an important political speech.

But the problem remained, and the amendments to the Con-

[18] *Lincoln's Speech at Peoria, 1854, op. cit.*, p. 199.
[19] *Ibid.*, p. 202.

stitution which purported to solve it by bluntly proclaiming that the Negro was a man and, as such, free and equal to other men produced no real solution. What they did was to raise a new obstacle to any rational settlement by ensuring that force and fraud would be employed to prevent that answer from being accepted. The resulting situation was not and is not democratic: but it is the kind of deviation from democracy which Marx or Lenin rather than Hegel can explain. For the plain truth is that government by consent is not and never will be accepted by everybody in any community all the time. This does not imply, as sincere Marxists would have us believe, that democracy is always of necessity a mere pretence behind which interested motives operate unchecked. It does mean that "a universal feeling, whether well or ill grounded, cannot be safely disregarded." The color problem is an instance of the way in which force irresponsibly employed interferes with the smooth running of the democratic machine, but, except in a highly democratic State, the American colored people would certainly not be nearly as well off as they are in the United States today.

Let us now turn briefly to the second charge against American democracy, namely, the alleged vindictiveness which it has displayed against "advanced" or "left-wing" political opinions. Here again, the case is not a frivolous one. There have been numerous unquestioned instances in which the freedom of teachers, in particular, to express their political views has been restricted; the proceedings of the Dies Committee against "un-American activities" would certainly not bear full examination; and the treatment accorded to Sacco and Vanzetti, to mention only a single case, was no model of what democratic justice ought to be. But once more it would be a grave mistake to suggest, as has often been done, that any or all of these departures from democratic standards are the product of State worship. There is not the slightest reason for claiming that they prove anything except that many rich men disapprove of socialist doctrines and some of them are none too scrupulous as to the methods they employ to make their disapproval effective. This lack of responsibility, and not a faith in organic nationalism, is what produces these manifestations—which, incidentally, have always been given the widest publicity and have invariably been severely criticized without penalty by important sections of the American press and public. They demonstrate that democracy does not operate without quite serious lapses, not that it does not function at all, nor that the United States provide no genuine instance of it.

Additional confirmation, if any is needed, of the statement that the United States fulfil very closely the requirements of liberal-democratic theory may be gained by some reflection on an objection which may easily be made to it. The Constitution, it may be agreed, was invented by democratically minded men to meet their special requirements in the way of government by consent. This would account well enough for the fact that it worked in the early days, and might also, without placing an excessive strain on our credulity, explain its acceptance by their descendants who, after all, came of the same stock and inherited the same traditions. But what about the immigrants? Vast numbers of these in the nineteenth and twentieth centuries came from countries which we have already characterized as thoroughly organic in their traditions and outlook; and it is surely too much to suppose that these transformed themselves into natural democrats in the course of an Atlantic crossing, prolonged and harrowing as that experience undoubtedly was. This criticism misses two essential facts. In the first place, a large number of immigrants, and those the most influential, migrated because the political atmosphere of Europe was intolerable to them. They went to America because they were democrats, and therefore reinforced and did not weaken the prevailing currents of thought and opinion. And, secondly, since immigration became easier and less automatically selective, strenuous and consistent attempts have been made by the American authorities to recondition newcomers to the "American way of life." These attempts are not always entirely successful. A minority refuses to be absorbed at all and, in times of crisis in particular, behaves rather as part of a Polish, a Zionist or a German State than as a collection of Americans. But this tendency seldom survives into the second generation: or, if it does, it recurs only in an attenuated form. It would probably be agreed that neither in 1917 nor in 1941 did first-generation German emigrees as a class prove wholly reliable citizens of the United States.

We may thus fairly conclude that immigrants to America, especially those from the notably organic States, have not been easily absorbed into the system except when they were arbitrarily self-selected as peculiarly suitable for this purpose, and also that education and environment are normally capable of producing such assimilation in succeeding generations. It may be that none of the evidence I have brought forward will be found wholly convincing, and I should myself be the first to admit that the best of all arguments for holding that American democracy is a reality and not a pretense is that provided by direct experience. The Lincoln Memorial might very easily conduce to State worship, but in fact it does nothing of the kind. It just does not feel at all like the Lenin Mausoleum. Equally, on a different plane, the attitude of an American toward minor government functionaries would not come well from a convinced believer in the god-State. The German attitude toward them was, and probably still is, extremely different. Perhaps the most striking evidence which can be obtained of the total incompatibility of outlook on the State and its importance which separates the United States from the organic Powers is to be found in the extent to which most American representatives have found life in Russia, Germany and Japan so uncongenial as to be almost intolerable. They have felt toward it a kind of moral aversion, almost completely independent of political views in the narrow sense. American socialists have found Moscow as distressing as American conservatives found Berlin. Nothing much of a practically inconvenient nature has happened to them: they simply find State worship shocking, and their reaction to it is what one might expect of a devout churchman introduced unexpectedly into a Black Mass. Genuine hatred of the god-State in all its manifestations, political, judicial, and military, is imbued in Americans; and it is the best of all evidence that their own State is essentially democratic.

Possibly I have underestimated the significance of the contrary evidence. It would be rash to deny that victory has been followed by rather an outburst of American flag-waving and some pronouncements which have been made about "the American Century" and the "sacred trust" of the atomic bomb have the authentic note of the god-State about them. Time will show whether these are symptoms of an alteration in American outlook and practice in favor of an organic political theory. I do not think that they are.

GREAT BRITAIN

The English certainly believe that their system of government is democratic. They are so convinced of this that suggestions to the contrary give rise to amusement rather than to irritation. And if the democratic State is defined as we have defined it, namely as a State in which government is based on consent, it is obvious that the institutional basis for such a State is found in Great Britain. Some of this machinery has already been specified, but it is as well to recapitulate it here. The House of Commons is elected on a very wide franchise and at frequent intervals. It is liable to be dissolved before the end of its period of election, and members of it are therefore bound to keep the views of their constituents pretty constantly in mind. Subject to this condition, a Government with a majority in the House of Commons can, if it chooses to do so, have the final say on any issue, since the House of Lords has no longer anything but nuisance value to oppose to it. The power [20] of a House of Commons majority, however, does not extend to the oppression of minorities. Britain is the only State in which the minority in the legislative Chamber is actually recognized as a force complementary to the Government and not merely a hindrance to it. The Leader of the Opposition is himself a paid official of the State. Indeed, it may be argued that British, like American, tenderness for minorities of all kinds is excessive. The rights of the individual are safeguarded to a point at which criminals and seditious movements are given more scope than many would consider to be reasonable. It is frequently impossible for the police to get a man convicted of an offense which nobody can seriously doubt that he has committed; and the Russians are not alone in wondering whether the legal revival of a fascist party in Great Britain, within a few months of the end of a war to destroy fascism elsewhere, really makes sense. However this may be, there is no doubt that it is uncommonly difficult to deprive the Englishman of his life, liberty, or property, with or without due process of law.

In spite of all this, many Americans are seriously convinced that Britain is far from being a genuinely democratic country; and many citizens of the Dominions cherish something more than a suspicion that on this point, at any rate, the Americans are right. There are, too, in England itself, quite a number of people who admit that they are none too certain about it. This skepticism is too widespread to be ignored. The grounds for it need examination and discussion.

To some extent they are plainly historical. The British State

[20] See below, p. 203.

is not a device constructed for a specific and recognized purpose in the obvious sense in which this is true of the American
State. The constitutional changes inaugurated by the Revolution of 1688 were solid, but they were not spectacular. There
was no dramatic movement at which a number of delegates
constituting a National Convention put their names to a
stirring pronouncement to inform humanity that it had another last chance to mend its ways. Consequently, the surface
effects were not very striking. There were still a monarch and
a House of Lords; legal and constitutional forms remained
pretty much as they had been; and the Church of England
suffered no harm. There is no doubt that the continuance of
these institutions without seeming alteration has given rise to
some confusion of thought, especially in countries which have
experienced revolutions of a somewhat different type; for,
whatever their true importance may be, these institutions do
provide quite unmistakable parallels to some of the trimmings
which we usually find on the typical organic State. The coro-
nation of a British monarch looks more akin to the ritual
ceremonies of Moscow and prewar Nuremberg than it does
to the inauguration of a President of the United States. This,
however, would be agreed by those who know the facts to be
merely a superficial point. What is more solid is the allegation
that Britain, though nominally and institutionally democratic,
is essentially a class State. Critics differ as to whether the class
distinctions are fundamentally social or economic. On the
whole, Russians prefer the latter interpretation, while Anglo-
Saxons go for the former. But the general charge is clear. It
is that Britain has succeeded only in establishing political
equality; and that this, in the absence of social and economic
equality, is certainly important but is not enough to constitute
a genuine democracy.

The short reply to this objection is that what the English
are interested in is government by consent. They believe that

they have got the reality of such government, whereas arith-
metical equality, whether social or economic, is in itself no
more than a symptom. Therefore they are far less excited about
social distinctions than are the Americans, and attach less
importance to wide differences in wealth than the Russians
do. But this is not the whole story. A better answer is to say
that what the English really mind about is not equality as
such, but is fairness. Fairness is not exactly the same as justice.
It is more individual. Justice produces an approximation to
it, and laws are respected in so far as it is commonly believed
that they do, on balance, produce generally fair results. But
in the end, fairness is achieved by the use of individual judgment and not by the application of a mathematical formula.
This evidently raises moral issues which are more fully treated
in Chapter 5. The upshot here is that consent implies fairness,
since nobody would consent to an arrangement which was
unfair to himself; and it should be added that the English as
a whole are uncomfortable at arrangements which they feel
to be unfair to other people.

As a consequence of this view, it is widely held that class
distinctions based on birth or on inherited wealth are inherently unfair and therefore bad; but they were not very
strongly objected to as long as it was felt that they were accidentally fair in their operation. And this condition was satisfied if the distribution of power which resulted from them was
a fair one. Power is quite a different thing from strength or
force. It is not even legalized force, though legality is an
element in it. Power is more accurately the control of force
authorized by consent. And it is therefore essential to the
British conception of democracy that power should be fairly
distributed and fairly used. This, again, implies responsibility
on both sides. For power used irresponsibly is no longer power.
It is simply force, which may command obedience, but not
respect. Hence you lose your power and with it much, if not all,

of your strength when you behave irresponsibly. It would be unkind to cite cases in which this has actually occurred in British public life. But striking instances of it will be readily called to mind.

To sum up, we may say that the class distinctions to which foreign critics attach so much weight are common objects of condemnation by the English themselves. But the condemnation is less wholesale because it rests on different grounds. It arises primarily not because such distinctions involve inequality, but because the kind of inequality which they involve is increasingly felt to be unfair and therefore bad. The "old school tie" has lost most of its power; and it has lost strength because it has lost power. It is a common defect of oversimplified Marxist analyses of the British situation that they overlook this fact.

In the light of this general account, it is not difficult to explain the retention of "undemocratic" phenomena, of which the monarchy is the most striking, if not the most important. These are anachronisms, no doubt, but they are not bad, provided that what they symbolize is not force but power. Indeed, they are tolerable and may well be considered praiseworthy. It should, incidentally, be noted that the Romans in their better moments were perfectly clear as to the distinction between power and force. I do not suggest that the British now have a monopoly in it, but I believe it is more fundamental to their moral and political beliefs than it is to those of other nations, and even of most other democracies. But even if this general defense is allowed to be sound, it will be said that the British, like the Americans, have still a good deal to explain away. The democratic slate is not as clean as it might be. This is not a matter for any great surprise. The question is not whether lapses can be found, but is whether they are on such a scale as to prove, as some would claim they do, that British democratic pretensions have no secure base. Broadly speaking

the charges are that British colonial imperialism is quite inconsistent with any belief in government by consent, and that
class distinctions at home, whatever may be said about them
on the theoretical level which we have already discussed, are
quite important enough in practice to make nonsense of any
suggestion that the government of England is government by
the people. Neither accusation can be viewed with any com-
placency.

The first is particularly awkward, for, whatever may be
said to the contrary, the British jingo period of the eighties and
nineties had a theory behind it as well as an economic motive,
and that theory was definitely organic. It is interesting and, I
think, not unimportant, to notice that the philosophy of Hegel
achieved its most distinguished support in England during the
same period. Bosanquet's *Philosophical Theory of the State*,
which is still the standard English work on the organic political hypothesis, was first published in 1899. Rudyard Kipling
expressed the same view in a different medium: and there were
many lesser lights.

It is difficult to assess this outburst with any great confidence.
The Diamond Jubilee came as close to State worship as the
English had been for some centuries and must, I suppose,
have encouraged the belief which the idealist philosophers, at
any rate, wanted to entertain, that England was a good organic
State at heart in spite of all appearances to the contrary. It
would be possible to hold that this view had something in it
if the whole attitude on which it depended for its plausibility
had not collapsed so ignominiously in the aftermath of the
Boer War. But it did. And since the attempt of Sir Oswald
Moseley and his followers to revive it in the nineteen-thirties
was a total failure, though the circumstances of the time were
such as to make its chances of success not unpromising, it is
fair to suppose that the earlier and more lasting British flirta-
tion with organic theory and practice was not taken quite seri-

ously by the great majority and was hurriedly given up as soon as its less attractive implications could no longer be concealed. It would certainly not be easy to believe that such a radical change in established beliefs and practices could have been so rapidly brought about if its character had been fully realized, or that, having once been brought about, it could have been so easily and painlessly reversed. But, whether this is so or not, it must be admitted that the ideology of jingoism was genuinely antagonistic to that of democracy, and that the English, to the extent to which they accepted and believed in it, were giving up their democratic beliefs and traditions.

Apart from this, however, it is well known and undeniable that there are plenty of murky spots in British colonial and Indian administration. Some of them are less murky in truth than propaganda about them would suggest, but they are there all the same. Taken together they might be held to constitute a failure of democracy, but not a betrayal of it. We have never said, as the Germans did in effect of their treatment of the Jews, "Yes, we have done it; and we meant to do it, and we are proud of it." The position is rather that British administrators have generally been skeptical as to the possibility of exporting democracy to people whose outlook and traditions have nothing in common with it. Sometimes they have attempted, according to their lights—which have not invariably been very bright—to encourage and promote the theory and practice of government by consent. But the material they had to work with was often unpromising, and the demands of economic exploitation have frequently made it necessary for government by more or less naked force to be imposed. In other words, the explanation of British colonial misgovernment, where it has occurred, must be sought for, like the explanation of the most discreditable aspects of American handling of the color problem, in Marx rather than in Hegel. Lenin, as was so often the case, knew what he was talking about when he attacked capitalist imperialism; but he made a bad mistake in supposing that his criticism of it was the whole story. At any rate, he was not alone in his denunciation of it; and if the crimes and blunders of the British in dealing with their color problem have caused less stir in England than those of the Americans have in the United States, that is due to a geographical accident. We have a vast color problem on our doorstep, but the Americans have one firmly installed in the dining room.

The second charge, namely that the operation of democracy in England is so much at the mercy of social snobbery and economic inequality as to be ineffective, contains only a grain of truth. It was largely the case in the nineteenth century that social standing and the wealth which was closely connected with it by inheritance and marriage, did more to determine the individual's importance in the State than any inherent merit could do. It was, therefore, a common experience to find that those who controlled effective force had neither the morals nor the intelligence to make use of it in a responsible fashion. There are, however, two methods of dealing with such a situation. The simpler is to ensure, as far as can be done by electoral and other institutional arrangements, that no individual shall control any effective force at all. All individuals then become irresponsible provided that they keep within the law. This solution, which has, on the whole, been favored in the United States, tends to the identification of force with power.[21] The alternative is to entrust power to responsible people; and there is no automatic method of ensuring that this is done. It presupposes, on the one hand, an electorate which is sufficiently educated and experienced to exercise real judgment in its selection of rulers; and, on the other, potential rulers outside the class of the well-born and wealthy. These cannot be produced overnight, or even in a year or two. On their own

[21] See below, p. 245.

principles, therefore, the English were justified in continuing
to vote for old school ties, who at least had some traditional
knowledge of how to govern, until fairly general education and
experience of government had produced an efficient alternative. The worst that can be said is that they were unduly
hesitant in making up their minds that such an alternative
actually did exist, and no doubt economic forces and "sinister
influences" had something to do with prolonging this period
of hesitation. But the influence of these is frequently overes-
timated. As soon as it is understood that equality for its own
sake is not the ideal of British democracy the necessity for
them as secret forces brought in to account for the apparently
inexplicable behavior of the electorate disappears almost completely.

One further point deserves a little notice. It has sometimes
been suggested that in the 1939–1945 war the English, under
stress of circumstances, were constrained to abandon democracy and to adopt instead the political theory of their enemies.
There is literally nothing in this. Mr. Churchill as Prime Minister never enjoyed anything approaching the position of a
Führer, and, although the area of government control was
considerably extended and parliamentary control over the
executive was considerably weakened in order to meet the
emergency, it is fair to say that no changes in principle were
made. Some superficial resemblances to the kind of political
arrangements which normally go with an organic outlook
could no doubt be pointed out, but they were never more than
superficial. A few feathers have been lost here and there, but
the Trade Unions, the Churches and even the political parties
were all intact at the end of the war. The appearance of a sort
of General Will was encouraged on propaganda grounds, but
it was only an appearance; and great skill was shown by all
concerned in avoiding issues of principle which would inevitably have shown that it had no substance. Compulsory

transfers of labor on a large scale, for instance, would have produced a real crisis and were avoided even at some cost in national efficiency in the narrower sense. Indeed, it is fairly certain that any extension of compulsion or infringement of individual rights beyond what was generally recognized as the unavoidable minimum would have been resented and even resisted except during the very brief period of total emergency which followed the fall of France. And even then, nobody really felt happy about the employment of 18B.

The conclusion is that the English State, in spite of some appearances to the contrary, does satisfy the requirements of the democratic theory. There is no good ground for asserting that its political institutions are a pretense behind which an organic or a force State is concealed. Inevitably there are elements of force about it, and there is no point in denying that it has experienced at least one period during which its citizens appeared to lean toward a change to organic beliefs and practices. Democracy, however, is the equilibrium position to which the English tend to return, and this, as will appear later, is entirely consistent with their moral sentiments.

To confirm this view, it is useful to compare the democracy of Great Britain with that of the oldest established democracy of Europe, Switzerland. The differences are obvious. The Swiss have no Empire, they are professional neutrals, and they are entirely devoid of any monarchy or aristocratic trimmings. They are thus evidently not guilty of the major offenses against democratic orthodoxy with which the British have been charged. As they make use of a highly developed Federal system of government and are racially and linguistically not unified, one would naturally expect that their democracy would resemble that of the United States rather than that of Great Britain. Curiously enough, the opposite is the case. The Swiss are not particularly devoted to equality as an end in itself. They take for granted, in very much the same way as the majority of the English do, that, provided the reality of government by consent exists, they can always have as much equality as they want. In fact, they disposed of irrelevant social distinctions more expeditiously than the English did; but it should be observed that they also had a far easier problem to solve. It is less risky to operate the kind of democracy which assumes general responsibility in a small community than it is in a large one. Generally speaking it is true to say that the Swiss, like the British and unlike the Americans, are quite happy to base their political system on personal and local loyalties. They know how to be independent without being irresponsible, and are therefore not unduly impressed by the sanctity of rules.

What this comes to in the end is that the Swiss, in spite of geographical and institutional differences, resemble the English in distinguishing very sharply between power and force. They have no respect for the latter, and even the Germans noticed and took account of this fact.

I cannot see any reason why the Swiss and the English should resemble one another in this matter, but the resemblance is important if only because it should remove any suspicion that special pleading is required to justify the democratic pretensions of the English. Nobody is likely to question seriously the claims of Switzerland to be a democracy, and it seems to me clear that if the essence of the Swiss claim is examined, it will be agreed that the claim of Great Britain is fundamentally identical with it.

CONCLUSION

The preceding sections cannot avoid criticism for two kinds of omission. In the first place it will be said that the States considered are selected on no principle. They are just an arbitrary collection, and a hopelessly incomplete one. For it is surely obvious that, at the very least, Japan should be included among organic, and France among democratic States. Even then, it seems highly doubtful whether all States, past and present, could be tidily classified in this way, and it is certainly not obvious that States do not change their character. This might be admitted to be necessarily a slow and painful process. Nevertheless, the belief "Once a democracy, always a democracy" is not one which could be lightly accepted. Furthermore, the organization of those States which have been considered has been most inadequately discussed. Nothing has been said about the comparative positions of communities other than the State, although it is clear that the treatment accorded to such institutions as Churches, Universities and Trade Unions should differ widely between organic and democratic States. International relations, too, have been almost entirely left out. Yet here, also, significant differences in international behavior between States of different types ought surely to be discoverable.

I agree with all this, but would say that the criticism is not relevant if the aim of the chapter as a whole is borne in mind. My purpose has not been to provide a full analysis of the organization or institutions of any State, or to classify every actual or possible State under the appropriate theories. The question to which I wanted an answer was this: "Can it reasonably be maintained that all or any actual States satisfy the requirements of the three great political theories?" The answer appears to me to be that some are genuinely organic and some genuinely democratic. "Genuinely," however, must be taken in a strictly empirical sense. It means simply that the vast majority of the members of these States demonstrate both by their pronouncements and by their actions that they embrace organic or democratic beliefs. I do not see that it is possible to establish more than this, and therefore regard the claim of any of the theories to demonstrate its validity as a myth. For the States which we have considered here are certainly among the best available examples from which instances of undiluted organism and democracy, to say nothing of Marxist force States, could be selected. Yet it is clear that all contain elements of pure force, and that the democracies exhibit some organic tendencies, which may not be important but which are there all the same. Organic States show fewer impurities on the surface. But they do show some. And their avowed policy of repressing heretics may well encourage the belief that more may exist than meet the eye. However this may be, it is perfectly certain that States in which there is far greater confusion and uncertainty could easily have been selected. In France for instance, since the Revolution of 1789, organic theory and sympathies have been more than casual and temporary divergencies from an overwhelmingly democratic consensus. There is thus no point in prolonging the catalog, since it is abundantly clear that no single political theory can establish even a plausible claim to universal validity on empirical grounds. We should not add anything important to the argument by piling up more democracies and more organic States; and to show, as we could show, that many States are in such a confused or immature condition as not to be genuine instances of any theory, would merely complicate discussion of the main issue without altering it in any important point. I have therefore limited the discussion to a selection of modern Western States and have paid no attention to Ancient, Medieval or Oriental systems.

The problem which remains is this: Since no one theory will cover all States, *the* theory of *the* State is a delusion. This being so, since political and moral theories are mutually interdependent, we must face the fact that different people hold really and radically different views about right conduct. Hence, it is futile to expect States of different types to agree on moral questions, whether these affect only their own citizens or involve international relations. This is not a matter of ignorance

or imperfect information either about facts or about principles. It arises from a fundamental disagreement as to the
kinds of act which are moral. Quite simply, anybody who is
a willing and not a recalcitrant member of an organic State
believes sincerely that the General Will of that State is paramount: and he will act on that belief not apologetically or
with a sense of guilt, but as a perfectly honest crusader in a
good cause. It is quite unprofitable and even meaningless to
say that he ought not to think and act like that, just as it is
futile to tell a genuine democrat that he ought not to attach
the importance which he does attach to the rights of man.
These are questions of moral faith, or sentiment; they cannot
be solved by the application of pure reason.

It is not my intention here to inquire as to the way in which
this difference between States originates. That is a matter for
anthropology and scientific sociology to settle. Clearly it is of
great importance that it should be known, since until we are
informed about the cause, we cannot usefully do much to
modify the facts, even supposing we consider on other grounds
that this would be a good thing to do. At present, however,
there is no satisfactory evidence for asserting that the prevalence of one particular political creed rather than another
depends on economic, geographical, historical, or genetic factors. Possibly all are to some extent involved. But, whatever
we may think (or wish) about the explanation, it is suicidal to
ignore the fact.

Since there is not and is not likely to be any convincing evidence on this point, it is rash and quite unnecessary to assume
that every German and every Russian is irretrievably committed at birth to willing, lifelong membership of an organic
State. To say even that he is naturally, that is, genetically,
especially prone to do so is to go well beyond what the facts
will warrant. It is safer, and quite sufficient, to hold that, unless he is by nature quite abnormally resistant to environ-

mental factors, he will certainly be all but irrevocably committed to it at a very early age. Basic political creeds may not be actually imbibed (as Bradley thought they were) with mothers' milk: but children are none the less indoctrinated with them in practically every other way. Such overwhelming environmental influence cannot be eliminated by the simple adoption or imposition of novel State machinery. It can be disposed of, if at all, only by the annihilation, not merely of the apparatus of the State, but of practically every form of existing social organization.

As against this, it may be said that organic and democratic States are related to one another not as different types but as inevitable stages in the growth of a single species. Many ingenious theories have been propounded which claim to show that the organic State is only an immature democracy—and *vice versa*. I do not think that any doctrine of this kind will hold water. The trouble is not merely that *Kulturgeschichte* is a boomerang, since it is just as easy to argue that democracy tends to develop into organism as it is to show that the reverse is the case. It is rather that history will not support either view to the exclusion of the other. What is more important, however, is that, apart from our moral views, we have no logical ground on which to maintain that either change is for the better.

This brings us to a further consideration on which it is essential to be perfectly clear. I have not argued, and I do not believe, that organic States are necessarily bad or that democratic States are necessarily good. By "good" and "bad" in this context, I mean no more than "unlikely (or likely) to attack, directly or indirectly, the economic or political safety of other States." It is easy to argue "Germany was aggressive; Germany was an organic State: therefore all organic States are aggressive." But it is not good logic. Similarly, "The United States is peace-loving; the United States is a democracy: therefore democracies are peace-loving" is more creditable to the hearts than to the heads of those who believe it. Hegel thought that organic States were necessarily and rightly warlike, but I cannot see that he proved his point; and I can find no convincing reason why democracies as such should not be aggressive. There are plenty of other and better explanations of German bellicosity and democratic pacifism in the interwar period. I suspect, however, that the illogical link-up has been made because of the common confusion between philosophical, economic, and political terminology which I shall now try to elucidate.

Political Catchwords

So far I have refrained as far as possible from using current terms such as "fascist," "totalitarian," and "communist." I have employed "liberal" and "democratic" only in a well-defined sense. Socialism and capitalism have not figured much in the discussion, though I have been unable to keep them out of it altogether. In spite of, or perhaps because of this reticence, it may seem that what I have written is, after all, thinly disguised party politics, and that political philosophy is, as I have suggested at the beginning that it might be, simply the formulation in abstract and therefore unfamiliar terminology of party programs which can perfectly well be discussed and criticized without this additional complication. Have we at the end of all this proclaimed anything more startling than that Britain, the United States, Switzerland, and some other countries are democracies and that, as such, they differ very sharply from totalitarian regimes, whether fascist or communist in complexion? In a sense I should be prepared to admit that I have done no more than this. But two points should be noted here: In the first place, it is of importance that we should clearly recognize what does constitute a democracy, both in theory and in practice, and in the second, it is of even greater importance that we should be in no doubt as to what is inessential to it. Strictly speaking, there is only one question here, but for purposes of exposition it is convenient to keep the two sides of it distinct from each other.

My contention is that the terms in common use in day-to-day political controversy, partly as a result of carelessness and partly from design on the part of those who employ them, tend hopelessly to confuse the issue on both these points and are, therefore, best avoided when clear thinking is required. Fundamentally, there is no difficulty beyond that of definition. If "totalitarian" is defined as equivalent to "organic" in the sense in which I have used the latter term, and if "fascist" and "communist" mean simply "right" and "left," then there is no reason to quarrel about their employment. Such definition, however, would not really be a practicable proposition. Whatever we may say, these words have now got themselves associated with emotional reactions which make it impossible for them to be employed in rational discourse. In time, perhaps, they will be fit for use again. We should remember that "democratic" has not always been respectable. Mr. Gladstone protested that he was not a democrat. Even "liberal," which now seems harmless enough, was dynamite in England in the years before 1914. So "totalitarian," "fascist," and "communist" may at length recover their status and become words rather than slogans. But it will take some time. For the moment we have to admit that, as generally used, they have no strictly defined meaning at all. In spite of this, they generally suggest something, though they are riddled with ambiguity and uncertainty. The best that can be done in the way of provisional definition of them appears to me to be this:

Totalitarianism suggests (a) dictatorship, (b) some kind of centralized planning and control of industrial development and production, (c) concentration camps. The point on which I want to insist is that none of these are necessarily involved in any of the types of State which we have considered, and one only is definitely excluded from any of them. Even this may be an overstatement. Democracy and dictatorship are in principle irreconcilable. There is, however, nothing to prevent a democracy, without betraying its principles, from entrusting the executive with virtually unrestricted powers to cope with an extreme emergency. This would certainly have been the case in this country if a German invasion had materialized in 1940 or 1941. Organic States, on the contrary, tend to demand Dictators as a habit.[22] This is about all that can safely be said about (a). The existence of a dictator in any country is suggestive, but nothing more than that.

As regards (b), there is no necessary connection whatever between government by consent and either a socialist or a capitalist economic organization. The State is a trustee, and it may or may not be entrusted with the responsibility for owning or controlling the Post Office, the B.B.C., the coal mines, or any other service whatever. All that can properly be argued is that the concentration of force in private hands which capitalist ownership of these resources entails will probably be abused. In other words, the amount of irresponsible force which the capitalist system produces, unless it is controlled, normally (though not necessarily) produces results which are incompatible with government by consent in the full meaning of the term. Whether this is so or not is a question which needs serious discussion. But it cannot be discussed *in general*. The answer must depend on the particular circumstances of a particular country at a particular time. Otherwise the question is purely one of relative efficiency, which is entirely an economic matter. Beyond this we can say only that, because of the individualist basis of democracy and the consequent suspicion that the State will aways tend to exceed rather than to fall short of fulfillment of its functions, there is always likely to exist in democracies a prejudice against State ownership and control, which is by no means confined to those people who

22 But see footnote 7 on p. 164 above.

are likely to suffer from them financially. Conversely, organic States are likely to favor such control in principle, though they will not necessarily go very far with it in practice. Its extent here depends solely on what the dictator or (if there is no dictator) the government considers to be in the national interest at the moment.

Finally there are the concentration camps. Here again there is no case for holding that these and other repressive measures are necessary products of organic States and are equally necessarily excluded by democracies. Democracies, as the early history of the New England States abundantly proves, can be very harsh with dissenters; and even 18B. bore extremely heavily on some of the victims. But although democracies may be frightened or foolish, they do not thereby cease to be democracies. Equally, an organic State may find it safe and desirable to act with great tolerance under some circumstances. "Totalitarian" is, therefore, not a useful word for political philosophy to employ. In so far as it has any definite meaning, it denotes, not a State of a special type, but rather a number of arbitrarily chosen characteristics which any kind of State may have, though they are certainly more prevalent in organic than in democratic regimes. It may also be remarked that dictatorships and concentration camps are usual, though not inevitable, institutions in any State to which the force hypothesis has a high degree of relevance, that is in any State, whether organic or democratic in general outlook, which is in a thoroughly unhealthy political condition.

"Communist" and "fascist," as nontechnical terms, suffer from almost exactly the same defects as does totalitarian. In so far as "communist" means "Marxist," it is a definable and useful term. But in ordinary discussion it seldom signifies anything as precise as that. Indeed, like "fascist," it has degenerated to the point at which it is practically equivalent to "the kind of political view which I do not like." In democratic countries both terms are used in this way. The favorable epithet with which they are contrasted is then either antifascist (but not communist) or anticommunist (but not fascist). In the Russian vocabulary of political catchwords, "communist" is now more or less equivalent to "democratic" (in the Russian sense) and means "anyone who supports the home or foreign policy of the U.S.S.R." "Fascist" (or "Nazi") is applied to anybody who questions the complete wisdom or unselfishness of those policies.

It is not necessary to pursue these variations any further, but it may be added that everything which has been said here about "fascist," "communist," and "totalitarian" as useless words applies with even greater force to "bolshevist" and "bolshevism."

All these terms, in spite of their total unsuitability for anything but propaganda, are none the less frequently intended to mean something by people who say and write them; and, as we have already noticed, what they are supposed to mean is unquestionably regarded as important. It is not, however, as may be incautiously supposed, anything much to do with particular types of political or economic organization. A capitalist in this language is not "One who has capital; *esp.* one who has capital available for employment in reproductive enterprises." [23] He is the creature denounced by Karl Marx who thrives by exploitation of his fellow men. In other words, soapbox political terminology is a bane to political philosophy because, although it is ostensibly political, it is really concerned with a different but related subject. It is effective solely because it covertly appeals to the major moral issues which give rise to political theories, and not to those theories in themselves. I have already indicated what those issues are. In the next chapter I shall deal with them at greater length.

[23] N.E.D. *Capitalist.*

CHAPTER 5

Politics and Morals

*When you pronounce any action or character to be
vicious, you mean nothing, but that from the constitution of your nature you have a sentiment or
feeling of blame from the contemplation of it.—*
HUME.

No UNIFORMITY EXISTS in the relations maintained by contemporary States between the State and the individual, and
none of the political theories can lay claim to any confirmation
by experience of its general validity. At most it might be said
that States are all essentially alike, though admittedly they look
very different from one another. Even this cannot be argued
without gross torture of the observable facts. No doubt, facts
are sometimes misleading, and any amateur psychologist with
a political axe to grind will find little difficulty in persuading
himself that they can in the end be reconciled with his theory;
but the only evidence which can be adduced in favor of such a
view is a firm conviction that it must be correct, since if it
were not, a political theory which is known to be universally
applicable must be given up altogether or drastically modified. This attitude is reminiscent of the procedure of pre-
Copernican astronomy with reference to the movements of
heavenly bodies. If we claim to know by revelation or intuition
that the earth is the center of the solar system and that the
planets revolve about it in circular orbits, we have a number
of tiresome observations which do not conform to this view
to explain away. This can be managed by human ingenuity if

enough supplementary hypotheses are also accepted. The result is exceedingly complicated, but it will fit the facts because it is designed to do so. But more and more facts keep coming to light, and more complicated epicycles are required to accommodate them. In the end, even the most patient find that their credulity has been overstrained. They look for a simpler solution and, to get it, they are prepared to admit that the basic assumption of the theory is not a revelation after all.

The best ground we can have for supposing that a theory is suffering from epicyclic degeneration is that it becomes less plausible the more carefully and fully we investigate the facts; and this fate certainly awaits any theory which sets out to expound the relation of *the* State to *the* individual. When we know very little about a particular State, it is easy to believe that, although superficially it is democratic or organic in character, it is actually founded on pure force. As far as a large number of States, including those of South America and the Balkans, are concerned, I am fully conscious that my ignorance makes me open to this kind of argument. I have no direct acquaintance with these States, and they do not offer, as Russia for instance does, a mass of literature and political speculation which can act as a partial substitute. But even when the most severe restrictions are imposed on unsupported guesswork and attention is confined to Britain, Germany, and the United States, I find that increasing knowledge progressively confirms my belief that radically different relations between State and individual exist and are generally approved in them.

It may further be taken as established that these radical differences show no tendency to disappear in the course of time. It might be true that all States, in spite of their present differences, were inexorably tending to turn themselves into democracies or proletarian dictatorships. But there is hardly a shred of genuine evidence on which any such conclusion can rest, and there are strong reasons for holding that precisely the opposite is the case. Both democratic institutions and State worship appear to be more and not less well founded in the countries which favor them than was the case a hundred or even fifty years ago.

But some will maintain that these conclusions, even if they are sound, are not to the point. We can satisfy ourselves on rational grounds, it can be argued, that one type of State ought to be universal, since one type only admits of the full realization by the individual of all his capacities; and this type will then stand as an ideal which we can strive to realize for ourselves, and which we can assist and encourage others to achieve. It would be satisfactory if we could go beyond this and demonstrate historically that the ideal is in process of being generally attained. We should like to show that all States, past as well as present, can be arranged in a series of more or less perfect, in accordance with the degree to which they show a democratic or organic character; and to prove that there is a process from the less to the more perfect. This process need not be continuous. There might be setbacks and disappointments. We could accept these with resignation, if the existence of a broad evolutionary stream could be philosophically proved. If, however, this is denied to us, we could still be reasonably satisfied by the establishment of a well-accredited universal ideal.

This aspiration has been common among political philosophers ever since Plato wrote the *Republic*. Its attractions are evident. It would, if fulfilled, give us certainty, which is always welcome in a very uncertain world, and it would also provide us with an excellent argument for imposing our own political beliefs on other people. We have already seen, however, that it cannot possibly be fulfilled within the boundaries of political theory. All the main hypotheses can be consistently stated and all can produce instances (though the force hypothesis is here in a somewhat different position from the other two) to show that they are not mere abstract speculations. They cannot, as political theories, be required to do any more than this. It is of no assistance to any of them to demonstrate that some of their opponents have failed to be consistent. It is only too easy to show that particular writers have done their job indifferently. Their statements may be muddled and even self-contradictory. But to point this out, though it is both useful and important, does nothing to refute the main doctrine. Rousseau was not a consistent organic theorist, and Marx was not a Marxist. But if we are talking about political ideals, what we want to know is whether we ought to consider the State or the individual to be supremely important, which is quite another question.

In other words, if the view that one type of State is "best for man" is to hold water at all, it must rest on a system of moral philosophy which is itself firmly established. Political institutions are no more than symptoms of the political theory on which a given State is based, and politcal theories inevitably take for granted moral views about the importance of the individual. If then we are to go beyond our present position, which is that the three political theories can all claim at least a measure of *de facto* validity, and to assert that one of them ought to be valid of all States without exception, we can succeed only by proving that one account of the value of the individual is definitely right and that the others are definitely wrong. If we could be convinced of the incompatibility of one or more of the theories with standards of conduct which we accept on other and unassailable evidence, then, although we have been constrained by the facts to admit that States of this type exist, we should nevertheless maintain that they are immoral institutions which ought to be abolished. That is what is meant by claiming that any war has been fought with a moral and not merely an imperialist aim.

It will be immediately observed that this claim can be substantiated only if it is proved that all normal human beings are fundamentally agreed as to the solution of moral problems. Alternatively, it might be shown that, as far as the worth of the individual is concerned, disagreements are merely superficial. They could then be removed by more careful analysis and honest appreciation of the facts. We have already, in investigating the validity of political theories, found grounds on which this assumption must be seriously questioned. If such agreement exists, it is certainly well concealed. None the less, the belief that it does exist has been and still is widely and authoritatively held, and cannot safely be discarded without further examination. It is not enough to point to the evident fact that actions commonly deemed right in one age or country are universally condemned in others. This might be due to lack of care or insight. Many truths which are quite obvious to those who have taken the trouble to find them out are not obvious or even intelligible without a good deal of effort by the ordinary man.

The conviction that general agreement will always be found, at least between civilized and educated people, as to what ought to be done in a particular case has been widely held by moral philosophers. Exceptions to the rule are inevitably admitted, but are commonly held to be of small importance as far as moral theory is concerned. It would be easy to cite many statements of this conviction, but one taken from the works of Bradley will be sufficient to illustrate what is meant. At the end of a severe criticism of the utilitarian morals expounded in Sidgwick's *Methods of Ethics*, the following passage [1] occurs: "I hope the reader will not go away with the idea that I wish to represent our author as a revolutionary character, or his book as 'dangerous for young persons.' I do not suppose there is any serious or, I might say, any difference of opinion between us as to what in particular is right or wrong, for we both substantially accept the doctrines of ordinary morality.

[1] BRADLEY, *Mr. Sidgwick's Hedonism* (1877), p. 50.

The difference is one of principle, not detail. I object not to the things he teaches us to do, but to the spirit and the way in which he teaches us to do them. It is not the particular conclusions of his casuistry, but the whole principle of it, that seems to me both false in theory and corrupt in practice. And if we consider not our author himself but his main doctrine, we must say more. Deduced by a man of practical good sense, the conclusions of the hedonistic art of life would never seriously conflict with common morality. There are good psychological reasons for that. But once admit the principle, and what is to happen if men with no sense or hold on real life, but gifted with a logical faculty, begin systematically to deduce from this slippery principle? Is this not a danger, and is it a wholly imaginary danger?"

Bradley's doctrine is this: There is complete agreement between Sidgwick and himself as to the behavior proper for a moral man in any particular set of circumstances. But unfortunately some men are immoral. Whether their immorality is due to lack of insight or to radical badness of will is not relevant. But it is necessary to ask whether Sidgwick, by his explanation of the character of moral acts, may not inadvertently have provided such men with intellectual support for their evil doings. The possibility is indeed one which ought not to be neglected, and Bradley might well have reflected on the use to which his own Hegelian type of theory could be put by the unscrupulous. But this is by the way. What is really astonishing is that Bradley, who, as we have already seen,[2] was an ardent, if not entirely consistent, advocate of a strong organic political theory, should seriously have supposed that there could never be serious disagreement between himself and Sidgwick, who was an equally ardent liberal, on the merits of a particular case. It is surely evident that they could never, except by accident, have come to the same conclusion on any

2 See above, p. 163.

specific problem in which the right of the individual to justice was in conflict with the claims of his State to loyalty.

If, however, it is as easy as that to dispose of any belief in the community of moral views among all but the illiterate and the depraved, it seems at first sight inexplicable that such an illusion should have dominated the thought of serious moralists as it unquestionably has done. It is, in fact, not so strange as it appears, and can be explained partly by a traditional but ill-advised use of the word "moral" to cover acts which are essentially different from one another, and partly by the historical development during the Christian era of common standards of everyday conduct in the countries of Western Europe. These points are very closely connected with one another, and I shall examine them together.

It is a common complaint that the problems which writers of standard works on morals attempt to solve are usually so trivial as not to be worth discussion, or so abstract and peculiar as to have no bearing on ordinary life. To make this objection clear, I will quote two instances of the kind of inquiry against which such criticism is directed.

The first is taken from a discussion [3] on whether acts are right in themselves or because of their consequences, and the obligation primarily considered is that of keeping promises. In the course of his inquiry the author asks whether my promise to return a borrowed book is fulfilled if I send it by a messenger to the lender or hand it to his servant or send it by post; or whether, strictly speaking, I have kept my word only when the lender actually receives it. The latter is found to be the correct answer. "Our duty is to fulfil our promise, *i.e.,* to put the book into our friend's possession. This we consider obligatory in its own nature, just because it is a fulfillment of promise, and not because of *its* consequences. But, it might be replied by the utilitarian, I do not do this; I only do something

[3] W. D. Ross, *The Right and the Good*, pp. 42–47.

that leads up to this, and what I do has no moral significance in itself but only because of its consequences. In answer to this, however, we may point out that a cause produces not only its immediate, but also its remote consequences, and the latter no less than the former. I, therefore, not only produce the immediate movements of parts of my body but also my friend's reception of the book which results from these. Or, if this be objected to on the grounds that I can hardly be said to have produced my friend's reception of the book when I have packed and posted it, owing to the time that has still to elapse before he receives it, and that to say I have produced the result hardly does justice to the part played by the post office, we may at least say that I have *secured* my friend's reception of the book. What I do is as truly describable in this way as by saying that it is the packing and posting of a book. (It is equally describable in many other ways; *e.g.*, I have provided a few moments' employment for post office officials. But this is irrelevant to the argument.) And if we ask ourselves whether it is *qua* the packing and posting of a book, or *qua* the securing of my friend's getting what I have promised to return to him, that my action is right, it is clear that it is in the second capacity that it is right; and in this capacity, the only capacity in which it is right, it is right by its own nature and not because of its consequences."

The second comes from a passage [4] on the difference "between a right and a moral action—between doing what is right and doing it from a motive which makes the doing good." This is illustrated by the following problem: "Let us suppose a man X employed in some position of trust, the Secretary let us say to a Colonial Governor, but also an intimate friend of another man Y living in the Governor's jurisdiction. Y reveals to X, as between friends, and after letting him know that he relies on their friendship for the information he would give him to be

[4] *Some Problems in Ethics*, H. W. B. JOSEPH, pp. 31–33.

treated as confidential—perhaps after first securing from him the assurance that he might so rely—a scheme that he is hatching which the Governor, if he knew of it, would undoubtedly hold it his duty to prevent. He reveals the nature of the scheme to X finally, let us say, by letter, and on the very eve of its execution, so that X may be unable to demand release from his promise to treat the information as confidential before imparting it to the Governor, if this is to be done in time for the execution of the scheme to be stopped. In such a situation, X might well hesitate about his duty, especially if he himself thought that the execution of the scheme would bring on balance great advantage, and that the Governor, though bound, if he had wind of it, to stop it, would not be sorry that it should be executed without his getting wind of it."

It may well seem that any attack on these and many similar examples which occur in books on moral philosophy is grossly unfair and involves a complete misunderstanding of what their writers had in mind.[5] An instance, it will be said, should not be taken seriously. It is invented simply to make the author's meaning clear, and, therefore, it is extremely improper to assume that in his opinion all moral problems are of this somewhat trivial kind. I agree that in certain circumstances this would be a legitimate objection, but I do not think that it will hold in this case.

My point is this: If we agree that acts are right or wrong, moral or immoral, in virtue of their conformity to a general rule, and if that rule is such that it can be applied to all acts, irrespective of their importance or triviality, then any instance is as good as any other to help in the elucidation of the rule. But this condition is satisfied only if there is no genuine difference of opinion between honest men as to the particular acts which are to be grouped together as moral and immoral. Otherwise there can never be agreement as to the nature of

---

[5] Cf. STEBBING, *Ideals and Illusions,* Chap. III.

the general rule which is to be formulated. Unless we can recognize the members of the class of things we are trying to classify, our definition of it is not likely to be helpful or undisputed. It appears to me that moral philosophy frequently goes astray in this respect, and the tendency to argue about what are admittedly trivial cases is a symptom of what has happened to it.

A moral issue is something extremely important. It is an issue on which people are prepared to risk losing their lives, or at least to incur real sacrifice as distinct from minor personal inconvenience. To regard an issue as being moral, therefore, means to accept it as sufficiently weighty to deserve full and careful consideration. I must at least contemplate allowing the system of relationships which mainly makes up my life to be broken up rather than give way about it. It is consequently incorrect to say that what philosophy is concerned about is not the importance of an act but simply the rule or principle involved in doing it, and that this is equally well exemplified by the keeping of dinner engagements and by the keeping of a promise to abstain from the employment of atomic bombs. I believe that the method of approach to which I have drawn attention, and the kind of treatment of moral problems to which it has given rise, involve an inadequate view of the nature of moral action and a consequent divorce of moral from political philosophy which has seriously weakened both studies.

In my view there is a distinction not merely in degree but in kind between the acts of revealing prematurely the deliberations of an unimportant committee and dining out on impending military operations. The former is a breach of good manners and mildly reprehensible; the latter is morally wrong. In other words, acts must be judged by their consequences, but, unless those consequences are of substantial importance, to describe the act as moral or immoral is to debase a valuable word and to introduce confusion into the discussion of a vital question. I go so far as to say that in cases where a genuine moral choice is involved no accumulation of nonmoral considerations is of decisive importance; and it is thus erroneous to say that the principles involved in the latter are indistinguishable from those involved in the former. I should prefer to reserve the term "moral" for matters of first-rate importance and designate the relative trivialities in a different way. There are, however, objections to this, and it is probably better to speak of first- and second-order moral problems. This is what I propose to do. Broadly speaking, then, first-order moral problems are those which involve the life and happiness of myself or of people whose life and happiness I regard as not less important than my own. Second-order problems are those which affect the convenience and comfort of myself and of other people. There is no theoretical line which can be drawn between these classes—which is the reason why it is customary to call both of them by the same name. And it is possible for people who are both civilized and educated to disagree with one another (a) as to whether a particular act involves a moral decision or is simply a question of manners; (b) as to which of two or more possible moral decisions is right. As regards (a) it is sufficient to point out that there is no general agreement as to whether or not fornication raises a moral problem; and as regards (b) it would be widely agreed that the proper method of dealing with conscientious objectors in time of war does raise a moral problem, and that there is nothing approaching universal agreement as to the solution of it.

If I am right about this, my objection to many standard moral theories is that they have concentrated on the method of appreciating second-order problems to a degree which has almost precluded them from considering first-order problems at all; and, mainly as a result of this concentration, they have been led to the false conclusion that all relevant problems are really of the second order, and that therefore no serious differences about what ought to be done in a particular case arise between normally intelligent people who are not morally blind or incurably vicious.

This view is greatly strengthened by the fact that, over a wide area which, until quite recently at any rate, comprised all Western Europe, the United States and substantial parts of the rest of the more or less civilized world, there was relatively little disagreement about second-order problems. This is not in itself very surprising. It is, as many writers have pointed out, generally advantageous to the vast majority that people should pay their bills and keep their engagements, even when it is rather inconvenient for them to do so. At this level it is rather academic in the bad sense to dispute as to whether their motives for doing these things are desire to promote their own general happiness or respect for a revealed or reasoned system of moral laws. It will be widely agreed that as a matter of fact they do behave like that, and that it is a good thing that they should do so. If nothing more were involved in morals, we should really have very little to worry about.

It would be satisfactory to believe that this is the case, and in the days when peace rather than war was the normal condition of most of the world, it was not too difficult to hold such a view. Under moderately civilized conditions, the first-order moral questions which ordinary people have to deal with are not numerous, and this is especially true of moral philosophers as a class. As Professor Broad has said, "Fellows of Colleges, in Cambridge at any rate, have few temptations to heroic virtue or spectacular vice." [6] It should further be remembered that the first-order questions which most of us have to solve in a reasonably tranquil life are often concerned with

[6] BROAD, *Five Types of Ethical Theory*, p. xxiv.

sex, sex problems, unless presented in the peculiar language of psychoanalysis, are generally regarded as unsuitable for discussion in books about morals. The field remaining is small in extent, and its neglect is therefore not surprising.

This failure to distinguish at all carefully between acts which merely involve our convenience and comfort and acts which are moral in the strict sense was much encouraged, especially in this country, by the political stability of the nineteenth century. Partly at least as a consequence of it, Englishmen even during the nineteen-thirties were singularly blind about what was happening in other parts of the world. Generally speaking, the attitude of the Germans toward second-order moral problems was perfectly respectable even under the Third Reich. They usually paid their private bills. Hotel staffs were honest and efficient. And ordinary people habitually spoke the truth, returned borrowed books and kept dinner engagements. It was, therefore, not immediately obvious that the attitude toward most first-order moral problems which German political theory implied and which the vast majority of Germans indorsed was one which the vast majority of Englishmen regarded as an abomination. It was of course equally difficult for the Germans to do the calculation in reverse. Many of the Nazi leaders as well as the middle classes as a whole evidently supposed that a common mistrust of Russian ideas about sanitation would infallibly unite the English and the Americans with the Germans against the Bolshevist barbarians.

This discussion has been something of a digression from the main theme, and the problems raised in it are left for fuller discussion later on. I have introduced the general problem of moral standards at this point because of its importance in connection with the relation between political and moral theories which I now propose to consider. Naturally I do not imagine that I have refuted any moral theory which assumes that universal moral standards exist and that the aim of moral

philosophy is simply to investigate and elucidate them. Any
such refutation is impossible in principle. Rationalist theories
in morals, as in politics, cannot be refuted if their authors
work sufficiently hard to make them internally consistent. All
that can usefully be said about them is that they do (or do not)
fit the facts, and the facts in question here are the moral judgments of individuals. What I have done is simply to disagree
with the statement that all educated men either have or can
achieve, if they will only take the trouble to do so, an agreed
view on first-order moral questions. I have not yet put forward
any detailed alternative to this view, but have merely asserted
that, in my opinion, the distinction between first- and second-
order problems is vital; and I have suggested that divergent
political theories are based on the divergent views which men
hold on first-order moral problems. I might, perhaps, add that,
for this reason, I do not agree with the current belief that
political philosophy is a rather unimportant adjunct to morals.
On the contrary, it is in political theory and practice that the
most intractable moral problems occur, and it may even be
that, in the last resort, these are the only moral problems which
are incapable of solution by reflection and discussion. Now it
is clearly useless for anybody who holds, as I do, that there are
no first-order moral principles which it is logically necessary
for every mature human being to accept, to attempt any
demonstration that one of the political theories which have
already been considered is morally superior to the others. All
that I can profitably do is to state my own grounds for regarding the moral basis of the organic State and the force State as
unacceptable. This is not difficult. What is harder is to explain
the important difference which exists between the moral basis
of democracy as it exists in the United States and is often
advocated elsewhere, and democracy as it is found in Great
Britain. In the course of the latter exposition I hope that my
own view of the nature of moral action will become clear, but

I may say at once that that view makes no claim to universal validity.

THE MORAL BASIS OF THE ORGANIC STATE

In the organic State there is no distinction in principle between moral and political obligation. "The good man" and "the good citizen" are equivalent terms. Consequently there is not a great deal to be added here to what has been mentioned already as to the moral obligations to which the members of such a State are subject. The answer to the question "What ought I to do?" must always be "What your position in the State demands of you," and to the further question "Why ought I to do what the State requires of me?" there is no answer. The question is simply meaningless. If we wish to be rather more practical and ask "How do I know what it is that the State requires of me?" the answer is twofold. In the first place there are the laws and decrees issued on behalf of the State by the government. It is my duty to obey these since they are the expression of my own real or genuine will. In addition there are other obligations not laid down in laws but none the less sanctioned by the General Will of society. These embrace what are commonly considered as moral rather than political obligations, such as truth-telling, cleanliness and so on. The reason why these are not made matters of legislative enactment is not that they are outside the competence of the State. No activity can be that. They are omitted either because enforcement would be administratively impossible or because legislation is unnecessary, since sanctions are adequately provided by public opinion. This theory necessarily ignores the distinction between first- and second-order moral problems. As a substitute, we are offered something very different, namely a *de facto* distinction between the departments in which any particular State does and those in which it does not consider that legislation is worth while. There is admit-

tedly some connection between these distinctions. Any competent organic State must suppress, as far as it can, disagreement on some first-order moral problems. There can, for instance, be no haggling about the obligation to obey the law.
But pogroms and the murder of political opponents may be
encouraged.

None the less, it may happen that the practical effect of
an organic State on a particular individual may be very slight.
Such a State has no need, except in times of stress, to interfere
perceptibly with the choice of its citizens in minor matters.
It is on the whole more likely than is the democratic State to
indulge in "red tape" and restrictions, but this is merely an
irritation, not a moral problem. Reflection shows, however,
that, although this seldom appears on the surface, nobody can
be a sincere, as distinct from a reluctant, member of such a
State unless he genuinely believes, among other things:

1. That the State has absolute right, as distinct from overwhelming strength, to compel him to sacrifice his life and happiness for any purpose which, in its judgment, is worth while.

2. That he has an absolute obligation to inform against and
join in suppressing any of his friends and associates who contest
the claim of the State to dispose of them in this way.

He may regret the State's decision that he must divorce
his non-Aryan wife, but he has no right to question it on moral
grounds, and still less to disobey or evade it, even if he is able
to do so without fear of detection. To put it bluntly, the individual can have no conscience of his own at all. He does not
surrender it to the State, since he never had it to surrender; his
belief that he had is revealed as mere delusion, as the erroneous setting up of an abstract particular in conflict with the
concrete universal.

I find this moral outlook intolerable. If I were compelled to
exist in a regime in which it was generally accepted, I might

be able, at least for a time, to avoid coming into conflict with
the State on a first-order moral issue, and I have no great confidence that, when in the end such an issue was inescapable,
I should do what I conceive to be my duty and face the concentration camp. But it is important to remember that organic
States, though identical in their underlying moral assumptions, are very different in their practical aims. I, for instance,
agree in general with the internal aims of the U.S.S.R., and
since the majority of its acts can be justified on other grounds
than those on which it would itself defend them, my difficulty
in reconciling myself to its behavior is greatly reduced. This
does not alter the fact that my agreement is only accidental.
It merely makes possible the postponement, perhaps for a long
time, of any clash of principles.

It is here that we must look for the explanation of what
would otherwise be an extraordinary phenomenon. For everyone who is acquainted with their work is well aware that the
leading writers of the organic school, especially in Britain
and the United States, have been broad-minded and humane
men who would have been as horrified as anybody at Belsen
and Buchenwald. They accepted the theory of the organic
State on the understanding that it would in practice be more
and not less liberal in its treatment of individuals than were
the capitalist States of the nineteenth century. It would be
wrong to ignore this point of view. A democratic State which
is in a bad way and which, because of a widespread divorce of
strength from responsibility, operates on the lines of a re-
actionary force State, is not an attractive institution. It may
be, and often is, so deplorable in its operation as to justify almost any method of getting rid of it. Marx saw this and advocated revolution. Others looked for a less desperate remedy.
Most of them did not fully realize (though both Bradley and
Bosanquet were sometimes uneasily conscious of it) what their
cure entailed. They hoped that the god-State would be a good

god-State and that the conscience of the individual could thus survive in appearance (since there need be no practical conflict) even though in reality it had been completely superseded.

This was not an outrageous hope, though it was overoptimistic to a degree which can only now be thoroughly appreciated. But those who held and propagated it might well have reflected more carefully than they did [7] on the possibility that the moral reeducation of their countrymen (which they were advocating) might easily lead to an exchange of the frying pan for the fire. They assumed much too readily that pogroms and lynchings could never be the expression of the will of more than an inconsiderable fraction of a civilized community, and believed that the *real* will of any mature State would always be to behave in such a way as to win the moral approval of its best citizens. How mistaken they were! Organic States, even when their aims are laudable, are at least as likely to underwrite the morals of Himmler as those of T. H. Green.

THE NONMORAL BASIS OF THE FORCE STATE

Although there are no States based on force in the strict sense, there are certainly governments which, for the time being, maintain themselves almost solely by the employment of overwhelming strength. Such governments have admittedly no moral basis whatever. They make no claim to the allegiance of their subjects and rely entirely on fear for the attainment of their purposes. Their principle was nicely stated by Hilaire Belloc's Captain Blood: [8]

> *Whatever happens, we have got*
> *The Maxim Gun, and they have not.*

[7] See above, p. 221.
[8] *The Modern Traveller*, p. 41.

There is nothing morally repulsive about such a State unless it claims that its oppression is based on divine authority, or, as Hobbes maintained, on an initial contract which could never subsequently be revised or reconsidered, although those who were bound by it had never been parties to it. In the absence of such inventions, nobody is supposed to have any moral obligation to obey the State, and anyone who feels that he ought not to do so is at least entitled to rebel and take the consequences. He is not required to denounce himself as a criminal and consent to his own execution.

None the less, those who have consciences and regard them as important would do well to remember that any government which rests on force alone is almost certain sooner or later to produce legislation which conflicts with those consciences, and the probability of such an occurrence is quite enough to make life at best a rather uncomfortable and hazardous affair. The nearest thing to a force State which exists in practice is a military occupation; and this, even if it starts out with good intentions not to oppress the governed unnecessarily, is faced with a dilemma. It must become either tyrannical or ridiculous. In the nature of the case it cannot rule by consent of the governed and be told how to behave by the civil authorities. It must command and not request, or it degenerates into a farce. But when it simply commands without discussion and backs its commands with machine guns, it is a pure despotism, and it is a virtual certainty that a considerable number of people will consider it their duty to undermine it and defeat its aims. They may do this either as individuals in obedience to their personal convictions or as an organic society realizing a general will. In either case the result is the same. The occupying force is driven to multiply restrictions and embark on harsh repressive methods to maintain its own prestige and safety. It thus increases still further the number of its active opponents.

The moral theory of the force State is purely negative. Its operation is inevitably such as to ensure that some at least of the first-order moral obligations of its citizens can be fulfilled only at the risk and probably at the cost of life and liberty.

A qualification similar to that made in the case of the organic State is necessary here. A democratically minded member of the industrial working class might easily find that a Marxist dictatorship of the proletariat did not for a time require him to do anything morally unpleasant. Many perfectly respectable people "collaborated" with the German occupation forces on similar terms. But this situation cannot be permanent. Only those who have no morals can accept a force State, even as a temporary measure, without asking for very serious trouble. "These are my principles, but, if you find them unsatisfactory, I am quite prepared to change them," is the right frame of mind in which to advocate the establishment of such a State, unless, of course, you propose to be its sole ruler.

Two further points deserve some attention. A consistent force State eliminates political obligation altogether, and this, as far as I am concerned, is a mistake. I do not agree that I have a perfect right to break laws whenever I find it convenient to do so, and I do recognize a moral obligation to "fight for King and Country," provided (which is all that the much-discussed and misunderstood motion of the Oxford Union maintained) that this does not entail belief in a superpersonal god-State. Furthermore, I do not think my belief that it is a good thing to keep laws (of which I shall have more to say later on) can be analyzed into a belief in the virtue of immediate or enlightened self-interest. It pays me to defraud the income-tax collector and the customs official. But they are not activities of which I should be particularly proud, even if I could carry them out without fear that the police would find out about them.

A force State, however, like an organic State, has no respect for honesty or for justice as such. It is not a trustee, though its rulers might well decide, as rulers in a dictatorship of the working class would presumably do, that some forms of injustice, such as the exploitation of man by man, must be prohibited. But they certainly would not hold, as Locke did, that the primary function of the State is to make possible and to protect fair dealings between individuals. Admittedly "fair dealings" is here a vague term. But, whatever may be the precise definition of it which we choose to accept, it would be idle to expect that fairness can have any importance as an end in a State whose avowed object is to promote a strictly sectional interest with complete disregard for the interests of everybody else.

THE MORAL BASIS OF THE DEMOCRATIC STATE

A. RADICAL DEMOCRACY

Attention has already been drawn to an important distinction within democratic theory between the view advocated by radical supporters of the natural and inalienable rights of man and the more qualified position maintained by Locke and his successors. Generally speaking, the difference is that which distinguished radical from liberal theory in this country in the nineteenth century. Both doctrines are unquestionably based on consent, and it may therefore easily be supposed that they rest on common moral beliefs. This is not quite correct. The divergence of moral principles involved in them is considerable, and although it does not normally lead to disagreement, except on second-order questions, it is liable to do so.

In this section we shall be concerned with the moral basis of the radical democratic State which is exemplified by the United States of America and supported by many whose views deserve the greatest respect in England and in other countries.

Some, indeed, would argue that this moral theory and the type of State which exemplifies it alone deserve to be called democratic in any genuine sense, and that anyone who has doubts on this point must be a thinly disguised fascist or communist agitator. I do not agree with this. The radical democratic State has many excellent points, but I do not consider that its principles are above criticism. To explain its character we need a fairly detailed exposition of a philosophical argument which was mentioned somewhat incidentally at an earlier stage.

The fundamental difficulty which we have found in the moral presuppositions of nondemocratic States is that they claim *de jure* or *de facto* to ignore or to override the moral convictions of the individual. The force theories make no bones about this and openly claim that the individual does not matter, at any rate as far as earthly things are concerned. Even if he happens to be a successful tyrant, he is still something thrown up by the laws of economic development, the dynamic of history, or, in the view of the older and simpler theory which accepted hereditary monarchy, just plain luck. In contrast to this the organic theory makes a pretense of recognizing his importance. The State gives expression to his real will and alone makes possible his full development. But this is all just a sham. In the end we find that he has no genuine standing and can rightly be sacrificed whenever the interests of the State require. To all these contentions the theory of the radical democratic State is fundamentally opposed. It is assumed as self-evident that all men are created equal and that the primary function of the State is to protect this sovereign equality. The Rule of Law is invested with peculiar sanctity just because it is held that the Law guarantees the inviolability of the individual and may be relied upon to insist that every man should be treated as an end in himself, not as an instrument for promoting the well-being of any other man or group of men. The State is thus invented to guard the life, liberty, and property of the individual and so to maintain and uphold the essential equality of all individuals in matters of primary importance. This is certainly a great deal, and at first sight it may well appear that radical democracy is built on a very solid moral foundation. The question, however, is whether it genuinely provides the final or the best political system for those who regard the individual as the fundamental political unit. I do not think that it necessarily does this. There is something wrong, and I believe that it arises from the way in which the individual himself, rather than the State which he creates, is conceived.

When we say that the rights of the individual are paramount, we may mean one of two rather different things. We mean either his rights *qua* man or his rights *qua* John Smith. This sounds a complicated and quibbling distinction, but it is important. Like so many of the ideas of western philosophy, it is a consequence of the line of philosophical inquiry inaugurated by Plato and Aristotle, and it can be understood only in relation to their method of approach. What the Greeks were the first to notice, or at least to take seriously, was that we have to classify in order to think. We cannot get along without talking about groups of things such as cows and tables. It also seemed reasonable to Greek philosophers to say that, unless our classification and, therefore, our thinking is just a game or a practical device (and they did not think this was the case), there must be some characteristic genuinely possessed in common by the things classified together. We may not and often do not know exactly what this something is, but the aim of our philosophical thinking is to find it out. We do know that there is something which belongs to all the cows and something different which belongs to all the human beings, and it is because of that that Elspeth is a cow and John Smith a human being. The general view which can be developed out of this idea has been severely criticized both as logic and as

metaphysics, and I am not here concerned either to attack or
to defend it. What matters is that, although it has been almost
completely abandoned by modern science, it has retained
much of its influence as far as speculations on political theory
are concerned. What is even more important is that it has
a tendency, when developed along lines which became popular
in the seventeenth and eighteenth centuries, to give support,
not to the organic theory of the State, which Aristotle himself
favored, but to a strict radical view.

The explanation of this development is as follows: Scientific
thought in Western Europe during the seventeenth century
was almost completely dominated by new theories about the
nature of the physical world of which Newton's *Principia* was
the climax. The basis of these theories was that Aristotle's conception of the universe, though sound in principle, was im-
mensely overcomplicated. The classification of things into
cows, tables, etc., is perfectly sound as a matter of convenience,
but what makes Elspeth a cow is not the possession of an oc-
cult quality called "cow-ness" or "the idea of cow," it is simply
the arrangement of a large number of minute particles or
atoms in a particular way. This arrangement can be completely
stated when we know about the essential properties of atoms
and the laws in accordance with which they behave. What
Newton did was to formulate a simple system of laws which
enabled this to be done. In other words, he stated in quite
general terms what the essential qualities of atoms were and
what were the laws governing their movements. And the
theory worked. It provided explanations, which could be ex-
perimentally verified, of the movement of the planets, the
nature of light, and, to some extent, of the character of organic bodies. There was no obvious reason why it should not
be extended to cover the entire field of knowledge, and it was
confidently expected that this was only a matter of time.

In its simplest terms, what the new science maintained was

something like this: "It is true that there are essential properties which make things what they are, and these must be
clearly distinguished from accidental differences. We shall find
out about these essential properties, which are the only genuinely scientific basis of classification, when we really know
in greater detail than is yet available about the nature of
the atoms of which things are constituted, and of the laws by
which those atoms are controlled."

It is obviously only a step from this view about the physical
world to a correspondingly atomic view of Society and of the
State. One has merely to assume that individual men are just
like individual physical atoms in a Newtonian system. Each
of them will then have essential characteristics, and we shall
take it for granted that their behavior, like that of the physical
atoms, is determined by universal laws. The simplest assumption is that the relevant laws are those of classical economics,
and on this view, which has been widely held, some form of
force State tends to emerge. If, however, as was more generally
believed, it is part of the essential nature of man to be the
bearer of rights and not simply to be moved by external forces,
a more complicated theory is needed. We have then to say
that men *ought* to be respected in virtue of their humanity,
and that their right to be treated as ends and not merely as
instruments is as much an essential part of their nature as
being extended and mobile are essential parts of the nature
of a physical atom. It is fairly clear that this view does not
square comfortably with the materialist theory of the nature
of the physical world, and we may be driven in the end to
admit that we cannot explain how it makes sense to say both
that I am, like any other physical body, just a collection of
atoms pushed about by physical laws and that I am, as a human
being, something which ought to be treated with respect and
thus regarded as entirely different from any physical object.

But, in spite of this difficulty, it is still possible to formulate a system of laws which ought to hold for men as such.

By continuing along this line, we fairly soon arrive at a complete leveling theory as our political ideal. It can be argued with a good deal of persuasiveness that the characteristics which have been supposed to justify the enjoyment by some men of special advantages, especially birth and inherited wealth, are obviously mere accidents which involve no rights. Hence those advantages ought to be abolished. Men, considered simply as men, are identical. Consequently they are fundamentally equal, and all inequalities which exist between them are instances of injustice. It is hardly surprising that this extreme but perfectly logical development of physical theory as applied to human relationships failed to win universal acceptance. In practice it was modified by radical reformers in Britain and the United States into the more moderate ideal of equality of opportunity. But substitutes of this kind, although they have practical advantages and enable the principle of equality to win more general acceptance than it would otherwise obtain, are none the less based on the assumption that human beings are in some intelligible sense really equal. Accidental defects or original sin may obscure this equality, but the primary aim of political institutions is to restore it to the fullest possible extent. When this is accepted, a further point arises. Equality of opportunity is all very well. If thoroughly carried out it can, at least theoretically, ensure that nobody is penalized for lacking the external advantages of rank and fortune. But it may be doubted whether this is enough, since aptitudes as well as inherited advantages are accidents. It is unfair that individuals should enjoy a rent for their superior ability.

Nobody would claim that this aspect of radical theory has yet been very prominent in the political practice of any democratic State. It is, however, frequently urged, though usually not very clearly stated, as the moral basis for advanced New Deal and social security legislation, and it really does follow from the idea of men as isolated individuals with specific natural rights which belong to them essentially and which it is the function of the State at all costs to maintain. An odd result of the wholehearted adoption of this view is that institutions which start by preventing the strong from exploiting the weak may well end by drastically curtailing the claim of individuals to control their own lives, and may make it very difficult to preserve the kind of freedom which it is an important function of any democratic State to maintain. It is often noticed that the State in which equality is regarded as all-important and the full-blooded organic State are liable to have a good deal of superficial likeness to one another.

The explanation of all this is that, by concentrating on the alleged characteristics which human beings possess in common and, in particular, on their fundamental equality and the natural rights which can be inferred from these, we deliberately ignore as accidental and, therefore, irrelevant, the particular characteristics of John Smith. And when they are ignored on these grounds, it is impossible to get them back into the picture again. Smith has now become an atom which behaves in accordance with fixed and unalterable psychological laws. This situation is not modified, though it looks as if it might be, when we attempt to help out the radical State by introducing a new set of laws, namely those of morality. Certainly we can now say, though perhaps without much confidence, that the operation of economic tendencies ought to be tempered for the benefit of the weaker members of society. But even if agreement can be obtained as to the practicability and justice of such a course, it remains true that the individual as an individual is not significant. He remains entirely abstract and noneffective. And if we further ask for the grounds on which we ought to obey the moral law which demands this action, there is no answer except a motiveless respect not for Smith *qua* Smith, but for the "humanity" of which Smith is a particular instance.

It is true that the economic implications of this belief have so far not made a great deal of headway even in the United States. But the social and political consequences of it seem to me to be widely spread and deeply rooted. It is, indeed, very generally accepted as the true moral basis of society. To sum it up briefly, one may say that it is self-evident to much United States political thought that men (and also collections of men *vis-à-vis* one another) should be conceived as qualitatively equal. It is then merely an accident that they are quantitatively different. Political institutions should ignore as irrelevant differences in wealth, power, and aptitudes, and should concentrate wholly on the essential identity of human beings as such.

This is a weighty and respectable theory, and it is probably no accident that it is most clearly exemplified in the nation whose members in every generation have been drawn from such widely different environments. They have been almost compelled to accept it in order to achieve the basis without which unified society would be impossible. Nor is it sensible to ask whether it is correct or not. The United States are a society of that kind just as clearly as Russia and Germany are societies of an entirely different kind. But it is also true that this outlook is not universal, and that the radical democracy of America is no more a suitable article for world-wide export than are other types of political theory. It is not self-evident and it is not even true that all men are created equal. It *is* true that all American citizens are to an astonishing extent *made* equal, in the sense in which most of them think it important that they should be equal, by the political institutions of the United States. It is also true that with this equality goes, and I think goes necessarily, an acceptance of uniformity in taste, beliefs, and behavior, together with a respect for quantitative greatness (the only kind permitted by the theory) which other people who have not been carefully imbued with the moral view on which it is based are liable to find irksome and to consider (quite wrongly) to be rather childish.

Radical democratic theory, then, cannot be criticized for undervaluing the individual. It values him very highly. But it does so for what seems to me to be the wrong reason. John Smith matters, not because he is this particular individual with definite hopes, fears, and attachments, but because he is a specimen of the idea of humanity. Thus, although the process by which the conclusion is reached is quite a different one, the result has one vital feature in common with those attained by other theories: In the radical democratic, as in the organic and force States, the individual as such is not genuinely given any importance at all. He does not act. He behaves. This is not obvious, because it is concealed by the linguistic associations of terms in common use, but it inevitably emerges when the implications of the view are brought to light.

For what this theory does is to define as accidental, and therefore nonessential, all those characteristics of the individual which make him capable of self-determination. But those are just the characteristics which make responsibility possible. Certainly any individual's control over his environment is very incomplete, and, if we concentrate on this incompleteness, it is not difficult to forget about the control altogether and to assume that he is wholly dominated and pushed about by economic and psychological laws and forces over which he has literally no control at all. For those who are prepared to accept this view, the ideals of radical democracy will be perfectly satisfactory, provided that such a democracy possesses a moral backing of a more or less theological kind. In the absence of such backing, its degeneration into a force State is almost inevitable. But for my own part, although I cannot prove that all human beings are wholly or mainly self-determining, I am convinced that some of them are, and it is with these that I am here concerned. Now to be self-determining is to have the potentiality of consciously exercising force, and the common feature of the views so far discussed is that, because they agree in attributing to the individual the status either of an adjective or of an atom, they take no account of this.

Radical theorists agree in regarding obligation as obedience to or acquiescence in an external law, and in treating the spontaneous exercise of force by the individual either as illusory or as disreputable. This is not always made explicit. It is largely concealed by the very sharp distinction which is frequently made between bare physical coercion and pressure of other kinds, ranging from actual blackmail and economic tyranny to skillfully conducted press or wireless propaganda and "sales talk." But if we go rather more deeply into the matter, it is surely evident that on strict organic theory, no agent other than the State ought to bring pressure of any kind to bear on anybody to do anything, and that, on a strict radical view, not even the State has this right. On a force theory, no problem arises, since rights are by definition excluded from it. Now it is clear that the rigid separation between different forms of coercion and "persuasion" cannot be maintained as a matter of principle. The most that can safely be said is that physical violence is more repugnant to many people than other types of pressure are, partly because it is more blatant and partly because it openly violates what they regard as the minimal natural right of the individual, which is to dispose of his own body. It is also noticeable that this separation is more firmly insisted upon by radical theory than by other views. This is not accidental. Organism divorces reality from efficacy in the individual. But it unites them again in the State. Radicalism in theory carries the divorce to the limit. Hence, in order to avoid chaos, it is compelled to smuggle some sort of control in again by the back door, and a restricted right of constraint, both by the State of individuals and by individuals of one another, is surreptitiously introduced under the guise of a moral obligation to promote universal happiness or to improve other people. What these principles actually do is to borrow from organic theory the claim of the State to force people to be free, and to confer it either on everybody as a natural right or on selected peculiar people of whom the author of a particular theory is one.

It may be doubted whether a State, whatever its machinery, which is genuinely based on this view provides government by consent in the fullest sense of the term. It may produce highly efficient and even popular government. But that is not the point at issue. In so far as individuals are spontaneous and therefore essentially force-exercising agents, the only government by consent which they can have, far from excluding the use of force, necessarily implies it. This is not paradoxical. Unless individuals really are only exemplifications of universals and instances of laws, it is obvious. For to be an individual is to do something, and to do something is to exert pressure of some sort deliberately on other similar but not identical individuals. If this is agreed, it is clearly a mistake to suppose that the use of force is in itself either good or bad. It is a common characteristic of all deliberate action and cannot conceivably be praised or blamed in abstraction from the details of a particular act. Equally, it is not sensible to say that some forms of constraint are intrinsically bad while others are good or at least harmless. The question is never whether force or some particular species of force is being employed, but whether it is being responsibly employed. And that is a question which seldom or never admits of a simple rule-of-thumb answer.

To say that "All power corrupts" is, therefore, nonsense. If

the distinction made above [9] between power and force is accepted, it is self-contradictory; but even if no difference between them is admitted, it is still foolish, unless it is intended
to mean that responsibility is either an illusion or a bad thing.
Certainly it is possible to employ force very badly, but to re-
nounce force completely is not to be good. It is to be non-
existent.

B. Individualist Democracy

Radical democracy exalts the rights of man but has very little
confidence in his competence. It respects him, but it mistrusts
him profoundly. Hence its idea of a well-ordered State is that
of a State in which laws rather than individual judgments
control action. The law achieves a kind of independent reality
to that which it controls. Individualist democracy takes a different line. For it, rules are important, but they are not as important as all that. Their binding force depends not merely
on their being enacted by consent (which is the common doctrine of all democratic States) but on their continued capacity
to produce good results. It is, therefore, no accident that constitutional changes are technically much simpler to introduce
in England than they are in the United States. There is a
corresponding and connected distinction between the functions which opposition and discussion are supposed to fulfill.
For radical democracy these are wholly concerned with the
clarification of problems and the education of disputants.
In a thoroughly mature community in which men were fully
aware of the probable consequences of different courses of
action, it may well be doubted whether such preliminaries to
legislation would be required. Hence, though they are essential to democratic government, it is a defect in human
nature which makes them so. If we really knew the laws of
economics and psychology, there would be no ground for op-

[9] See above, p. 199.

posing rational proposals for legislation and little except details to discuss about them. In other words, what divides men is ignorance, not genuine disagreement.

For individualist democracy, on the contrary, the purpose of discussion is very largely to discover where disagreement lies and to produce a compromise which will work. It is assumed that people do differ on important, though not on vital issues, and it is not believed that agreement is possible if only sufficient facts are available. Hence opposition, whether in the House of Commons or in less important governing bodies, is not merely the negative of government. It is complementary to it. This is somewhat obscured by the dictum that the function of an opposition is to oppose, which suggests that any criticism is better than none. What it means is that an Opposition, at least ideally, is an alternative body to the government with a coherent and different policy of its own to recommend, and that its criticisms ought to be consistent with its own policy and not merely designed to make difficulties for the fun of the thing. I do not mean to suggest that all opposition in the United States is factious, or that in England it is invariably high-minded. But it is certain that the creation of a Leader of the Opposition as a paid government official would be inconceivable as an innovation into the United States Constitution.

This may be summed up by saying that in an individualist democracy competition is a good thing; and also that it is a very different thing from war. In a radical democracy, on the other hand, just because so much weight is attached to rules, all competition tends to be cutthroat. Provided you keep within the law, you can do what you like and you will be applauded rather than blamed for escaping the notice of the referee.

It may be thought at this stage that I am making a great deal of trouble on a minor point, and am straining the facts

in order to establish a major difference between American
and British democratic theory on a finespun metaphysical
distinction between two philosophical views about the nature
of the individual. I agree that the difference has so far been
stated in too abstract a fashion to be convincing, and shall,
therefore, devote the remainder of this section to a further development of it. In the course of this, I hope that the specific
character of individualist as contrasted with radical democracy will be more clearly shown. It will then be possible to
explain in the section which follows the moral beliefs on which
the former is founded.

The area of human life over which a democratic government, whether radical or individualist, can exercise effective
control is theoretically indeterminate. If its creators believe,
as most of the Fathers of the American Constitution did, in
the importance of laws rather than of individual judgment in
determining human action, they will do their best to determine this area precisely and to make the method by which it
can be altered a laborious one. But whether this is done or
not, it is to be expected that democratic governments will not
infrequently make mistakes as to what their constituents require them to do. It is useful to consider some of the leading
reasons for this tendency. Government by elected representatives is always difficult in that it is strictly impossible for anybody to "represent" the views even of a single client, though
for practical purposes this difficulty is capable of being overcome. But nobody, even with the best will in the world and
with the best available information, can do better than to
make an intelligent guess at the answer to any particular question which will best satisfy a multitude of competing constituents. This problem is obvious, but none of the suggestions for solving it such as the referendum, proportional
representation, frequent elections, etc., have any noticeable
tendency to produce the desired result, except in small societies

where the problems under discussion are simple and manage-
able. Up to a point, the extension of the franchise till it is
virtually universal is a useful method of constraining representatives to remember and take account of varieties of
opinion which otherwise they would be likely to neglect. But
there is and can be no hard-and-fast rule about it. Everything
depends on variables like the level of education, general political maturity and common sense of the mass of the population.

Furthermore, the variety of interests which political representatives have to take into account and, as far as may be,
reconcile, makes the emergence of some sort of party system
essential to the operation of democratic government. Unless
the government produced by a general election is agreed as to
what legislation is to be passed during its lifetime and as to
the general principles on which that legislation is to be based,
it is practically impossible for anything to happen at all.
Even if no major legislation is in prospect, the carrying on
of foreign policy and day-to-day internal administration is
barely possible unless some fairly general principles are accepted without discussion by those responsible for making
decisions. It is only in times of emergency so great as to over-
rule differences on second-order moral principles that this
condition can be dispensed with. But there are inherent dangers in a party system. Parties tend always to become more or
less autonomous associations for advancing the interests of the
sources from which they get their funds. Hence they may come
to represent adequately only a comparatively small part of the
total population, and also to embody in their policy compromises due to the conflicting interests of their supporters, which
are out of harmony with public opinion on more general issues. This very often matters comparatively little, but it is
liable to be of great importance. A democracy has no General
Will, and it is the function of the democratic State to evolve

a workable policy out of the will of all. But it is very unlikely
to do this unless the balance of power in the representative
assembly reflects, at least approximately, the balance of economic strength in the community as a whole. It tends to do
this, since party funds do the reflecting more or less automatically, and in any case the next election has always to be
borne in mind. But the possibility of maladjustment is there
all the same. What Marx did was to concentrate attention on
what is likely to happen to a democracy in which economic
and political strength have become divorced, and it is clear
that a strong party system, unless it is intelligently managed,
can contribute a lot to bringing such a situation about. Parties,
too, contain or are associated with pressure groups of various
kinds, temperance, religious, and so on. Whether these are
thought to be a good thing or not will depend on whether
the radical or the individualist theory of democracy is held.

If we consider that government by consent implies pressure,
then they are good in principle. But they are none the less
liable to get out of hand and to force a government into taking
action which does not correspond to the distribution of forces
in the community as a whole. There is nothing wicked about
this. It is simply an instance of the way in which democracy
is liable and indeed bound, from time to time, to get the
wrong answer—and too much can easily be made of it. The
British electorate, for instance, was not "stampeded" by the
alleged Bankers' Ramp of 1931. It was faced with a choice
between two exceedingly unpalatable alternatives. Possibly
the Labor Party, deserted by its leader and by many of its
prominent ex-ministers, would have done less badly than the
Conservatives did, but the propaganda leveled against it was
by no means the only ground on which a rational man might
have distrusted it. This does not mean that wild political
propaganda is desirable, or that its occurrence contributes
anything to the health of a democratic State: it means only

that the importance of such propaganda may easily be exaggerated. The American Presidential election of 1944 and the British General Election of 1945 both showed its limitations very clearly. But it is true that skillful propaganda backed by substantial funds can be a menace to any democracy which is not firmly established and politically educated.

These and other difficulties are the commonplaces of any democratic political theory. The point in mentioning them here is to emphasize the fact that the measures taken to deal with them are essentially different for radical and for individualist democracy. The former, based, as it has to be, on abstract moral principles, must regard all forms of pressure as disreputable in principle; but preaching about ethical codes is not regarded as a form of pressure, even when the threat of concrete sanctions is known to be in the background. Hence the normal tendency is to attempt to improve the workings of democracy by improved legislation. If your elections go wrong, you need a better electoral law, a better voting procedure, or a more complicated method of representation. This corresponds to the underlying doctrine that, among rational beings, there is a system, if we could only find it out, which would make democracy function automatically. Individualist democracy, by contrast, has relatively little faith in any machine.

The difficulties of democracy so far considered are certainly not negligible, but they are still in a sense questions of detail. The fact that they can arise at all implies that democracy is operating, though that operation is not smooth. It is only when we push matters a stage further that the gap between the radical and the individualist outlooks becomes clear. We have to ask whether circumstances can arise in which any sort of democratic government is literally an impossibility. Radical theory cannot consistently admit such a case. If it appears to have arisen, this must be because people are misinformed as to the facts or are being exploited by unscrupulous agitators. It is certain that a formula can be found to deal with the situation and enable democracy to get started again. But on an individualist theory, none of this is self-evident. Consider, for instance, a community, such as that envisaged by Marx, in which there are two groups of individuals whose aims and interests are actually and not merely apparently incompatible. In such circumstances, it may be held, and on an individualist theory it need not be disputed, that, the more the opponents know about one another, the more difficult it is for them to produce a working compromise. There is no longer any basis of consent to hinder majority rule from degenerating into majority tyranny, and the moral basis of any kind of democracy is destroyed. This is, no doubt, an extreme case, and a radical theorist must deny that it ever happens. But if he is mistaken about this, it follows that situations do occur in which compromise is hopeless and nothing remains but to shoot it out. Discussion and "reeducation" are both futile, since irreconcilable moral sentiments are involved, and these do not yield to argument.

Certainly political differences are often much less intractable than they appear to be at first sight, and any individualist may admit without difficulty that they can often be resolved or accommodated by competent government or international policy. But he must also insist that some are genuinely intractable and cannot be dealt with in this way. Whether we approve of it or not, a very large proportion of the human race are prepared to fight (a) for whatever form of liberty is the basis of their whole system of thought and action; (b) for their material standards, when these cannot be much reduced without serious detriment to (a). Democratically minded people do not usually go to war for causes other than these. But, for reasons already mentioned, they are liable to think that fundamentals are being threatened when they are not.

Unless this problem is faced, and radical theory is bound to argue that it does not exist except as the accidental result of imperfect education and political institutions, there is substantial danger in a world in which powerful States are still unalterably opposed to democracy in either form, that short-run policies will lead to disaster.

The individualist conclusion must be that democracy never works, or can work, automatically. It is a practicable form of government only for people who by education, tradition and experience have acquired a well-developed sense of personal responsibility and are therefore prepared to take trouble and accept some sacrifices in order to make it work. There is no substitute for this in the long run, though a presentable alternative can be achieved by formulating moral maxims and constitutional devices. These, however, will not be operative, even in the short run, unless they are supported by a genuine belief in their sanctity. Without this condition, democracy is simply unworkable, and it is of no use to tell people who have no strong belief either in the value of man as man or of man as individual to behave as if they had. They cannot do it and had much better not try. The only solution is for them to have dictators and to pray that the dictators will be sensible.

Individualist theory, then, may be summarily restated as follows: The individual is supposed to be real, and to be real *qua* John Smith and not simply *qua* member of the human species. This in itself implies that disagreements between men are not mere illusions which can be dispelled by appropriate treatment. They are real too, and the primary function of the State is not to make them disappear or to absorb them in a superior general will, but to recognize and, when a properly constituted majority considers it necessary, to control them. It is thus a device invented by a group of individuals to supervise and to direct the uses to which they put their power. But it is a good and not a bad thing that they should possess power. The State, on the other hand, has no general authority to use the force entrusted to it for any purpose other than that for which it is specifically granted, and is simply a group of individuals appointed to perform a determinate task. The citizens thus retain their power as individuals and rightly claim to exercise it in accordance with their own judgment. But because their views on second-order moral problems do not by any means coincide, they recognize that there must be limits to the manner in which their discretion is used, and those limits are not restricted to what the law will enforce. They must be and are expected to be recognized by the individual judgment. The proper limits of State action, therefore, constitute a practical and not a theoretical problem. There must be compromises, and consequently some sort of rule in accordance with which compromises are to be reached and enforced is necessary. The aim is simply to produce a political organization which will be effective in enforcing such limitations on private discretion as are accepted by the majority as reasonable in the circumstances of the case. But there is no golden rule for deciding in general what the proper limits are. The State has to confine its activity to regulating matters which all or most of its members at a particular time consider to be sufficiently important to justify the use of coercion to produce appropriate action about them. If it does or claims to do more than this, it will be a State of a different type.

The main objection which any radical theorist will level at this sort of State is that it is deplorably subjective. It admits and even approves of precisely those elements of personal preference and individual caprice which good government ought to strive to avoid. This charge of subjectivism has some force, but whether it is fatal is a matter of opinion. It is on this point that radicals and individualists are in real disagreement, and argument will not help to settle it. It is an elementary truth that any system which encourages individuals to accept responsibility must at the same time make it possible for them to use their strength wrongly. But it is not obvious, at any rate to me, that any useful safeguard is provided by laying down eternal rules and making individuals completely irresponsible provided they are not detected in breaking these rules. Puritanism and rugged individualism (which is not at all the kind of individualism that individualist democracy postulates) go well together. But there is always a tendency for the rugged individualism to be the senior partner.

* * * * * * *

The difficulty of formulating the moral philosophy on which individualist democracy rests is not that it is highly intellectual. Quite the reverse is the case. The trouble is rather that it is not intellectual enough, and, when it is stated in terms which are philosophically satisfactory, it is very easily transformed into some variety of organic or radical theory. This may be because any view which takes the individual seriously is necessarily muddled and requires to be tidied up and transformed before it is philosophically presentable. And it may be true, too, that the kind of democracy which takes such a view for granted should properly be regarded as an uneasy compromise which must either accept pure radical doctrine or disappear as democracy altogether. But I do not think that either case can be made out except on the strength of a psychological belief which, although it has been consciously or tacitly accepted by many writers in Western Europe since the end of the sixteenth century, is unproved and by no means in conformity with all the facts.

This assumption is that the self can be analyzed without remainder into sense, thought, and will. These are defined as entirely separate and distinct from one another, and each is complete in itself. We are not concerned here with the implications of this view in logic and the theory of knowledge, but solely with its consequences as regards action. Even here, I shall avoid going into any details and shall simply state dogmatically the inevitable result of accepting it. This is that moral philosophy has to arrive either at an intuitionist or a utilitarian conclusion; and these, although much controversy was engendered about them in the nineteenth century, are not really very different from each other. Either will serve perfectly well as the basis of radical democracy, and both ignore the individual as such altogether. For both regard him as analyzable into a more or less complicated contrivance whose behavior is either mechanically determined or completely unpredictable. We have in fact two choices. If we concentrate on sense, we can say that what produces action is always and necessarily a desire to get something. Desire for pleasure or for happiness is the only operative motive. Thought broods in a helpless sort of way over a lot of discordant desires, and may possibly strengthen one by bringing to light the consequences of others. But it "is and ought only to be the slave of the passions." Strictly speaking, will does not come into the picture at all. The strongest desire is bound to win. This, however, is too simple to be very widely accepted, and it is usually argued that, in some sense or other, I ought to act in accordance with one desire rather than another. I ought, for instance, to promote the greatest happiness of the greatest number. Will can then be introduced as a kind of extra motive which makes it possible for action to happen even contrary to desire.

Although this statement of the theory is far too condensed to be acceptable, it contains the essential point, namely that desire moves me to action, reason calculates the probable consequences, and will somehow supervenes to bring the action about or to stop it.

The alternative offered by intuitionism is that reason as well as desire provides an operative motive. I know that I ought to behave in accordance with a certain moral law, *e.g.,* to pay my debts. This knowledge is in itself a motive to act, even though I do not desire to act in that way. The function of will is then to determine action in accordance with reason; that is, to enable reason to overcome desire. And a good will is a will which does this. A bad will, on the other hand, suppresses reason and gives rein to desire. Here again I have oversimplified the view, but the point is clear. We now have reason and desire as conflicting motives with will as a sort of arbitrator to decide between them.

What is common to both views is that they break the individual up into pieces, or faculties, and then find extreme difficulty in putting him together in any way which will enable what happens to be intelligibly called *his* action. It would more reasonably be described as the product of his desire, or his reason, or his will, than of himself as a whole.

It is the contribution of Hegel that he challenged this view, and Bradley, as his disciple, provided in *Ethical Studies* one of the most thorough and damaging criticisms of the basis of radicalism which have been produced.[10] Hegel's conclusion, however (and Bradley with some heart-searching and qualification, followed him on the main issue) was that the conflict between intuitionism and utilitarianism could be resolved only by accepting the principle of the organic State. What this means is that the analysis of the individual into sense, thought, and will is implicitly accepted. It is then argued that he can get over the incompleteness which this analysis involves only by recognizing that his reality lies, not in himself, but in the State of which he is a member.[11] I am not interested here to decide between the theoretical merits of "abstract individual-

---

[10] *Ethical Studies,* Essays 3 and 4, contain the full statement of what I have briefly summarized here, and the reader is referred to them for further information on the implication of this kind of moral theory.

[11] *Ethical Studies,* Essay 5, from which I have already quoted, elaborates this contention.

ism" and "the concrete universal" (which is the organic State) as systems of moral philosophy. My purpose is simply to show that by rejecting one of them we do not automatically commit ourselves to the other. It is perfectly possible to start with a different psychological analysis of the individual and to work out a theory of action not identical with that on which radical democratic theory is founded and which organic theory claims to supersede or "transcend." There is no reason why I should not claim to be capable of exercising judgment, which is something different both from sense and thinking and not analyzable into a combination of the two. By "judgment" here I do not mean judgment in the technical sense in which it is contrasted with inference. I mean simply what is generally known as the capacity to "size up" a situation. The existence of such a capacity is commonly admitted when we are discussing esthetic appreciation (though attempts are often and unsuccessfully made to analyze it into a combination of sense and thinking), but even those who accept it as a fact in esthetics are often anxious to dispute its existence as far as moral situations are concerned. None the less, it keeps cropping up in various thinly disguised forms in moral theories, especially in those of the English Schools. Bradley, for instance, attaches far more importance than a good idealist or organic thinker might be expected to do to what he calls the moral consciousness of the plain man. In the last resort, his reliance on the validity of this kind of appreciation of the situation even leads him to question and to disavow as a final solution the organic State which his intellect has so readily accepted. And supporters of both the theories which Hegel claimed to supplant are in much the same position. They disagree as to what makes right acts right, but, when it comes to knowing what I ought to do in a particular case, the "immediate" or "intuitive" judgment of the ordinary man is what counts. It is true that under the influence of their psychological assumption they conceive this judgment as concerned only or mainly with finding out what rule the particular act exemplifies, and thus minimize its importance. But the fact that in some form it is so generally accepted suggests strongly that it is not, and is not genuinely regarded by the authorities as being, simply confused thought or sophisticated sense.

Returning now to the moral philosophy which individualist democracy must rest on, it is evident that for it the individual is real in his own right. It will not do at all to conceive him as somehow reconstituted out of a collection of desiccated faculties, or as important simply because he exemplifies a universal "manness." Nor can we seriously maintain that he is morally meritorious simply because he conforms to a collection of laws, irrespective of whether he actively consents to them or not. On the contrary, the individual must be regarded, not as a subject of moral laws, but as a responsible agent who normally obeys rules to which he has consented, and who is for that very reason entitled and obliged to break them when his moral judgment finds them inappropriate to a particular situation.

It is not unduly hard to develop a moral psychology on these lines. We do not require to discredit either sense or thought. Both of them are essential, since, unless we are going to overestimate (as intuitionist morals often seem to do) the universal competence of the ordinary man without any special training to get the correct answer in particular cases, we need to admit that previous thought and experience are essential to the exercise even of a natural ability to make sound judgments. There are naturally good men just as there are natural game-players, but without training they are unlikely to get very far. But we need to insist that thought, sense, and judgment are activities of the self. They do not constitute the self in the sense in which bricks and mortar constitute a wall, but are ways in which the self is active. To make this clear, we can drop the notion of will altogether. What is commonly described by this name is simply the self. It is *I* who finally act against or in accordance with my own moral judgment, and we merely confuse the issue by inventing a faculty called will which is thought of as a part of myself to do this for me.[12] There is nothing in this which would require us to say that all human beings are either by nature or by training equally competent in all kinds of activity, or to deny that natural ability which is not exercised is likely to atrophy. Hence it is not impossible that national training and education should be so devised as consistently to discourage the use of individual judgment in moral questions and to produce thereby a situation in which moral theories other than the one we are now considering are substantially valid for large bodies of people. We might expect in such cases to find that judgment had become relatively unimportant in determining action and that authority in some form was necessary to fill the gap created by its ineffectiveness. If human beings made themselves irresponsible (or are made so by their environment), they need laws imposed on them from outside by Church or State to keep them more or less respectable. Probably we could go much further than this and argue that, unless they deliberately train themselves to *be* responsible, implicit obedience to such laws is about the best that they can hope to achieve.

But, whatever we may think on this issue, it is clear that any system of morals which takes the individual seriously must face the problem of subjectivism. We may easily be frightened at the outset by the threat of moral chaos. If every individual is the sole and final judge of what he ought to do, shall we not find it impossible to set any sort of limit to personal eccentricities, and, in particular, as far as political philosophy is concerned, shall we not find it impossible to produce any satisfactory answer to the question "Why should I obey the laws

12 BRADLEY's *Vulgar Notion of Responsibility, Ethical Studies*, Essay 1, comes very close to this.

of the State?" Radical democracy, as we have seen, can deal with this with the help of a universal moral law. It can say "It is self-evident that you ought to keep your promises, and your relation to the State is in the nature of a promise or contract to obey its laws. Hence you ought to obey them, even when it does not pay you to do so." If, however, we are going to do without belief in an eternal and universal moral law, the problem of political obligation at once becomes acute. For it may well be thought that no moral theory which does not include a doctrine of natural rights can make democracy possible at all.

The problem of individual democracy, then, is to regard the individual as a responsible agent and at the same time to retain political obligation. It is possible to state a moral theory which will do this, but before we attempt to do so, it must be recognized that we are going to rely more on moral sentiments and less on moral laws than it has been popular to do since the eighteenth century. I am not suggesting that the doctrines of Shaftesbury, Hume, or Hutcheson as they stand are adequate to meet our requirements. But there is no harm in remembering that an influential school of British moralists to whom the existence of a faculty of moral judgment was a well-attested fact really did exist before the principles of '89 were formulated and before the self-evident truths of the American Declaration of Independence became the rallying cry of those who disapproved of the absolutist State which Aristotle's political theory was generally invoked to support.

Individualist democracy, as we have seen, requires a moral theory which accepts the individual as real, not as man, but as John Smith. But it is not necessarily committed to the assertion that all members of the species *homo sapiens* are responsible moral agents. Except in some special metaphysical sense in which all are believed to possess souls this contention is, and is bound to be, denied in practice. Infants, lunatics, and other classes of human beings, while they are normally thought of as having some special rights as compared with animals and inorganic things, do not, on any known moral or political theory, enjoy the same rights as normal adults do. There are wide differences of opinion as to the extent of the class within "human beings" who are, or ought to be, entitled to full status as moral and political individuals. For instance, even in what is known as western Christendom neither women nor black men are universally admitted to this class. Nor is there general agreement as to the rights which human beings excluded from the privileged class ought to enjoy. It has to be admitted that the firmest believers in self-evident or innate human rights are bound to explain away as best they can the obvious fact that the class of human beings and the class of "bearers of natural rights" are not, even on their own theory, exactly coextensive.

There is thus nothing new in maintaining that, although individuals are real and do not need to participate in some wider whole in order to achieve reality, the grounds on which it could be argued that all human beings are individuals are inadequate. The matter can be settled only by definition, which is unhelpful, or by judgment on the particular case, which is not capable of determination by a formula in advance of experience. There is no *a priori* reason for holding that all (or no) black men, Germans, or British citizens under the age of twenty-one are fully certified moral agents. There are obvious difficulties about this, but I shall not stop to consider them here. Some of them at least will be solved in the course of the subsequent discussion.

To hold that individuals are real in themselves implies that they cannot be analyzed without remainder into relations. It also means that societies or collections of individuals can be analyzed without remainder into more or less complex relations between the individuals who compose them. We do not have to maintain that all societies are like this, but merely that there are at any rate some individuals or people and therefore some societies of which it is true. To avoid possible confusion, however, it is best to be rather more precise and to assert that all societies are analyzable into relations which individuals create or have created. The system of a society persists and has to be accepted by newcomers—or ignored by them at their own risk. It is a fact which the individual may like or dislike, but he cannot annihilate it simply by disliking it, although it is itself a human product. There is nothing difficult or mysterious about this. We can, if we like, invoke a general will or group mind to explain it, but there is no need to do so. Bradshaw may be the product of the general will of a community of railway directors, but its existence and objectivity can be accounted for on other grounds, and the theory which I am developing would be bound so to explain it. I do not need to deny (a) that joint plans (like the Allied invasion of Europe in 1944) are often so complex that the notion of a common will producing them has great plausibility, especially for those who see only the finished product; or (b) that in some cases where subindividuals are concerned, the group mind and the organic society may actually be more than metaphors.

What follows from this is that, although the individual is real as such, the individual in abstraction from all social relations is only a limiting concept. Ultimately what it means is "the individual in isolation from any moral environment," which is not a discoverable or even an intelligible state of things. It seems, therefore, meaningless to inquire what obligations the man on the desert island would have, and we may doubt whether he could significantly be said to have any, except in so far as he persisted in regarding himself as being in social relations, temporarily broken off, with other human beings. But, however this may be, I do not think that any system of obligations which might hold in these peculiar circumstances would be important. Nothing would follow from it as to what is the case under quite different conditions, and there is not the slightest ground for holding that it would constitute the fundamental system from which the more complex systems of civilized life are developed. It might well be completely discarded in a different environment.

If we accept these conclusions, we cannot claim to know that any kind of action is necessarily or universally obligatory on all individuals. Reflection on man *qua* man, though it is of importance at a later stage, is useless as a starting point, since what is in question is not the rights of man but the rights of John Smith. The notion that I can infer the second of these from the first must be considered as a misapprehension based on a partial view of the facts. Unless it is self-evident that the identity of man *qua* man is more than a piece of logical classification, nothing follows from it as regards the rights of individuals. I can, indeed, obtain a theory of natural rights, but this is nothing more than a number of propositions which are self-evident only because they are tautologies. They add nothing to the definition of man as the bearer of universal rights which has been itself accepted without evidence, though their analytical character is obscured by linguistic usage.

In other words, unless we accept by an act of faith the proposition that all men are created free and equal, we can get nowhere by this kind of rationalist procedure. And it is equally impossible to reach universal moral rules by contemplating the individual with whose character and beliefs I am best acquainted, *i.e.*, myself, because I can do this only in the context of, and not in abstraction from, a specific set of social relationships.

It is hardly necessary to point out that attempts to produce a moral or political system by starting from assumptions about "human nature" in the abstract are equally unpromising. The proposition "human beings always follow what they believe to be their own greatest interest" is either a tautology or it is false. It is a tautology and therefore useless as a basis of actual obligations of any kind if it means simply that "what I do" is by definition "what I think it will pay me to do." But no other meaning can be produced which the facts will accept unless unhelpful phrases like "unconscious desires," which will explain anything, are taken seriously. Here, too, it should be observed that unanalyzed slogans like "Life, liberty and pursuit of happiness" are highly dangerous because they are liable to conceal real differences of view under a familiar verbal formula.

The common belief that any theory which denies the existence of eternal laws must abrogate moral and political obligation altogether and involve complete chaos as far as human relations are concerned, arises only because of a question-begging assumption. If we take it that human conduct either is or ought to be subject to precise universal laws of the same kind of generality as those postulated in Newtonian physics, and that the only alternative to this kind of "realm of law" is complete anarchy in which all occurrences are random and unpredictable, then the alleged consequence follows. Otherwise it does not. It is clear, however, that individuals, provided they are genuine individuals and not spiritual atoms, will not be subject to law in this sense. Their actions may be predictable statistically, and they may be susceptible of intelligent forecasting as a result of insight and experience. But that is another matter. The situation we have to contemplate is one in which actual individuals, each with his own determinate character, act in an equally determinate environment. We cannot then have any complete view either of what any of them ought to do or will probably do, either by analysis of the individual or by analysis of the environment or by considering both together as an abstract or scientific whole. Every actual situation is unique, and therefore the conception of human beings simply as members of an ideal "Kingdom of ends in themselves" will never help us in determining particular obligations. For these depend on particular relations to other particular individuals which are by no means wholly definable in general terms. In other words, my moral and therefore my political obligations arise from particular relationships to other individuals; and those relations are describable in terms not of general laws but of particular judgments.

In so far as the individual is real and is a definite and not an abstract person, it is to be expected that he should attach peculiar importance to his own well-being and to that of a limited number of other definite individuals with whom his personal relations are very close. At least, it is in no way surprising that this should be so, and, as far as I am concerned, it is actually the case. Beyond this, there are numerous other individuals with whom I have social, economic and official relations and whose well-being, though to a much smaller extent, I regard as important. Thus one achieves a system articulated into a large number of different groups, friends, family, trade union, business associates, and so on. These groups are liable to overlap in the sense that one individual can be a member of two or more different groups. The resulting system is extremely complex, and it is unnecessary and even futile to look for a quantitative analysis of it. I do not find that I can ever attach any meaning to the statement, "The well-being of A is twice as important to me as that of B." It is also, as far as detail is concerned, a constantly changing system. There is, however, a high degree of general stability about it, and this stability shows a fairly steady increase, so that in time the general shape of it becomes very difficult to upset or even seriously to modify. This being the case, I find it easy enough to assume that all other individuals have roughly similar systems, in some of which I am included.

Now for me, my own system of personal relationships is fundamental, and no obligation is real except as an element in it. This is where I differ from intuitionists and utilitarians, who conceive such systems as merely accidental, and organic theorists, who concede them reality only as elements in the larger and more integrated whole which is the State. I imagine that the same is true of other individuals whose constitutions are fairly similar to mine. But observation suggests that there are wide variations in this matter. Some systems seem at least to be a good deal wider and more complex than mine, others to be narrower and more simple. It is, of course, theoretically possible that all, or all normally constituted, individuals should be either complete egoists or complete altruists. But I see no evidence for believing this. To me, it appears that egoism and altruism are both limiting types which in practice do not occur. Neither I nor anyone with whom I am acquainted regards the well-being of all individuals other than himself either as being equally of supreme importance or as being in all cases equal to o. Furthermore, nobody appears to feel the kind of moral obligations which either view would presuppose, or, what is even more significant, to be ashamed that he does not feel them.[13]

My moral obligations, then, arise from the values I set upon the well-being of myself and other individuals within a system of relationships which is much too complicated to admit of any diagrammatic representation, but is in practice not usually at all difficult to work. Only very small areas of the whole system are normally involved in a particular decision, and the relevant parts can generally, though sometimes only at a cost, be abstracted without loss from the whole.

The moral view which I have outlined is not at all new. It has much in common with many moral-sense and intuitionist theories and is also, or so it seems to me, very close to what

---

[13] A good analysis of the facts is given by BARBARA WOOTTON, *On Public and Private Honesty*, Political Quarterly, Vol. XVI, Number 3. As the article assumes the standpoint of radical democracy, the author considers that they are a sign of immorality.

Locke and some of his successors really had in mind as the basis of their political theories. They stated it, however, rather carelessly in terms of the current doctrines of social compact and natural rights, which were very far from being clearly thought out, and thereby laid themselves open to charges of hypocrisy which had little or no justification in fact. They simplified their view largely for purposes of exposition but partly because they did not fully appreciate the implications of the radical theory to which on paper they committed themselves. Their practice, however, was not consistent with radical views. In particular, their emphasis on property in the widest sense, though it has led to odd and unforeseen consequences, was a greatly needed antidote to the leveling implications developed later by more abstract writers. To put the moral position shortly, I see no reason to deny to any individual the right to maintain unimpaired his own system of personal relations; and this includes the right to obtain and enjoy the material resources which are needed to make such maintenance possible. Nothing much is gained by calling this a natural right, though perhaps the qualification is worth having since it indicates that such systems of relations are the foundation of first-order moral obligations. Once this is admitted, it follows that I can never make much headway with the question "Ought I to do this?" unless I have a clear idea of who will be affected by it, and to what extent.

It is obvious that no foolproof method will suffice to answer questions of this kind. Clashes of opinion are inevitable, since the line between first- and second-order problems itself cannot be drawn in any hard-and-fast way. All that can be asserted with safety in general terms is that I am ready to accept considerable restrictions in detail so long as the general pattern of my system is not destroyed. But there comes a point beyond which further concession is worse than resistance by force to encroachment. This means that there is a wide, though not

an unlimited, area within which compromises between the
maximum claims of conflicting interests are acceptable. The
highly complex interlocking between the systems of individuals to which I have already drawn attention itself makes
such compromises inevitable and easy, as a rule, to obtain.
There is always likely to be a large amount of discoverable
agreement over fairly well-defined geographical areas because
of social and economic relationships within those areas. There
is thus a strong tendency for groups of individuals to solidify
into independent societies. But as soon as quite a low level of
complexity is exceeded, some controlling organization to regulate and, when necessary, to enforce compromises on second-
order questions is an obvious requirement which may be explained by the emergence of a group mind, but which does
not imperatively call for any such metaphysical support.

It may, perhaps, be thought that I have overstated the case
and have attached too great weight to the alleged readiness of
individuals to compromise on all issues but those which they
regard as fundamental. To this there are two answers: In the
first place, I am not attempting to formulate a truth about
human beings as such. I do not think that any proposition of
this type can claim more than restricted and empirical validity.
All I am directly concerned with is the general moral view of
the majority of people in this country here and now. In the
second, I find that, under the conditions in which I am interested, it is impossible for me to reject all compromise and
promote my own system with total disregard for those of other
people, even if I considered this a profitable line to take. The
reason is not fear of police intervention. It is that my system
is not and cannot be a closed one. To maintain it, I have to
take into account the systems of other people who form part
of it but whose own systems extend beyond it. If the welfare
of X is a matter of primary importance to me, I cannot adopt

a course of action detrimental to Y, who is essential to X, even though Y is to me personally indifferent or mildly unpleasant. It is from this point of view that the operation of economic and geographic factors on human obligations becomes clear. No system or collection of systems is completely closed. But there are well-marked coagulations which are national and regional communities. Even under modern conditions of transport and communication, the vast majority of individuals do not extend their systems beyond the Nation-State to any appreciable extent. Hence toward people outside it their sense of responsibility amounts to very little, and the more remote from direct or indirect personal links they are, the more closely does it approximate to zero.

Many will, no doubt, say that, although the outline I have given is not an unfair account of the moral standards which the English on the whole accept, it is none the less quite wrong that they should do so. If it is true that I ought to feel equally responsible for the well-being of all human beings without respect to age, sex, color, or creed, I cannot evade this proposition simply by being conscious of an overriding obligation toward an arbitrarily selected group or groups of individuals. I have already disposed of this point in principle by denying the validity of universal laws of morality, except in so far as these are mere tautologies. Something more, however, needs to be said on this point in order to make the position clear. We still have to explain how this kind of moral outlook can give rise to any effective consciousness of political obligation. How does it escape from complete subjectivism in politics and morals? I think that a reasonably satisfactory answer can be given on the following lines: The State is a practical device, and the ground on which the laws of the State and moral laws can be obligatory is identical. We cannot always study in detail the merits of each particular case, since we have to act, and

opportunities for successful action are often fleeting. Furthermore, the particular case is sometimes so complex that no
amount of reflection will enable us to pass a judgment about it
of whose rightness we are certain beyond the possibility of
doubt. For the most part, then, it is sensible to act as *if* certain
moral principles were universally valid (though we know that
they are not) and *as if* the laws promulgated by the State were
always the best compromise possible between conflicting interests in the circumstances, though they are clearly too abstract and take too simple a view of human nature to be
finally authoritative. It is therefore an obligation to obey them
except when I know sufficient about the particular case to be
certain that the law or principle is wrong; that is, when it
conflicts with my own first-order moral judgments. If laws are
conceived in this way, it need not surprise us to find that they
are inadequate and in conflict with one another in particular
cases. The only ultimate court of appeal is thus my own judgment, or conscience, if that word is preferred, but that judgment itself is frequently that I have no adequate grounds for
forming a decided view on the merits of the case and am therefore under an obligation to accept the judgment of someone
who is better informed than I am. The general assumption has
to be that laws, whether moral or political, are made and enforced by people who are reasonably well informed and reasonably honest. This is enough to give them a strong *prima facie*
claim to be obeyed, subject always to a liability to morally
legitimate infringement when circumstances warrant this.

Political and moral laws thus become valid in general, but
they are not absolute—and neither can be operative except in
a society of individuals who have considerable confidence in
one another's judgment. This happens only when it is generally recognized that individuality implies both power and
responsibility, and that these are inseparable and proportionate to one another.

CONCLUSION

To what conclusion about political philosophy does this investigation lead? Briefly stated, I think that it is as follows: Although it is convenient for many purposes to segregate moral from political philosophy and to treat each of them as a "subject" which can be studied almost completely in abstraction from the other, such segregation, unless it is watched with the utmost care, is practically certain to involve trouble. Political philosophy when narrowly defined deals solely with hypotheses. That is to say, it can do no more than take for granted accounts of the nature of society and of the individual provided from other sources, and work out a consistent theory or theories as to the relation between States and their members which these accounts involve. It may then ask whether experience provides instances of the realization of any or all of these theories. Further than this it cannot go without accepting or inventing a view about morals.

No considerable writer on the subject has been prepared to accept this limitation, and it is neither possible nor desirable that it should be enforced. For, as we have seen, the great political theories grow out of and give expression to moral beliefs or sentiments. None of the important questions in political philosophy can be answered without reference to these beliefs; and no moral doctrine can be seriously estimated or criticized without full consideration of the political theory which derives from it. It is a disastrous consequence of the policy of segregation, when it is taken seriously and not regarded merely as a device to simplify exposition, that this essential interconnection tends to be overlooked or suppressed. But since neither the moral nor the political aspect of the problems under discussion can be eliminated without robbing the other of all significance, there is a strong tendency to introduce a kind of dummy as a substitute for the missing reality.

To put it differently, political theorists who want to avoid discussions on morals and also to recommend one political theory rather than another as the sole truth, frequently make highly uncritical assumptions as to the universality and necessity of the moral sentiments which underlie that theory. They take it for granted that men either are or (more plausibly) that they ought to be invariably treated as ends and not as means; that the whole is (or ought to be) superior to the part, and so on. Moralists, on the other hand, frequently postulate, without necessarily being aware that they do so, the kind of political theory which will at least make it possible for a special kind of morality to be acted upon without immediate suicide being the consequence. In an aggressively organic State not many people can be moral on the lines suggested either by Kant or by J. S. Mill. To do so involves consequences, not merely for the agent but for his associates and, ultimately, for humanity at large, which are seldom or never taken into account by those who advocate such principles in the abstract.

Thus political theorists are liable to accept without question the moral background which suits their favorite theory; and moral philosophers often take for granted the political foreground which enables them to generalize their private moral beliefs.

As a result, too little attention has been paid to the question whether any one political or moral theory can rightly claim universal acceptance. For one who has complete faith in the capacity of rationalist thought to explain the universe, including human behavior, it is a foolish question; and it is no less foolish for the confirmed anti-intellectualist who asserts as self-evident the complete supremacy of an entirely irrational will or life-force, or whatever is for the moment the popular catchword. I cannot agree that the matter can be so easily settled, and, although it is impossible here to go fully into the problem of moral standards, I shall attempt to make

rather more precise what was said about them in the previous
chapter.

Rules of conduct exist on three distinct levels, and the third
of these is in an entirely different position from the other two.
In any State at any time we can discover what I will call group
standards, national standards and ideal standards; and it is
not hard to explain what these involve. If we limit ourselves to
England at the present time, there can be no doubt that group
standards are a fact, or that they are different in different walks
of life. We are not interested here in "higher" or "lower"
standards, or in group as contrasted with general standards
of conduct, but simply in the fact that professional misconduct
does not embrace the same acts for a doctor, a turf accountant,
a lawyer, and a priest. Yet all have standards which they are
expected by their professional colleagues to reach. These
standards, too, would be completely meaningless if they were
not for the most part maintained by members of the group.
They represent what one may reasonably hope to find. Hence,
they are not ideal but average standards. Some practitioners
will consider it their duty not merely to conform to these
standards but to accept something more difficult as their tar-
get of achievement, others will regard them as unduly exacting
and will privately aim at something rather less tiring. The
standards are thus practical norms of conduct, generally accepted and attained with at least sufficient regularity to make
the censure of delinquents a practicable proposition. In some
cases the censure is given a legal basis, but this is not at all
essential.

National standards are very similar in principle. They are
the standards which a well-informed person will expect to find
prevailing. They, too, are an average, and it is a practical
necessity that they should be the standards which people on
the whole successfully achieve. Anything more difficult than
this, even if it were technically enforceable, would very

quickly require the moral condemnation of people who, in the general estimation, ought not to be so condemned. And this is not a practicable requirement.

What is noteworthy about group and national standards is that they are quite definitely factual. They may be easy or difficult to achieve, but there is no doubt whatever that they are not merely accepted but also, for the most part, reached by average individuals at the relevant time and place. They are not restricted to what I have called second-order moral problems, or manners, though these in the nature of the case are usually more prominent than first-order problems in any explicit formulation of them. It is quite impracticable to formulate or even to accept without explicit formulation any code of professional behavior covering the relation either of doctors or of lawyers or of bankers to their clients without assuming a view on first-order problems. For any professional man as such is in a position to some extent to "force his clients to be free," and his professional standards inevitably determine the extent to which, as a member of his profession, he is entitled to do so. It is evident that national standards are in exactly the same situation.

Ideal standards are a very different and much more difficult business. We can best approach them by examining a view which, though promising, is certainly erroneous. Whatever we hold about ideal standards, it is clear that they are universal in their application. They are not restricted to any place, time, or type of man, but hold of all human beings. This is evident from their formulation. They are imperatives addressed explicitly to men as such. "So act as to treat humanity always as an end and never merely as a means"; "Always do the act which will promote the greatest happiness of the greatest number"; "Always act in such a way as to realize your true self." All these admit of great variations in detailed application, but as principles they are strictly universal. At first sight we might suppose this to mean that they are very similar to the group standards of conduct we have just considered, but that they are more general in character. In other words, they may be thought to have the same relation to national standards as the latter have to group standards. The situation might then be summed up as follows: It is clear that, in the end, no State can permit the survival of professional codes which conflict with national standards. No consistent organic State, for instance, could tolerate the acceptance by doctors, bankers, or priests of a code which made it obligatory on them to refuse information which it was in the national interest that they should reveal. Equally, no democratic State could insist on revelation unless it had been empowered to do so by a properly constituted majority. If it were so empowered, it would have to insist; and, unless the relevant group standard were changed, those who adhered to it would then automatically become a conspiracy against the State. We might pursue this idea and conceive ideal standards as dominating State standards on similar lines.

What would this amount to in practice? Let us assume that an operative World-State has been created. The suggestion then is that world standards of moral conduct would also be evolved, and that these standards would be universally accepted and generally acted upon, just as we find that national standards are accepted and acted upon in existing Nation-States. We must further assume that defaulters, whether individuals or States, which fail either to accept these standards or to live up to them with fair regularity will be subjects of general moral condemnation and will, if they persist, be forced into conformity.

This sounds a possible program, but, if it is more carefully examined, it does not make sense. In the first place, on the face of it we are here talking, not about an ideal but about another average. What is proposed might well be a good thing

to do, but it would surely be good because it tended to promote ideal moral standards, not because it tended to stabilize
those already in existence. We shall return to this point later.
It is more immediately relevant to observe that no plan for
making any moral standard effective by the creation of a
World-State can possibly be carried out except by methods
which are seldom clearly envisaged by those who advocate it.
To fulfill the function assigned to it, a World-State has to be
a State. That is to say, it has to govern. Now we have already
seen that it cannot just be a State. It must be a State based
on a particular kind of moral sentiment, and it must govern
accordingly. It cannot permit the continued existence of
powerful subordinate bodies with moral standards different
from and in conflict with its own. It may, for practical reasons,
tolerate them for a time; but sooner or later, they have to go.
We have already seen in practice what this means. The German new order for Europe, and ultimately for the world, was
probably not explicitly intended to involve the complete
reconditioning of all countries from top to bottom on organic
lines. Whether it was or not, there was finally no choice about
it. The governing State had to govern, and it could do so only
in its own way. Much may be attributed to the fact that Germans are not very good at putting their views across without
the help of truncheons; but to stress this is simply to obscure
the issue. It was literally impossible for them to achieve their
purpose of creating a Superstate without getting their own
moral law accepted and acted upon by virtually all the members of the subordinate organizations. Broadly speaking, that
view was that the State is always right, has supreme authority
as well as supreme strength, and has, therefore, without consent by anybody, a moral claim to override the standards of
any person or community for the general good. Another organic Superstate might conceivably be more skillful at deceiv-

ing its members as to what its claims were, but sooner or later it would have to enforce them all the same.

A democratic Superstate would be no better placed. In one way its position would be less favorable, because infinitely more complicated. It is impossible to see how actual democratic machinery could function at Superstate level, though perhaps this is only a technical problem which could be solved by good will and intelligence. But it is at least certain that no organic State could be a member of a democratic Superstate, since the latter can govern if, and only if, its moral standards are generally accepted; which, in those conditions, they cannot be. Hence, it would be a practical necessity for the democratic Superstate to impose acceptance of its moral theory, presumably by a generous application of atomic bombs, on recalcitrant subordinates. The wheel would thus turn full circle, and it would now be the democrats who were forcing their opponents to be free.

This sounds extremely paradoxical. To understand how it happens, we need to return to the question of moral ideals. The Superstate, we have said, must govern. It can do so only if one set of moral standards is generally accepted, and therefore it must see to it that this condition is fulfilled. Its justification for ensuring this can be nothing other than the conviction of its rulers that one system of moral principles is not merely accepted but is ultimately and finally right. In other words, its political theory must be not merely a theory. There must be nothing hypothetical about it. On the contrary, it must be the indubitable truth about what the relation of individuals to society ought to be. Then only can it be maintained that any individual or body of individuals who fail to recognize this "ought" can properly either be constrained to behave as if they did, or be duly liquidated.

It thus appears that there can be no universal moral standards without a World-State to formulate and maintain them; and no World-State can be a State, that is can govern, unless it enforces the kind of moral theory which its own nature postulates. But, in the absence of any demonstration that one political faith is absolutely superior to the others, the idea of a Superstate as a voluntary organization is quite untenable.

CHAPTER 6

The Practical Problem

*Is it therefore infallibly agreeable to the Word of
God, all that you say? I beseech you, in the bowels
of Christ, think it possible you may be mistaken.—*
OLIVER CROMWELL.

IF THE CONCLUSIONS reached in the preceding chapter are accepted, their practical implications cannot safely be overlooked. In particular, it is of the first importance that their
bearing on the morality and usefulness of ideological crusades
should receive careful attention. There is no universally accepted standard of morals, and we have seen strong reasons for
supposing that no such standard will exist within any measur-
able time. There are, on the contrary, numerous States with
radically different moral sentiments and radically opposed
political theories based on them. There is, of course, no logical
reason for supposing that this position will continue forever.
It may be that within the course of a few centuries the human
race will work out a single moral and political system which
will be universally accepted. But we cannot here and now
envisage such a system, and, however much moralists may
deplore the fact, it is at the moment true that increased study
and reflection tend to exacerbate rather than to allay ideological differences. It is exceedingly difficult to avoid getting
impatient about this, as the Germans notoriously did. Many
intelligent Germans have long been convinced of the superiority of their own moral and political views over those of other
people and, in particular, over those commonly held in Eng-

land and the United States. They could not bear to wait until experience convinced the democracies of the futility of the democratic outlook. So they tried to spread their convictions by propaganda and, ultimately, by force of arms. It was not a success. Now it is up to the democracies, and in particular it is up to the Americans, to consider the line which they propose to take; and there are two questions, in both of which Great Britain is intensely interested, which demand to be answered. Both have to be answered in practice immediately, so it is as well to consider, at least in broad outline, the principles on which tolerable solutions may be sought. We must first ask whether, in view of what has already been argued, it can reasonably be held that democratic theory is a suitable article for indiscriminate export; and we must further inquire whether there is any hope that political theories which differ so completely about the answers to first-order moral problems as organic and democratic political theories have been found to do, can have practical effect given to them by States of first-rate importance without involving a final struggle for ideological survival between those States.

THE PROPAGATION OF DEMOCRATIC PRINCIPLES

We have already found reasons for holding that there is no simple method for changing the existing character of any State. It is not possible to convert a democracy into an organic State, or *vice versa,* by the device of adopting a new Constitution, a special type of electoral system, or a novel economic organization. It may be admitted that, when the basic moral outlook required to realize either type of State is present, constitutional and economic measures will help it to find adequate expression. By themselves, however, they are of little importance. It may further be agreed that, as far as democracy is concerned, the moral basis is respect for human beings.

Whether this is felt because of a common humanity or is rendered to individuals as such is not relevant here. In either case, what we are concerned with is a conviction or sentiment which can neither be induced nor driven out by reasoning. This does not imply that it cannot be induced or driven out at all, since education is by no means entirely a matter of carrying conviction by means of argument. Psychological conditioning, however, is by no means fully understood as yet. It has been employed by educationalists for centuries, but we are still not at all clear either as to its potentialities or as to its limitations. Nobody doubts that something can be done by means of propaganda and specially arranged environmental conditions toward encouraging or eliminating State worship as an attitude of mind; equally, nobody would be anxious to pronounce an authoritative view as to how much can be effected by these methods, and under what circumstances. There seems no reason to doubt that conditioning is a simpler process than reconditioning, and that either process is more likely to be successful if it proceeds unopposed than it is if counterpropaganda for the opposing view has to be overcome. But this does not take us very far.

The problem of exporting democracy, that is, of educating or re-educating nondemocratic peoples to respect and maintain democratic ideals may conveniently be divided. We must first inquire as to the prospects of so-called "backward races." By this is meant peoples who are not yet sufficiently advanced in their political development to have acquired any type of highly developed State. For the most part such peoples are found in the colonial empires of the European Powers, though this description is not exhaustive. Secondly, investigation is needed into the position of those politically mature peoples who explicitly reject the democratic faith and embrace instead organic moral and political principles. As regards the "backward races," it is curiously difficult to get any really convincing evidence as to whether they are or are not essentially capable of democratic self-government; that is, of government by consent. This is not due to lack of pronouncements on the subject. There have been plenty of fervent declarations on both sides. The reason is rather that, for a number of more or less adequate causes, no really crucial experiment has yet been made. Some broad conclusions, however, can be drawn with a fair degree of confidence.

Experience has not confirmed the breezy optimism of the eighteenth- and nineteenth-century believers in radical democracy. The noble savage has turned out to be an entirely fabulous monster, and it is now demonstrably not the case that all human beings instinctively recognize and respect the inherent dignity of man unless they are warped and perverted by oppression and tyranny. Almost precisely the opposite is true. The democratic outlook never has been and still is not at all common, and it is fair to expect that undeveloped peoples, if left to shift for themselves, will tend to produce States which satisfy the organic rather than the democratic theory. It would be foolish to expect anything else. The organic State is the line of least resistance. It invites us to cast our burdens on it and abdicate (or never assert) any claim to make decisions for ourselves. So perhaps we hardly need an elaborate psychological theory about regressive tendencies to account for its popularity, though the Jungian psychology unquestionably throws much light on the whole question. In addition to this normal proclivity of human beings toward laziness and avoidance of personal responsibility, we have to face the fact that, in the absence of fairly widespread education, government by consent can in any case be little more than a pretense. Even if people who cannot read or write have the most admirable moral sentiments, they cannot give any worthwhile expression to them. An essential presupposition of democratic government is lacking. There is no similar requirement in the organic State. Literacy may there very well be economically advantageous (as the U.S.S.R. has discovered), but it is not politically indispensable. Hence it may be taken as a virtual certainty that democracy will never break out among backward peoples unless it is strongly encouraged to do so. There is no good ground for holding that its growth cannot be stimulated sufficiently to produce good results; but it never has been so stimulated. There has been plenty of passive official benevolence and some valuable active work, mainly by voluntary bodies. But, taken as a whole, it must be admitted that, in the absence of prolonged and strenuous effort on a big scale, no convincing conclusions have been established.

This is due, at least in part, to the fact that deliberate inculcation of respect for the inherent rights of individuals is not exactly consistent with the requirements of intensive economic development. The English and Americans, to say nothing of other democratic States, have on the whole, and in a general way, wished to spread their democratic beliefs among less favored peoples. They have not so far wished sufficiently hard to overcome the opposing tendencies of economic and political vested interests. It is fair to add that these vested interests are not always as black as they are painted. They, or their representatives, are closer to the problem than their critics; and the latter habitually underestimate the difficulties. The cry for democracy overnight can very easily (and not unreasonably) provoke the countercry for "no equality in Church or State." Unquestionably the educative work, both moral and technical, which is necessary to make self-government a practicable proposition for peoples who are politically primitive is a major undertaking; but there is at least no obvious reason for thinking it impossible. The backward races will quite certainly get a developed political philosophy from somewhere sooner or later, and it is hard to see any grounds on which the States which have incurred responsibility for them can, without absurdity, abstain from instilling the principles to which they themselves are committed. But political theories, as the English have learned from extensive and painful experience, take a long time to implant, and there is nothing to be gained by attempting to hurry the process. There is much to be said against the abolition of a working system, even if its basis is both primitive and peculiar.

The position of politically mature States is utterly different. There is here no deficiency to be made good. The question is not, "What moral and political ideals are the Japanese or the Germans to acquire?" since they already have plenty. It is "Can we eradicate their existing ideals and replace them by others more in keeping with our own?" In other words, can we "dis-educate" them from organic theory and "re-educate" them to democracy? Direct evidence on this point is nil. Psychological reconditioning on this scale has never been attempted, except by methods which are presumably not contemplated at the present moment. There are, however, a number of pointers which indicate that the prospects of success are so small as to be negligible.

The moral basis of democratic political theory is neither self-evident nor demonstrable. Considered as a theory, the organic hypothesis is at least equally well placed. It is, therefore, not to be expected that any conversion from one to the other can be effected by logical argument. There is nothing to argue about. We can exhibit what we take to be the superiority of the "democratic way of life," but if those who have previously rejected it continue to do so, we have no course left except to repeat the demonstration and hope for better results in the future. There is no absolute bar to progress by this method, but its hope of success in the absence of a vacuum demanding to be filled should not be put very high. Moral re-education is an extremely drastic project, and is one which is inevitably resented as impertinent. There are grounds for supposing that it will be accepted as a kind of profitable window dressing more frequently than it will lead to any genuine change of heart.

Thus the outlook would be poor even if no counterpropaganda were to be anticipated. When, however, we turn from re-education in general to that of the democratization of the world, or even of Europe here and now, it is obvious that this is most unlikely to be the case. Both on moral and practical grounds the U.S.S.R. has precisely the same incentive to restrict democratic missionary work as the United States and Britain have to promote it. There is every reason for believing that the Kremlin is well aware of this.

Against these difficulties there is little which can be said. The hypothetical liberal minority which may possibly exist in all organic States could be encouraged. But this minority has already turned out to be a poor affair in Germany, and in Japan it is hardly even that. Or it may be said that, while adults are admittedly unpromising material for re-education, the children offer better prospects. Possibly they do. We can assume with a fair degree of plausibility that the factors which produce State worship are mostly environmental, and, further, that they belong to the part of environment which is changeable at will, rather than to geographical or climatic conditions. But even this does not help us much. For it is certainly not just a question of schoolteaching that is involved. The environment is total and includes family and esthetic influences—indeed, the whole national tradition and culture. It may be that with unlimited energy and resources, and in the absence of any effective opposition, something might be achieved, but it is not easy to believe that short-run success would be impressive.

There remains what may be termed the middle class of peoples: those who are neither politically mature nor politically primitive. What are the prospects of democracy as far as they are concerned? There is not much evidence about this. Most of what there is comes from Central and South America and is not particularly encouraging. But, as far as the Balkans and the Near East, in which for practical reasons we are bound to be mainly interested, are concerned, the prospects are not bright. The shortage of education in the narrower sense is formidable; and there is no absence of political attachment, since Russian and German penetration have stimulated the organic rather than the democratic faith. The motive of economic exploitation, too, is strongly present, and is, as always, inevitably opposed to the establishment of government by consent in anything but a formal way. It is hard to imagine that under such conditions democratic institutions could, within any foreseeable time, be anything more than an expensive decoration.

Two other points deserve some brief discussion. It may be held that this estimate of the practicability of exporting democracy on a large scale is overpessimistic, since it ignores the possible influence of religious ideas on the situation. In Europe, at any rate, and in Germany and Austria in particular, there is a well-established Christian tradition to build upon, and this might surely be expected to give a better hope of success than I have allowed. Any such expectation seems to me to rest on a complete misunderstanding. There is no unanimity between Christian sects except on second-order moral problems. When it comes to questions affecting the duty of human beings to respect authority, whether spiritual or temporal, rather than the rights of the individual, little or no agreement between the Church of England, the Church of Rome, and the Lutherans is discoverable. Indeed it must be admitted that prodemocratic Christians are a small minority. This does not imply that most Christians are "profascist," whatever precisely that term is taken to mean. It asserts no more than that the moral view underlying government by consent forms no part of their doctrine and is liable on critical issues to be inconsistent with it.

The final point is this: It may well be argued that, even if moral re-education is a less difficult undertaking than I have suggested, the moral grounds for setting about it are themselves none too secure. The whole case rests on our primary conviction of the fundamental importance of individual rights; but that conviction is itself stultified if we compel, or attempt to compel, other people to adopt it. This is evidently a major issue which no easy generalization can settle, for "compulsion" is itself a vague and ill-defined term. There is always some involuntary element in being educated, and we should not make too much of this. Nevertheless it is hard to deny that there is a substantial difference between the degree of compulsion required to inspire primitive and advanced peoples with new moral convictions; and, whatever views we may hold about the propriety of enforcing religious discipline on our own children, it is uncommonly difficult, in the absence of agreed revelation or authority, to produce any moral justification for imposing it on the children of other people. However attractive the opportunity may look, those who support democracy would be well advised to exercise great caution about compelling others to come in. Otherwise they may easily find that they have lost their own soul and saved nobody by losing it.

It appears, then, that democracy is something which can be cultivated in new areas only with great difficulty and under favorable conditions. I have said nothing specific about the difficulties of transplanting the organic view, though it may be supposed that these are somewhat less formidable as far as politically immature peoples are concerned. What evidence there is, particularly the notable failure of the German new order to attract many adherents in countries where democracy was firmly established, suggests that, in such cases at least, no transfer from the democratic to the organic faith can in practice be achieved, even when substantial inducements are offered to bring it about. What is surprising is not that collaborators existed but that, even when German victory seemed a virtual certainty in 1940, they were no more than an important minority in any country in Western Europe.

The conclusion of this inquiry, then, is that there is a genuine and irreducible difference in fundamental beliefs between those who attach primary importance to the self-determination of the individual and those who acknowledge the superior reality of the State. There is no harm in describing this as an ideological conflict, as I have sometimes done, though I do not think the term a very happy one.

ARE IDEOLOGICAL WARS INEVITABLE?

This brings us to the second and more difficult practical problem which demands discussion here. For if, as I have argued, there are two radically opposed conceptions of the nature of man, and if each of them is sponsored by a first-class power as a matter of faith, we are bound to ask whether there is any prospect that States whose entire tradition and outlook are so opposed will find it possible to live peaceably together in the same world. In one sense it is true that wars settle nothing. People do not change their moral convictions because they have lost a battle. If, however, a policy of extermination is consistently pursued by the winning side, that side can in the end get its view accepted by eliminating dissenters. It may be that even this would fail. We do not yet know how far the beliefs in question depend solely on environmental conditions, or what those conditions are. But the method could certainly be tried: and, if no accommodation between different types of State is reached, there is every reason to expect that it will be tried. Hence it is of importance that as many people as possible among the potential victims should seriously ask themselves whether such a conflict is really necessary or not.

It is no use blinking the fact that what is now confronting us is the likelihood of a religious war, even though no theological issue is at stake. I mean by this simply that the emotions aroused by any threat to the authority of the State on the one hand and the freedom of the individual on the other are essentially similar to those which have characterized what have been termed religious conflicts for the last two thousand years. And, however much the true issue may be obscured by careless definitions, confused thinking, and reckless propaganda, it is none the less real. The more carefully people think it out, the more they will come to recognize that no compromise in principle can be reached. Discussion is futile, for there is no agreed basis from which it can start.

The outlook, therefore, is rather bleak. But it is by no means hopeless. We must remember that it was at least equally unpromising in Western Europe in the sixteenth and seventeenth centuries. For there, too, no compromise in principle was possible between the claims of the Church of Rome and those of the Protestant Reformation; and it was terribly clear that nothing short of the annihilation of its opponents would secure the victory of either side. Yet, in spite of a good deal of destructive fighting, Europe did not commit suicide. There was no compromise in principle, but methods were found by which conflicts of discordant principles could in practice be very largely avoided, and, on the whole, the settlement has worked quite well.

There are two lessons to be gathered from this as to the lines along which a *modus vivendi* for irreconcilable political faith can profitably be sought. In the first place it must be noted that the religious issue between Catholics and Protestants (and between Christians and Moslems, to cite another instance) is not by any means an extinct volcano. On the contrary, it is liable to become dangerously active at any moment.

But it is one of the obvious tasks of statesmen to prevent this from happening. It is not easy, but it can be done. The Butler Education Act [British] is a good example both of the difficulty and of the possibility of doing it, and numberless other instances of the same process in this and other countries could easily be cited. The problem, however, remains a problem and will continue to be one for as long as we can foresee.

The second point to observe is that the preservation of religious peace is possible only because both sides genuinely want to preserve it and are prepared to accept the sacrifices on second-order moral questions without which such preservation would be out of the question. What this entails is that propaganda and counterpropaganda should be kept within reasonable limits and that mutual abuse by irresponsible agitators should be disavowed or at any rate not encouraged by the authorities on either side. "No Popery" is still a possible slogan in many parts of England, but it is one which no sane person in any position of responsibility would dare to advocate, however strongly he felt on the religious issue.

Let us now return to the political question. There is, as far as I can see, nothing whatever to be gained at this stage by attempting to conceal what it is. The two surviving Great Powers in the world, namely the U.S.A. and the U.S.S.R., unquestionably represent the conflicting moral and political philosophies whose nature and implications we have now investigated. They cannot compromise on principle, and it is not merely waste of time but a perilous source of misunderstanding that they should attempt to do so. If the U.S.S.R. were really trying to be democratic in the sense in which the United States is democratic, or in any sense in which the word is commonly used in Western Europe, then it would have to be admitted that she is not doing it at all well. The case for spreading propaganda and information as to how to do it properly among Russians in and out of season would then be a strong one, and the Russians would have no just ground for being suspicious and exasperated about it. The other side of the picture is that if the British were attempting to arrange for themselves an efficient organic State, advice from Russia as to how to do it would not be interference with the political affairs of another country, but would be friendly assistance in an admittedly difficult job. We all lay ourselves wide open to this kind of argument when, in a mistaken attempt to promote international amity, we pretend that our disagreements on principle are not really very important. They are absolutely fundamental. But provided that the Russians and the Americans do not want to have a war about them, and there is not the faintest ground for supposing either that they do or that they will, there is no reason why they should have one. The conditions of preserving peace, however, do not differ in any important way from those which have been found necessary to avoid armed conflict on other issues in which equally strong emotions have been operative. These are, to repeat what was said above, restraint from provocation and excessive propaganda by both sides and, what is even more difficult, mutual acceptance of sacrifices on all nonessential matters. If every economic disagreement is to be worked up into an ideological controversy, the prospects of peace are negligible. Indeed, the opposite activity is essential. We must rather insist that principles are not involved when, in fact, they are, than risk admitting that they are when, in fact, they are not. Unfortunately, this is just what does not happen automatically. It is far less trouble to say that we do not disagree about principles and that, therefore, all problems can be solved by discussion, than it is to face the fact that only secondary difficulties can be solved in this way. What matters is to ensure that nothing but secondary difficulties needs to be settled, and to do this requires more self-restraint and common sense on both sides than is always forthcoming. It also needs a clear

understanding of precisely what the major issues about which
no compromise is possible actually are, for, unless we understand them, we cannot expect to steer clear of them. It is this
kind of understanding which a philosophical study of political
theories ought to provide.

CONCLUSION

The result of this inquiry as a whole can be stated in very
few words. It is that dogmatism about political, and therefore
about moral theories, is dangerous and should be avoided.
The temptation to indulge in it is strong, and it would be too
much to expect that the quest for certainty in these matters will
ever be abandoned. But it should at least be pursued with
great caution. There is, as we have seen, an ever-present tendency for those who hold strongly the moral beliefs on which
the organic and the radical democratic theories depend to
persuade themselves that they are in possession of a gospel and
not of a theory, and that it is their duty to propagate that
gospel at practically any cost. Force theorists are in a different
position. Yet it can hardly be denied that Marxists often speak
of their view in language more appropriate to evangelists than
to scientists expounding a hypothesis. What I have called individual democracy does not lend itself to this type of enthusiasm. It is on its own showing quite unsuitable for universal adoption. To compel people to act responsibly is a clear
contradiction, and to encourage them to accept responsibility
before they are capable of it is, to put it mildly, unwise.

This being the position, it seems to me reasonable to suggest to those who are emotionally convinced of the unalterable rightness of their own views that they should at least
think it possible that they may be mistaken. By this I do not
mean that they may be mistaken as to the nature and strength
of their own moral sentiments, for it is hardly possible to
be mistaken about these. It is, however, quite possible to accept

them as facts without going on to claim either that they are universally experienced, or that those who do not experience them are morally crooked and in need of straightening. There is quite good empirical evidence for maintaining that some States are democratic and others organic in character, but none for saying that any State is organic or democratic in any strict theoretical sense. This may seem a disappointing conclusion. It would be more satisfying to wind up with a tidy rationalist demonstration that one or the other type is necessarily the best for men as such; and that we ought therefore to strive to propagate this type even among those who are blind enough not to recognize its merits. But this, if I am right, is a perilous delusion. It is bound to breed crusades without end. So long as we recognize that our belief, however strongly we hold it ourselves, lacks demonstration, we may be tolerant toward dissenters. But as soon as we claim to know the right answer, it requires superhuman patience and forbearance to abstain from thrusting it on other people.

As soon as the empirical basis of all political theory is clearly recognized, there is no good reason why States of essentially different types should not coexist perfectly happily. All that is needed is that each should know where the others stand. We do, after all, achieve this sort of accommodation in our private lives without too much difficulty or discomfort. It is fortunately quite possible for two men to do business with each other even when they do not hold identical views on first-order moral questions. But they would not be able to do this if each of them perpetually suspected that the other was somehow attempting to undermine his morals under the pretense of doing a business deal. We can transfer this argument to the level of international politics. There are not very many States, and, as far as the preservation of peace is concerned, only two, or, at the outside, three of them matter much. Provided that the two will deal with one another on second-order problems (which are economic and therefore almost always capable of solution by discussion), no insoluble problem should arise. But it is obviously essential that neither the U.S.A. nor the U.S.S.R. should have any ground for suspecting that it is being sold an unacceptable political ideology by the other whenever it makes a sensible economic compromise. If both will not accept this limitation, there is nothing for it but to bring out the atomic bombs. I cannot myself see why both of them should not accept it. But the trouble, or perhaps it is the merit, of empiricism is that it prevents me from seeing any sense in embarking on ideological wars in order to improve the morals of people in whose moral welfare I am not greatly interested.

Index

A

Abyssinia, 127
America (see United States)
American Civil War, 3, 191
Aristotle, 5, 19, 65, 72n., 78, 86n., 110,
    114, 150, 182, 238, 262
    and the organic state, 68
    and Plato, 68, 70
    and Rousseau, 80, 82
    theories of, 68-77
Austria, 288

B

Balkans, the, 288
Bankers' Ramp of 1931, 251
Belloc, Hilaire, 233
Belsen, 176, 181
Birley, 191n.
Boer War, 201
Bolshevist Party, 169
Bosanquet, 41, 123, 201, 232
Bradley, F. H., 41, 163, 164n., 210, 220-
    221, 232, 258, 261n.
Britain (see Great Britain)
Broad, 227
Brogan, 191n.
Buchenwald, 176

C

Calvin, 82
Capital, The, 109, 111
Central America, 288
Chamberlain, Neville, 66
Chesterton, G. K., 72
Church, the, 59, 69, 204, 207, 288
Church of England, 198, 288
Church of Rome, 288
Churchill, Winston, 185, 204

Cicero, 142n.
Civil War, American, 3, 191
Comintern, 171
Communism, 10, 33, 34, 68, 117, 177,
    212
    (See also Russia, Political catch-
    words)
Communist Journal, 118
Communist Manifesto, 99n., 102,
    103n., 109, 115, 119-120
Communist Party, 159, 172
    (See also Russia)
Condition of the Working Class in
    England, 111
Consent theory (see Political theories)
Conservative Party, 185
Conservatives, 251
Constitution worship, 140
C.P.S.U., 186
Critique of Political Economy, 111
Cromwell, Oliver, 85
Czecho-Slovakia, 182

D

Declaration of Independence, 262
Democracy, 9, 10, 12, 26
    (See also Political theories; State,
    democracy in)
Democracy in America, 187n.
Democratic Party, 32, 191
Democratic theory (see Political the-
    ories)
De Officiis, 142n.
De Tocqueville, 187
Diamond Jubilee, 201
Dies Committee, 193
Discourse on Political Economy, 78
Dumbarton Oaks, 134
Duranty, Walter, 170n.

E

Empiricism, 17-22
Engels, 111, 120, 155, 156, 168, 171n.
England (see Great Britain)
Essay Concerning Human Under-
standing, 142n.
Essay, Epistle to the Reader, 131n.
Ethical Studies, 164n., 258, 258n.
Ethics, 69, 70

F

Fascism, 9, 10, 33, 34
(See also Political catchwords)
Federalist, The, 14n.
Five Types of Ethical Theory, 227n.
Force theory (see Political theories)
France, 207, 208
Franco, 184
Frankfurt, 179
Free State, The, 191n.
Führer (see Hitler)

G

General Strike of 1926, 42
General Will (see Rousseau)
Germania, 176
Germany, 6, 8-9, 153, 165, 287, 288
characteristics of, 179-182, 228
Labor Front in, 181
liberal movements in, 176-177
as organic state, 175-182
Peoples' Courts in, 181
Second Reich, 177
split-personality theory of, 177-178
Third Reich, 177
Germany: The Double History of a
Nation, 177n.
Gilbert, W. S., 74n.
Gladstone, 212
Goebbels, 182
Gondoliers, The, 74n.
Göring, 185
Great Britain, 33, 127, 140, 153, 211,
236, 287

constitution of, 68
changes in, 198
charges against, 201-204
colonialism of, 202-203
snobbery in, 203-204
as a democratic state, 196-206
organic theory in, 201-202
social distinctions in, 199-200
Greeks, 19, 164n.
Green, 123

H

Hamilton, 14n.
Handbook of Marxism, 116n.
Hegel, 13, 41, 42, 63, 68, 172, 182, 193,
201, 258
and Aristotle, 86
philosophy of, 86-97, 109, 145
and Rousseau, 88, 90
and later theories, 95-97
Hitler, 42, 83, 84, 165, 175-182, 184, 186
Hobbes, Thomas, 5, 26, 45, 69, 71, 98,
99, 111, 131, 135, 160-162, 234
and Marx, 100-102
philosophy of, 102-109
Hobhouse, L. T., 13n.
Hook, Sidney, 156
Hume, David, 85, 262
Hutcheson, 262

I

Ideals and Illusions, 224n.
Individuals and the State (see State)
Internationale, 171

J

Japan, 6, 165, 206, 287
Joseph, H. W. B., 223n.

K

Kamenev, 168
Kant, 274
King, 131n.
Kipling, Rudyard, 201

L

Labor Party, 251
Laird, 21
League of Nations, 41, 42, 43, 59, 127, 134
Lenin, 119, 160, 161, 167, 168, 170, 173, 177, 193, 202
Letters concerning Toleration, 130
Leviathan, 45, 69n., 102n., 103n., 104n., 105, 107, 108, 160
Liberalism, 32
Life of Locke, 131n.
Lincoln, 12, 129, 190, 191-192
Lincoln's Speech at Peoria, 1854, 192n.
Locke, 5, 64, 68, 121, 128, 145, 185, 188, 236
  and State of Nature, 132
  philosophy of, 130-144
Lord, 44
Ludwig, 177n.
Luther, 176
Lycurgus, 82

M

Maritain, 39n.
Marx, 26, 56, 71, 75, 87, 96, 98, 128, 145, 160, 161, 169, 171n., 193, 215, 219, 232, 251
  and Hobbes, 99-103
  philosophy of, 109-120
Marxism, 32, 39, 45, 56, 57, 60, 68, 111, 117, 151, 153-162, 167, 168, 170, 171, 173, 235
  arguments in favor of, 158-159
Metaphysical Theory of the State, The, 13n.
Metaphysics, 69
Methods of ethics, 220
Mill, J. S., 274
Modern Traveler, The, 233n.
Montesquieu, 188
Morals and politics, 216-230
Moseley, 201
Mr. Sidgwick's Hedonism, 220n.
Muhs, Karl, 120n.
Murl, 72n.

N

Nazi Party, 177
Near East, the, 288
Newton, 239
Nuremberg, 175

O

Open Society and Its Enemies, The, 13n.
Organic theory (*see* Political theories)
Orthodox Church, 167

P

Paris Commune of 1871, 111
Party programs (*see* Political philosophy)
Peter the Great, 171n.
Philosophy of Right, 13, 90
Philosophical Theory of the State, 41n., 201
Plato, 19, 26n., 36, 37, 68, 70, 123, 150, 218, 238
Poland, 182
Political catchwords, 1, 211-215
Political philosophers, 62-145
Political philosophy, aim of, 1-25
  importance of, 4-15
  and moral philosophy, 25
  method of, 15-17
  and party programs, 3
  and the State, 13
Political policy, 32
Political theories, 26-61
  chart of, 33
  common elements in, 28-29
  consent theory, 32, 33, 54-55, 57-58, 59, 123, 143
  democratic theory, 52-55, 58, 59, 120-130
  equations of, 32
  force theory, 32, 33, 51-52, 56, 97-141
  machine theory, 45-51
  Marxist (*see* Marxism)
  organic theory, 32, 33, 34-45, 56, 57, 59, 60, 71, 76, 86, 97, 141

Political theories (*continued*)
 and Catholicism, 39
 difficulties of, 44
 the individual and, 35-39
 moral basis of, 230-233
 and parties, 33
 Platonic, 68-69
  (*See also* State; Germany; Great
  Britain; Russia; United States)
Politics, 69, 70, 73, 86
Politics and morals, 216-230
 (*See also* State)
Popper, 13n.
Principia, 239
Protestant Reformation, 39, 43, 44
Prussia, 92-93
Public and Private Honesty, On, 268n.

R

Radical Socialist Party, 34
Rationalism, 15, 15n., 16, 17, 20, 23
 and empiricism, 17-22
Reformation (*see* Protestant Refor-
 mation)
Reichstag, 177
Republic, 26n., 37n., 123, 218
Republican Party, 32
Ribbentrop, 185
Right and the Good, The, 222n.
Romanovs, 172-173
Ross, 222n.
Rousseau, 45, 66, 105, 180, 219
 and Aristotle, 80, 82
 General Will theory of, 78-85
 and Hegel, 88-91
Russia, 6, 47, 56, 68, 113, 121, 153, 159,
 287, 292-293, 296
 the church in, 167
 Communist Party in, 172
 Constitution of, 172, 186
 Czar of, 167
 Marxism and, 167-171
 as organic state, 165-175
 Revolution of 1917, 167-170
Rutherford, 6
Ryazanoff, 120n.

S

Sacco and Vanzetti, 193
Scholasticism and Politics, 39n.
Second International, 157
Second Reich, 177
Second Treatise on Civil Government,
 68, 132n., 133n., 135n., 138n.
Security Council, 134, 134n.
Shaftesbury, 262
Social Contract, 80n., 88n.
Social Democrats, 177
Socialism, 10
Some Problems in Ethics, 223n.
South America, 288
*Speeches and Documents in American
 History*, 191n.
Stalin, 134, 159n., 165, 169, 172, 173,
 179
State, the, 20, 21n., 22, 26, 35-39, 208-
 211, 213
 based on force, 153-165, 235
 nonmoral basis of, 233-236
 definition of, 20-22, 34, 50
 democracy in, 120, 183-187
  individualist, 254-272
 moral basis of, 233-247
 moral philosophy of, 260-262
 practical problems of, 281-282
 propagation of principles of, 282-
  290
 radical, 247
 standards for, 275-280
 the individual and, 15, 26, 35, 38, 46,
  73, 216-222, 266-267, 271, 275
 as a machine, 97-102
 meaning of, 23-24
 and morals, 219-230
 organic theory in, 163-165, 166
 rights of, 65
 in theory and in practice, 146-215
  (*See also* Political theories)
State of Nature, 132-133
Stebbing, 224n.
Stephens, 191
Superstate, 278-279
Suvarov, 171n.

Switzerland, democracy in, 205-206, 211

T

Tacitus, 176
Theories (*see* Political theories)
Theory, 15*n*., 22, 62-63
Thesis on Ruerbach, 112*n*.
Third German Reich (*see* Germany)
Thrasymachus, 26, 123
Totalitarianism (*see* Political catchwords)
Toward the Understanding of Karl Marx, 156*n*.
Trade Dispute Act of 1927, 42
Trade Unions, 41, 42, 59, 204, 207
Trotsky, 168, 169
Two Treatises of Government, 130

U

United States, the, 140, 144, 153, 211, 236, 287, 296
  Constitution of, 14, 53, 68, 187-189, 194
  amendments to, 190
  Civil War in, 3, 191
  as a democratic state, 187-196
  immigration to, 194-195

powers in, 188-189
problems in, 190-196
  color, 190-193
  political, 193-196
U.S.S.R. (*see* Russia)
U.S.S.R., 170

V

Vatican, the, 39
Versailles Peace Conference, 5
Vulgar Notion of Responsibility, 261*n*.

W

War, ideological, 290-294
  political issues in, 291-292
  religious issues in, 292-294
Wehrmacht, 181
Weimar, 179
Weimar Constitution, 181
Wilson, 5, 129, 143
Wooton, 268*n*.
World-State, 277, 278, 280

Y

Yalta, 134

Z

Zinoviev, 168